W9-CEU-770

---Study the Principles Not the Problem---

Joe & Charlie's
Big Book Study
Workshop Workbook

A 19-Week "Active" Journey Through the Big Book of Alcoholics Anonymous!

IMPORTANT:

This workbook is meant to be used within a workshop setting, whether it's an entire group effort or just a few folks; make certain those attending are committed to stay the entire 19 weeks for optimal results for everyone involved.

Recommended Reading!

Look inside ↓

Flip to back

Joe & Charlie: The Big Book Comes Alive Paperback – December 27, 2014
by John Smith (Author)
⭐⭐⭐⭐ ▾ 4 customer reviews

› See all formats and editions

Paperback
$9.95

4 Used from $9.96
14 New from $8.62

The Joe & Charlie Journey to Recovery in THE BIG BOOK COKMES ALIVE is a book that you'll want to read for your own Big Book AA recovery as well as get for your friend too.

ORDER ONLINE TODAY!

©2001-2016 All Rights Reserved

2016 Step Workshop

Each week, during the beginning of each workshop session and after the break, please indicate your level of being "PRESENT". Use a number 1 through 10, with 10 being fully present.

Week #	Beginning	After Break
Week 1		
Week 2		
Week 3		
Week 4		
Week 5		
Week 6		
Week 7		
Week 8		
Week 9		
Week 10		
Week 11		
Week 12		
Week 13		
Week 14		
Week 15		
Week 16		
Week 17		
Week 18		
Week 19		

Keep Track of Your Progress for Optimal Results

The Big Book Workshop Format

Good evening, my name is _____, and I'm an alcoholic. Welcome to the *Big Book* Workshop. We as leaders do not consider ourselves to be the gurus of *The Big Book* of Alcoholics Anonymous. We do not consider ourselves to be experts in anything at all. For those who care to, please join me in a moment of silence to remind us of why we are here, and for the alcoholic who still suffers.

Please join me in the workshop prayer:

"God, let me set aside everything I think I know about you, AA, myself, and my disease, for an open mind and a new experience. Let me be honest and thorough. Amen."

For the first couple of weeks we will go around the room and introduce ourselves in order to get to know one another.

Purpose: It is the purpose of this workshop to experience the recovery process as outlined in *The Big Book* of Alcoholics Anonymous, either for the first time or again, so that we may better carry out and understand our primary purpose; to stay sober and carry the message to the still-suffering alcoholic.

We are here to talk about recovery only and to go through the Twelve-Step process as outlined in *The Big Book* of Alcoholics Anonymous. This is not an emotional or intellectual exercise. This is a spiritual exercise so that we can all recover and experience the recovery process as we read it together. It is recommended that anything that you hear here that cannot be reconciled in *The Big Book*, *Twelve and Twelve*, or any other AA-approved literature be simply ignored.

THIS IS NOT A CROSS-TALK WORKSHOP:

Questions should be saved for the end of the meeting or for after the meeting. Chances are very good that your questions will be answered at a later time during the workshop.

WEEK ONE – INTRODUCTION, OBJECTIVES, AND GOALS

STEP STUDY OUTLINE AND ASSIGNMENT SHEETS

The following is a suggested assignment sheet as outlined for use by this Step Study Workshop. It is suggested that before the study is completed, each member completes Steps One through Twelve.

PRELIMINARY: During the first meeting we will review this outline regarding the purpose, plan, and meeting format of the workshop. It is important that the commitment section of this outline be carefully reviewed and that you thoroughly understand that you are <u>committing to taking the Steps</u>. It is most helpful that everyone attend and be present as much as possible. It is also suggested that the homework be done soon after the class and then reviewed with your sponsor before the next workshop meeting. We will not be completing or reviewing the homework in this workshop. You will need to do your homework with your sponsor in preparation for the following week's meeting.

1. **PURPOSE**:
   a. To provide the person who has not worked the Twelve Steps with motivation and assistance in taking the Twelve Steps.
   b. To provide those who have worked the Twelve Steps with an opportunity and the motivation to do it again and to help those who have not yet taken the Twelve Steps.

2. **PLAN**:
   a. There is no designated seating arrangement, but the seat you choose tonight will be where you sit throughout the entire workshop. Additionally, your communication (before and after the workshop meeting, NOT during) with the other members of your table is crucial to your success here.
   b. During the introductory meeting, all in attendance will:
      i. **Commit** to stay with their table.
      ii. **Commit** to do all the steps as suggested in *The Big Book*.
      iii. Those who have previously done a workshop will be asked to **commit** to do it once more as part of their Twelfth Step.
      iv. **Commit** to attend the meetings except on rare and extremely unusual circumstances. <u>Each member really needs to attend and be present each week</u>. If you cannot attend, notify a member of your table or another workshop member and advise them of your situation.
      v. **Commit** to exchange phone numbers and making a phone call and/or personal contact with one or more members of their table during each week of the workshop and sharing your problems and/or experience with the assignment for that week.
   c. The time to complete the workshop is nineteen weeks.

STEP STUDY OUTLINE AND ASSIGNMENT SHEETS

3. **MEETING FORMAT:**
   a. The leader simply discusses the assigned material and shares their experience in applying it in their own life.
   b. It is suggested that each member come to the meeting having read and studied the assignment from the previous week pertaining to the portions of the *Big Book* and *Twelve and Twelve* as they relate to the Step under consideration.
   c. The function of the member is to apply the principles of each Step in their lives and share their experience in a discussion of each Step with their sponsor.
   d. It is suggested that each member obtain a 3-ring binder, an ink pen, a highlighter pen, and 3-hole paper or notebook to record your notes and complete assignments.

Meeting Reader Reads

The Big Book of Alcoholics Anonymous Preface states: ***"This book has become the BASIC TEXT of our society".*** The forward to the first edition states: ***"To show other alcoholics precisely how we have recovered",*** and additionally on page 29 in *The Big Book* it states, ***"Further on, clear-cut directions are given showing how we recovered".***

This is the task you are about to undertake!

PREFACE TO *THE BIG BOOK OF ALCOHOLICS ANONYMOUS* - HIGHLIGHTS
READ: Page xi, paragraphs 1 – 2
READ AFTER: Page xi, paragraph 2
BASIC TEXT: A "textbook" is a book that is used to transfer information from the mind of one human being through the written word, to the mind of another human being, thereby increasing the knowledge of the user of the textbook. A textbook is always written in a certain sequence. It assumes that the reader of the subject matter will know very little about it. It will start at a simple level and as the reader's knowledge increases, the material presented becomes a little more difficult.

The Big Book is a textbook written in a standard textbook format. It assumes that we know nothing about the disease of alcoholism. It starts by describing what the problem is, then describes the solution, and finally gives us a program of action so we can find the solution.

We believe that "The Doctor's Opinion" and the first four chapters in *The Big Book* prepare us for Chapter Five. If we go through *The Big Book* in this way, we will be able to see how each chapter dovetails into the next chapter, building information on information.

The other idea is that alcoholics haven't changed since 1939. Alcohol hasn't changed either. Therefore, we haven't found it necessary to change the program of recovery.

Workshop leader reads this page aloud – Attendees see page 5 *Big Book* Goals

Let's take a look at the Table of Contents from the book ***Alcoholics Anonymous*,** affectionately referred to as **"*The Big Book*"**. *The Big Book* is structured and laid out in a very particular manner. When we read the *"Doctor's Opinion"* and *"Chapter 1 – Bill's Story"* we are looking at the **problem**. More is revealed further on in *The Big Book*, most of the information about the <u>problem</u> is found here in these two chapters. If we can truly see the <u>problem</u>, then we will be able to see there are two parts: 1) the physical allergy, and 2) the obsession of the mind. We will be able to understand the <u>powerless condition of mind</u> and body and concede that we truly are powerless. This is **Step One**. Step One says we are **powerless**... if we are powerless then obviously the <u>solution</u> lies within **power.**

As we continue to study *The Big Book* we will learn there is nothing we can do about the physical allergy of the body; our only hope of recovery is through the mind.

"Chapter 2 – There Is a Solution", "Chapter 3 – More About Alcoholism" and, "Chapter 4 – We Agnostics" gives us this Information. from these chapters we learn that we might be able to come to believe that there is a Power greater than we are which can restore us to sanity. This is **Step Two**.

CONTENTS

Chapter	Page
PREFACE	xi
FOREWORD TO FIRST EDITION	xiii
FOREWORD TO SECOND EDITION	xv
FOREWORD TO THIRD EDITION	xxii
FOREWORD TO FOURTH EDITION	xxiii
THE DOCTOR'S OPINION	xxv
1 BILL'S STORY	1
2 THERE IS A SOLUTION	17
3 MORE ABOUT ALCOHOLISM	30
4 WE AGNOSTICS	44
5 HOW IT WORKS	58
6 INTO ACTION	72
7 WORKING WITH OTHERS	89
8 TO WIVES	104
9 THE FAMILY AFTERWARD	122
10 TO EMPLOYERS	136
11 A VISION FOR YOU	151

PERSONAL STORIES

PART I
Pioneers of A.A.

DOCTOR BOB'S NIGHTMARE ... 171
A co-founder of Alcoholics Anonymous. The birth of our Society dates from his first day of permanent sobriety, June 10, 1935.

So, if the problem is that we are powerless and the solution is a Power greater than ourselves, then the only other thing we need to know is, how do you find this Power?

> There is a specific order which the process goes; we must follow this order or we will not get the results others have.

Again, *The Big Book* gives us what we need...**a Practical Program of Action** which is laid out in "Chapter 5 – How It Works", "Chapter 6 – Into Action", and "Chapter 7 – Working with Others". These three chapters contain the remaining suggested steps; **Steps Three through Twelve** which **are the Practical Program of Action**.

If we **apply** this **Practical Program of Action** (Steps Three through Twelve), **in our lives**, then **we will find the Power which will overcome our powerless condition.**

It's just that simple!

The Big Book is written in a specific sequence to convey certain ideas in a precise order so that we may recover from alcoholism which makes *Alcoholics Anonymous* an especially fascinating book!

Goal One: Problem

Doctor's Opinion Chapter 1: **Bill's Story**	STEP 1 **POWERLESS**

Goal Two: Solution

Chapter 2: **There is a Solution** Chapter 3: **More About Alcoholism** Chapter 4: **We Agnostics**	STEP 2 **POWER**

Goal Three: Action Necessary for Recovery

Chapter 5: **How It Works** Chapter 6: **Into Action** Chapter 7: **Working With Others**	STEPS 3, 4, 5, 6, 7, 8, 9, 10, 11, 12 **HOW TO FIND** **THE POWER**

The Lack of Power is Our Dilemma, There is one Who has all Power, that One is God, … …may you find Him now.

FORWARD TO FIRST EDITION HIGHLIGHTS

READ AFTER: Page xiii, paragraph 1

The Big Book, "Forward to the First Edition" suggests two pertinent ideas:

1. This book was written by Bill W. and edited by forty sober people. When first published, there were more than 100 men and women who had recovered with the information as set forth in this book. They recovered from the same problems that we as alcoholics have today.

2. To show other alcoholics precisely how we have recovered is the main purpose of this book. Our book does not deal with membership or fellowship. It deals with **recovery only**. If we choose to do what the first 100 people did to recover, then we should expect the same results, which is recovery from the disease of alcoholism.

FORWARD TO THE SECOND EDITION
DR. SILKWORTH'S

DIAGNOSIS READ AT: Page xvi, 9 lines from the top
From this doctor, the broker had learned the grave nature of alcoholism.
In 1933, Dr. Silkworth treated Bill W. and explained what he believed to be the disease of alcoholism. He believed:
1. It was **NOT Lack of Will Power.**
2. It was **NOT Lack of Moral Character.**
3. It was **NOT Sin.**

Dr. Silkworth said: "Bill, I believe **alcoholism is an actual disease** and a peculiar disease."
1. It is a disease of the **body** as well as
2. A disease of the **mind**.

The doctor said, "Bill, when people like you drink, they react entirely different than normal people. Normal people take a drink and they get a slightly warm, comfortable, relaxing feeling. They may have one or two drinks and that's all they want to drink. But people like you drink a drink and you get a **physical feeling** in your body that produces a **physical craving** that **demands more** of the same. When you start, instead of one or two, you end up with three, four, six, eight, ten, until you get **drunk, sick, and in trouble.** This is **abnormal** and it only happens to **one out of ten people.** Therefore Bill, I'll say that **physically** you have become **allergic** to alcohol and react abnormally to it."

"Also, you have developed an **obsession of the mind**. Normal people do not care if they drink or not. They can drink today, tomorrow, or a month from now and it is not a big deal to them. But, people like you, Bill, have developed an **obsession of the mind** to drink. That **obsession** is so strong that it will make you believe something that isn't true."

"From time to time, you have been told that you cannot drink, and from time to time, you've known you cannot drink. From time to time you've even sworn off drinking. But the **obsession of the mind** is an idea that says you can now drink. This time it will be different. This time you will only take one drink. That **obsession** is so strong that it makes you believe you can drink and just before you drink you know it's going to be OK. It will always lead you back to taking a drink, then the drink will trigger the allergy, and then you will be unable to stop drinking. **People like you have become hopeless."** After this conversation, Bill left a hospital and stayed sober for a while. But his **obsession of the mind** told him he could drink, and he did. One year later, he was put back into that hospital under Dr. Silkworth's care again and this time the doctor **pronounced him incurable.** He left in the summer of 1934, knowing he could not drink, and **fear kept him sober for a while.** On Armistice Day, 1934, his mind told him he could drink. He took a drink and triggered the allergy and couldn't stop.

EBBY THATCHER'S OPINION

Ebby, who had been in the Oxford Group, came to visit Bill and gave Bill two additional pieces of information. Dr. Silkworth had explained the **problem**. Ebby T. said:

"Bill, the **solution** to that problem is **finding a power greater than human power**. People like us have become absolutely **powerless** over alcohol. If we are to recover, we have to find a **Power greater than alcohol**, greater than we are and greater than human power. If human power would have worked, we would have recovered a long time ago. Willpower would have done it, doctors would have done it, and ministers would have done it. But none of them have helped us. If we can **find the power greater than human power, then we can recover!** The Oxford Group has given me a **practical program of action** and they guarantee that if I **apply it in my life**, I would find that power and I wouldn't have to drink anymore. Look at me; I've been sober for two months."

Bill knew Ebby and how he drank. He knew a miracle had happened in Ebby's life. From these three pieces of information, he **recovered** from his disease!

1. He learned the **PROBLEM** from Dr. Silkworth.
2. He learned the **SOLUTION** from Ebby T. and the Oxford Group.
3. He received the **PRACTICAL PROGRAM OF ACTION.**

Bill applied the action in his life and found that Power and never had a drink again!

Bill W. got sober December 12, 1934 and passed away sober in January 1971, with thirty-five years of sobriety.

Closing: It is now time to end our meeting for this evening. After a moment of silence for the alcoholic who still suffers, please join me in reading "A Vision for You", found on page 164 of *The Big Book of Alcoholics Anonymous*.

*Close the Meetings with the Lord's Prayer and/or the long form of the serenity prayer.

THE BIG BOOK WORKSHOP HOMEWORK ASSIGNMENT

***NOTE: It is suggested that the homework be done soon after the workshop meeting and then reviewed with your sponsor before the next workshop meeting.**

1) Read **"Step One"** in the *Twelve and Twelve* book – *HIGHLIGHT ANYTHING YOU CAN RELATE TO!*

2) Read **"The Doctor's Opinion"** in *The Big Book* (1st Time) -- *USE HIGHLIGHTER!* (Just read and highlight the 1st time through the doctor's opinion.)

3) Read **"The Doctor's Opinion"** in *The Big Book* (2nd Time). Answer the work assignment questions below. Begin to write **"How You Were Powerless over Alcohol".** It is equally important to write any reservations you may have about the fact you are powerless over alcohol.

WORK ASSIGNMENT QUESTIONS
"The Doctor's Opinion"

Page xxv, paragraph 1

1. Are you interested in the doctor's estimate or the physical part of your disease...to discover the fact that you are powerless over alcohol after the first drink you take?

2. Was the testimony which came from medical men who have had experience with our suffering and our recovery helpful to you? **(MUST)**

Page xxv, paragraph 3

1. Are you the type who is hopeless? *(You want to quit and cannot stay quit. You drink when you are already drunk. You drink when you do not want to drink.)*

Page xxv, paragraph 5

1. Are you the type where other methods failed completely? (Nothing you tried worked?)

Page xxvi, paragraph 1

1. Are you willing to believe *The Big Book* as a remedy for you and can you rely on what these people who wrote the book say about themselves?

Page xxvi, paragraph 2

1. Do you believe that your body is as abnormal as your mind after the first drink? **(MUST)**

2. Did any explanation you got from yourself, or others, as to why you couldn't control your drinking satisfy you?

3. Did any picture view, which left out the physical factor, feel incomplete?

Page xxvi, paragraph 3

1. Does the doctor's theory that you have an allergy to alcohol and/or drugs interest you? Does it make good sense? Does it explain many things that you could not otherwise account for?

Page xxvi, paragraph 4

1. Do you believe that some form of a "spiritual experience" is of urgent importance to you?

2. Do you believe that any human can apply the power of good that is needed to produce this "spiritual experience"?

Page xxvii, paragraph 6

1. Can you believe that a Power greater than yourself is what is necessary to pull you back from the gates of death and as being the only possible solution?

Page xxviii, paragraph 1

1. Do you believe when you put alcohol and/or drugs in your body that the reaction is like an allergy and there is a craving for more? Has this craving happened to you with alcohol or drugs?

2. Can you safely use alcohol in any form? Did you form the habit? Could you break it? Did you lose your self-confidence? Did you lose your reliance upon things human? Did major problems pile up on you and become difficult to solve?

Page xxviii, paragraph 2

1. Did frothy emotional appeal from others work on you? Do you believe the message which can interest and hold you must have **depth and weight?** (depth = 'great detail' & weight = 'proof that it works'). Do you believe the message must be more than emotional? More than intellectual?

2. Do you believe that in order to re-create your life, your ideals must be **grounded in a Power greater than yourself? (MUST)**

Page xxviii, paragraph 4

1. Did you drink for the **effect** produced by alcohol?
   Did this effect become so elusive that after a time, even though you knew it was injurious, you could not **differentiate the truth from the false?**

2. Did your life using alcohol seem to be the only normal one for you?

3. **Untreated**, are you restless, irritable and discontented? Do you believe that in recovery, you must experience the sense of ease and comfort you got from drinking, and if not, you will drink again? Do you believe there will be little hope for your recovery unless you experience an entire psychic change?

Page xxix, paragraph 1
1. Do you believe that to attain this psychic change, there will be effort necessary and you will have to meet a few requirements and follow a few simple rules?

Page xxix, paragraph 2
1. Can you stop on your own?
2. Do you need help? (2 **MUSTS**)

Page xxix, paragraph 3
1. Do you believe that something more than human power is needed to produce the essential psychic change or do you still believe that you have the Power to quit drinking on your own?

Page xxix, paragraph 4
1. Do you believe your alcoholism is entirely a problem of mental control?

Page xxx, paragraph 1
1. Has this craving, at times become more important than all else?

2. Were there times you were not drinking to escape, but to overcome a craving beyond your mental control?

3. Were their situations which arose out of this craving which caused you to make the supreme sacrifice (to drink again) rather than to continue to fight?

Page xxx, paragraph 5
1. Have you identified your allergy to alcohol as a craving for more alcohol when you start drinking?

2. Do you believe this allergy differentiates you and sets you apart as a distinct entity?

3. Do you believe the only relief to this physical allergy is entire abstinence?

4. Can you do that on your own?

"Omitting NOTHING, we get going, writing down everything that comes to mind, illuminating every twist of our characters so that we can see our own truth before us in black and white."

WEEK #1 Appendix – "THE DOCTOR'S OPINION"

[Optional Reading: Additional Information from "Wikipedia" and the "National Institute on Alcohol Abuse and Alcoholism"]

Metabolism is the body's process of converting ingested substances to other compounds. Metabolism results in some substances becoming more, and some less, toxic than those originally ingested. Metabolism involves a number of processes, one of which is referred to as oxidation.

Through oxidation, alcohol is detoxified and removed from the blood, preventing the alcohol from accumulating and destroying cells and organs. A tiny amount of alcohol escapes metabolism and is excreted unchanged in the breath and in urine. Until all the alcohol consumed has been metabolized, it is distributed throughout the body, affecting the brain and other tissues.

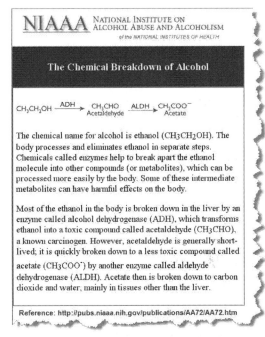

When alcohol is consumed, it passes from the stomach and intestines into the blood, a process referred to as absorption. Alcohol is then metabolized by enzymes, which are body chemicals that break down other chemicals. In the liver, an enzyme called alcohol dehydrogenase (ADH) controls the conversion of alcohol to acetaldehyde. Acetaldehyde is rapidly converted to acetate by other enzymes and is eventually metabolized to carbon dioxide and water.

Alcohol also is metabolized in the liver by the enzyme cytochrome P450IIE1 (CYP2E1), which may be increased after chronic drinking. Most of the alcohol consumed is metabolized in the liver, but the small quantity that remains un-metabolized permits alcohol concentration to be measured in breath and urine. The liver can metabolize only a certain amount of alcohol per hour, regardless of the amount that has been consumed. The rate of alcohol metabolism depends, in part, on the amount of metabolizing enzymes in the liver, which varies among individuals, especially in heavy drinkers and alcoholics.

WEEK #1 Appendix – "THE DOCTOR'S OPINION"

Drinking heavily puts people at risk for many adverse health consequences, including alcoholism, liver damage, and various cancers. But some people appear to be at greater risk than others for developing these problems. Why do some people drink more than others? And why do some people who drink develop problems, whereas others do not?

Research shows that alcohol use and alcohol-related problems are influenced by individual variations in alcohol metabolism, or the way in which alcohol is broken down and eliminated by the body. Alcohol metabolism is controlled by genetic factors, such as variations in the enzymes that break down alcohol; environmental factors, such as the amount of alcohol an individual consumes and his or her overall nutrition; a person's age; and for alcoholics how long their disease has progressed.

Differences in alcohol metabolism may put some people (especially alcoholics) at greater risk for alcohol problems, whereas others ("normies") may be at least somewhat protected from alcohol's harmful effects.

The Chemical Breakdown of Alcohol: Alcohol is metabolized by several processes or pathways. The most common of these pathways involves two enzymes—alcohol dehydrogenase (ADH) and aldehyde dehydrogenase (ALDH). These enzymes help break apart the alcohol molecule, making it possible to eliminate it from the body. First, ADH metabolizes alcohol to acetaldehyde, a highly toxic substance and known carcinogen (causes cancer). Then, in a second step, acetaldehyde is further metabolized down to another, less active byproduct called acetate (acetone), which then is broken down into water and carbon dioxide for easy elimination from the body.

Other enzymes: The enzymes cytochrome P450 2E1 (CYP2E1) and catalase also break down alcohol to acetaldehyde. However, CYP2E1 only is active after a person has consumed large amounts of alcohol, and catalase metabolizes only a small fraction of alcohol in the body [1] Small amounts of alcohol also are removed by interacting with fatty acids to form compounds called fatty acid ethyl esters (FAEEs). These compounds have been shown to contribute to damage to the liver and pancreas.

Acetaldehyde: a toxic byproduct — Although acetaldehyde is short lived, usually existing in the body only for a brief time before it is further broken down into acetate, it has the potential to cause significant damage. This is particularly evident in the liver, where the bulk of alcohol metabolism takes place. Some alcohol metabolism also occurs in other tissues, including the pancreas and the brain, causing damage to cells and tissues. Additionally, small amounts of alcohol are metabolized to acetaldehyde in the stomach and intestines, exposing these tissues to acetaldehyde causes damaging effects.

In addition, **alcohol directly contributes to malnutrition** since a pint of 86-proof alcohol (not an unusual daily intake for an alcoholic) represents about half of the daily energy requirement. However, ethanol does not have any minerals, vitamins, carbohydrates, fats or protein associated with it. Alcohol causes inflammation of the stomach, pancreas, and intestines which impairs the digestion of food and absorption into blood. Moreover, the acetaldehyde (the oxidation product) can interfere with the activation of vitamin.

WEEK TWO – "THE DOCTOR'S OPINION

READ AFTER: Page xxvi, paragraph 3

ALLERGY: We as laymen have a basic understanding and definition for the word "**allergy**". If you have an allergy to something, it would always be indicated or manifested by some physical reaction. For instance, say you are allergic to strawberries and you eat them. You break out in a rash. If you are allergic to penicillin and you take a shot, you will break out in welts all over your body. If you are allergic to milk or dairy products and you drink or eat them, then you get a form of dysentery. These are physical manifestations of an allergy.

When I came to AA they told me I had an allergy to alcohol and I could never drink it safely again. How can I have an allergy to alcohol? I drank a quart of it a day! How can you drink that much of something if you are allergic to it? Besides that, it never made me break out in a rash. It doesn't put welts on my body. I didn't understand and asked them to explain it to me. They said, "You don't need to understand. All you need to know is that you are allergic and you can't drink." Today I know why they told me that; because they didn't understand it either.

Being an inquisitive alcoholic, I needed to know. So, I went to a source which never fails me; *Webster's Dictionary*. I looked it up and it states: **"An allergy is an abnormal reaction to any food, beverage, or substance of any kind." An <u>ABNORMAL REACTION</u>!**

I tried to see where I was abnormal when it came to alcohol. To my amazement, I didn't know what was **normal or abnormal.** For me to find out, I had to go to those normal people; the nine out of ten people considered to be "normal, socially moderate, temperate drinkers"…Those who drink alcohol and do not get in trouble with it.

I asked if they would describe to me what happens when they take a drink. They said they get a warm comfortable relaxing feeling after one or two drinks… and they don't want any more for the rest of the night. I don't feel that way when I drink. I don't understand a warm, comfortable, relaxing feeling. I get a "get-up-and-go-somewhere-and-do-something" feeling. I think it is one of the reasons I love to drink. It makes me feel different than it does for a normal social drinker. They said something else that absolutely amazed me. When they have two or three drinks, they get slightly tipsy, out of control, and the beginnings of a nauseous feeling. They don't like that tipsy, nauseous feeling, so they only want one or two drinks. Today I realize that is a normal reaction to alcohol.

ALCOHOL IS A TOXIC DRUG. It is a destroyer of human tissue. Normally the **mind** and the **body**, when you put something in it that is going to destroy it, will sense what's there and react by wanting to "throw it up" and "get it out". <u>The normal reaction to alcohol is a nauseous feeling in the body</u>. My physical reaction, instead of nausea, is **a craving for more of the same**. That is a **physical craving** and it is so strong that it overcomes the ability of my mind to stop me after I start. I react abnormally. The difference between normal and abnormal is that the majority of people, (nine out of ten), don't get the **physical craving**.

We **react abnormally** in two ways: 1) **It makes us feel differently** than normal people, and 2) It produces the **phenomenon of craving**. That **physical craving** ensures we will continue until **we get drunk every time we take a drink**.

CONTINUE READING: Page xxviii, paragraph 1

Chronic: "Reacting over and over again"
Phenomenon: "Something we do not understand".
Craving: Usually you are dealing with the mind, **but in the context of *The Big Book*, you are dealing with the body**. Craving is what happens after we put one or two drinks in our body. It produces a **physical craving** for more of the same.

CONTINUE READING: Page xxx, paragraphs 1 through 5

During the era in which this book was written medical science had not yet uncovered the chemical breakdown that occurs in the body. That is why Dr. Silkworth called it a **phenomenon of craving**. Today, science has discovered the exact reaction that takes place when we ingest alcohol.

LEADER EXPLAINS DISEASE CONCEPT OF ALCOHOLISM: By reading pages 12–13 while the group looks at diagram on page 16.

NORMAL PERSON: For the normal social drinker, (this is approximately 8 people out of 10, today) you have a line on the drawing that represents these people who can drink safely and are at ease with alcohol. Alcohol is no problem for them. They take a drink and put it in their system and the mind and the body recognizes what it is. The enzyme production begins and the enzymes start to attack the alcohol and begin to metabolize or break it down.

The enzymes break it down to the first state, a chemical called **acetaldehyde**. Later, after a time, it is broken down to a chemical called **diacidic acid** and finally over more time to **acetone**. **Acetone** is rapidly broken down to a **simple carbohydrate** which is made up of **water**, **sugar,** and **carbon dioxide**. In normal people, the breakdown of **acetone** to **simple carbohydrates** occurs quickly.

The body can use the sugar. Sugar has calories and it has energy. Interestingly enough they are empty calories. They are not any of the things necessary for life, such as amino acids, vitamins, etc., but it is a form of energy the body can use. The body burns up the sugar and stores the excess as fat, the water is dissipated through the urinary and intestinal tracks, and the carbon dioxide is expelled through the lungs. For the normal person, alcohol is broken down (metabolized) at a rate of about 1 oz. per hour.

ABNORMAL PERSON: These are the 1-2 out of 10 who cannot drink safely or who have a **DIS-EASE** with alcohol. By the way, that's all the word **disease** means; something that separates you from a sense of ease, something that separates you from the normal thing that happens to most people. When we alcoholics put a drink in our bodies, the same thing starts to take place for all of us. The mind and body recognize what it is. The enzyme production starts and attacks the alcohol and breaks it down first to **acetaldehyde**... then to **diacidic acid**, and finally over more time to **acetone**. It seems that in the body of the alcoholic, the enzymes necessary to break it down from **acetone** to the **simple carbohydrates,** <u>are not there in the same qualities and quantities as in the body of the non-alcoholic.</u>

Therefore, the rate acetone is broken down to simple carbohydrates is a much slower operation which keeps the level of acetone up in our bodies for a longer period of time. **It is the acetone in our bodies that creates the <u>physical craving</u>.** For the alcoholic, alcohol is broken down (metabolized) at a significantly slower rate of ¾ oz. per hour, or ½ oz. per hour or even 1/5 oz. per hour depending on the enzyme production which is directly related to the stage of alcoholism we are in.

The medical profession today has proven beyond any shadow of a doubt that **acetone ingested into the human system**, that remains there for any appreciable period of time, **will produce an actual <u>physical craving</u>** for more of the same. As the **<u>craving</u>** is produced, the body then begins to say to the mind, "Let me have more of that stuff you just put in there." So, instead of having the one drink we intended to have, the body says, "Give me the second drink... the third drink... the fourth drink... the sixth drink." Now, **the first drink was caused by the mind**... **but those after, were caused by the body**.

We think that one of the most interesting things recently discovered is this: the medical profession has proven that **alcohol ingested into the human system** over a period of time **is an actual destroyer of human tissue**. As we drink more and more, we destroy more and more human tissue in all parts of the body. But it seems as though the first two organs of the body that are attacked, in most cases, happens to be the liver and pancreas. They have also proven today, that **the enzymes necessary to metabolize alcohol come from the liver and the pancreas**. As we drink we begin to damage the organs of the body, the enzyme production becomes less and less and less and the **phenomenon of craving becomes harder and harder and harder.**

So you see we not only have a **disease**, we have a ***progressive*** disease, guaranteed to get worse as time goes by because we are destroying the organs of the body that are necessary to metabolize alcohol. We also know that as we grow older, everything that the body produces begins to shut down. So, as we get older, **the enzyme production becomes less due to the age factor**. Therefore our **disease is a progressive disease whether we drink or not**. The fact that we are allergic to alcohol is academic, if we don't take the first drink. We need to understand that **<u>the main problem and the solution are going to be within the mind</u>**, even though the body is going to get worse with age. I think sometimes in A.A., we don't explain this to the new people about the physical factor of their disease.

Leader reviews and describes "Alcohol's Effects on the Brain and Behavior"

READ: Page xxviii, paragraph 4 to "Differentiate the true from the false".

We must understand, if we are going to deal with alcoholics, that **practicing alcoholics cannot differentiate the true from the false**. To most of them, what they are doing seems absolutely normal. To the alcoholic mind, it is all the normal people who are abnormal. We surround ourselves with people of our own kind, diluting our minds into thinking that we are different. As far as the practicing alcoholic is concerned, it is the normal drinkers who are abnormal.

We can see that drinking is injurious and gets us into trouble, but we really cannot differentiate the true from the false, because to us, we are doing what we consider normal.

An **obsession of the mind** is an idea so powerful that it overcomes all other ideas to the contrary. It's so strong that it **will make you believe something that isn't true**. When we drank we had a couple of drinks and it made us feel better. So our minds put those two thoughts together. Feel bad… take a drink and feel better. That is a **mental** addiction not a **physical** one. The mind says it's OK to take a drink and the mind really believes it is OK. The mind says it will be different this time… the mind believes it. That is **"BELIEVING A LIE"**.

Any alcoholic who believes he can drink successfully believes a lie.

The **obsession of the mind** causes us to believe a lie and take the first couple of drinks. As soon as we put the first drink in our bodies, the **allergy of the body** takes over triggering the **phenomenon of craving** and we cannot stop. The one thing that you and I can do for the practicing alcoholic is to help them see the **allergy of the body** and the **obsession of the mind** that they are experiencing. I didn't know about these two problems when I was drinking.

READ: Page xxviii, paragraph 4 at "To them" to end of 1st paragraph, page xxix

SUMMARY

IF YOU CAN'T DRINK BECAUSE OF THE

ALLERGY OF THE BODY .....AND

IF YOU CAN'T QUIT BECAUSE OF THE

OBSESSION OF THE MIND

THEN:

YOU ARE POWERLESS OVER ALCOHOL

READ:

Page 355, paragraph 2

"Study *The Big Book*, don't just read it."

"The explanation that alcoholism was a disease of a two-fold nature, an allergy of the body and an obsession of the mind, cleared up a number of puzzling questions for me. The allergy we could do nothing about. Somehow our bodies had reached the point where we could no longer absorb alcohol in our systems. The why is not important; the fact is that one drink will set up a reaction in our system that requires more, that one drink is too much and a hundred drinks are not enough.

The obsession of the mind is a little harder too understand and yet everyone has obsessions of various kinds. The alcoholic has them to an exaggerated degree. Over a period of time he has built up self-pity and resentments toward anyone or anything that interferes with his drinking. Dishonest thinking, prejudice, ego, antagonism towards anyone and everyone who dares cross him, vanity, and a critical attitude are character defects that gradually creep in and become a part of his life.

Living with fear and tension inevitably results in wanting to ease that tension, which alcohol seems to do temporarily."

The keys character traits of the untreated alcoholic are: Irritability, Restlessness and Discontentment. When in the state, we seek ease and comfort from it. Sometimes in sex, music, dancing, spending money, eating, gambling, etc. Eventually none of these will work well enough to subdue the dis-ease within and drinking will be the end result, we've lost the power of choice or control in the matter.

21

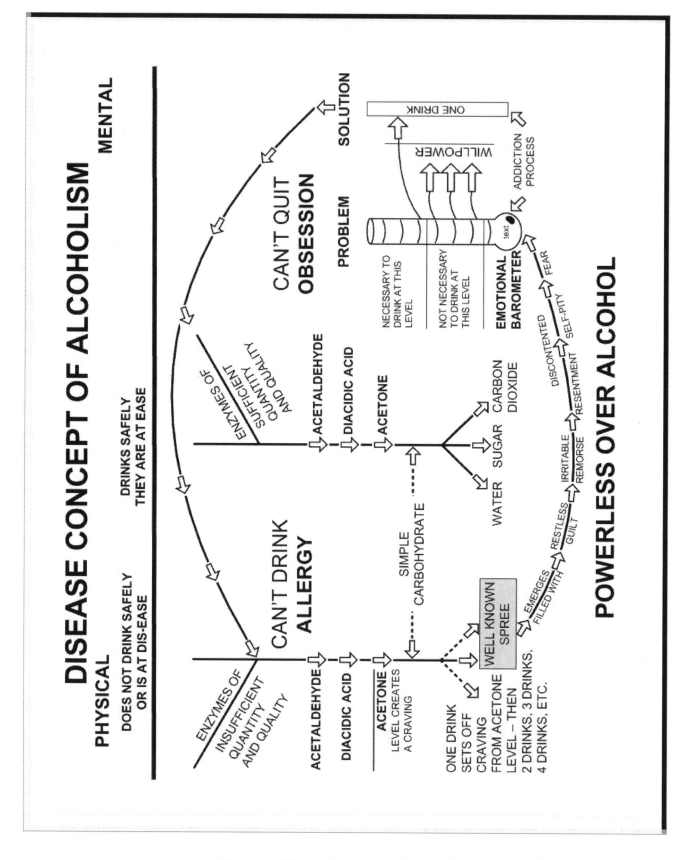

Figure 1 – Disease Concept of Alcoholism

Alcohol's Effects on Brain and Behavior

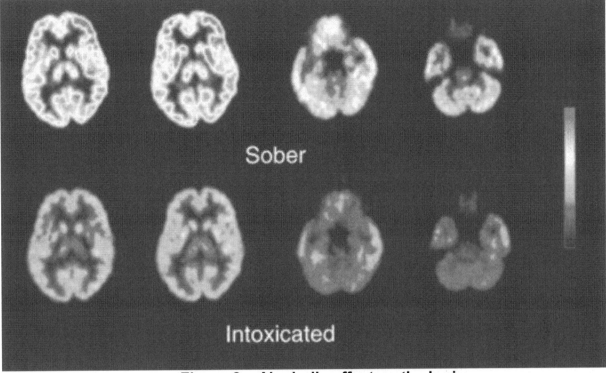

Figure 2 – Alcohol's effect on the brain

BRAIN AREA	EFFECTED FUNCTIONS	NORMAL: NON-ALCOHOLIC	ABNORMAL: ALCOHOLIC
As alcohol takes effect, it stimulates and suppresses different areas of the brain	This leads to: reduction in anxiety; euphoria; aggression and memory loss.	No Obsession	Obsessive
FIRST STAGE: DECREASED ACTIVITY			
Cerebellum	Controls basic motor function Controls balance Controls visual cortex (rear-brain)	OK, as long as rate of consumption is 1 drink/hr.	Once started, little or no control over the amount or rate of consumption. Obsession turns to craving.
SECOND STAGE: DECREASED ACTIVITY			
Midbrain (limbic)	Generates feelings of: Stimulation Pleasure Euphoria	Had enough	I like this feeling! (Craving takes over and is in control)
THIRD STAGE: DECREASED ACTIVITY			
Basal Ganglia	Disrupts: Normal Motor Skills Coordination Thinking	No Thanks… I'm feeling it.	I want MORE!
FORTH STAGE: DECREASED ACTIVITY			
Left Brain (Controls Language Processing) **Frontal Cortex** (Controls motor skills, and reasoning.)	Words become slurred. Vision is distorted.	Rarely reaches this stage. Remembers vomiting and hangovers.	Cannot stop drinking.

Table 1 : Effects on Areas of the Brain – Non-Alcoholic vs. Alcoholic

BIG BOOK WORKSHOP HOMEWORK ASSIGNMENT

***NOTE: It is suggested that the homework be done soon after the workshop meeting and then reviewed with your sponsor before the next workshop meeting.**

3. Read **Step One** in the *Twelve and Twelve* book – USE HIGHLIGHTER!!!
4. Read Chapter One, **"BILL'S STORY"** in *The Big Book* (1st Time) -- USE HIGHLIGHTER!!!
(Just read and highlight the 1st time through the Bill's Story.)
5. Read Chapter 1 **"BILL'S STORY"** in *The Big Book* (2nd Time). Be prepared to discuss this matter as it applies to your life in the second week. Continue to write how you are powerless over alcohol and how your ideas have changed as a result of reading "The Doctor's Opinion". Answer the work assignment questions below as outlined for "Bill's Story" and be prepared to discuss them.

WORK ASSIGNMENT QUESTIONS
"BILL'S STORY"

Page 1

4. Did alcohol work for you?

5. Did alcohol affect the way you thought and felt?

Page 3

3. Did alcohol take an important and exhilarating part of your life?

4. Did your drinking later assume more serious proportions?

Page 5

4. Did you ever ask, "Was I crazy?"

5. Did alcohol cease to be a luxury and become a necessity?

6. Did things gradually get worse?

7. Do you still think you control it? (Alcohol? The situation? Your life?)

Page 6

3. Did you ever feel remorse, horror and/or hopelessness the next morning after drinking?

4. Did you your mind ever race uncontrollably?

5. Did you ever seek oblivion?

WORK ASSIGNMENT QUESTIONS (Continued)
"BILL'S STORY"

Page 7

1. Can self-knowledge fix you?

Page 8

4. Did you ever feel lonely?

5. Did you ever feel fear?

6. Can fear keep you sober?

7. Did alcohol overwhelm you?

8. Was alcohol your master?

Page 10

1. What was your reaction to religion, the church, and God?

Page 12

NOTE: Note what happened to Bill's prejudice against "their God" when he began to apply <u>his own conception of God</u>.

4) Did you know that "**nothing more was required of me to make my beginning...**" than willingness or a willingness to believe?

Page 13

3. Can you admit for the first time, that of yourself you are nothing and without God you are lost?

4. Does Bill, essentially take the First through the Eleventh Step at this time?

EXERCISE:

Have you done the exercise with the first eight pages?

In so doing, in these areas as you relate to them, are you as hopeless as Bill?

If so, is there hope for you on page 17, paragraph 1?

Underline every sentence or phrase in Bill's story that you can identify with.

Identify with how he thought, how he drank and how he felt. You didn't do what he did, so don't compare your life to his life. Instead, look for the drama, chaos and calamity, look for the progression, look the thinking and the feelings that would always lead you back into your drinking.

Number them in the book. Then number your notebook and write a sentence or two on the 'why and how' you are identifying with it. Start becoming familiarized on these terms with your story and start learning what makes you alcoholic.

This is your homework. You should commit two hours to it. The more continuous the two hours are, the stronger your experience with the work will be. If you are riddled with distractions, your experience will not be as strong. Get focused, turn off all electronic devices, and get to it.

Write three instances where you experienced the phenomenon of craving of Alcohol. Where you started to drink and were unable to stop despite everything; you had appointments to keep, etc.

1.

2.

3.

In your notebook write your drunk-a-log. Write your own version of Bill's story for yourself. From your first drink, the progression of your drinking career, to your bottom. Include mostly only those circumstances as they pertain to your drinking. i.e.; being homeless is a byproduct of drinking, so it would be included. Your baseball fantasy is not, except in where alcohol took that dream away. Keep it short and to the point, be careful not to over emphasize or belabor the point of the matter, which is to see for the first time the progressive nature of the illness.

WEEK THREE: CHAPTER ONE – BILL'S STORY

LEADER READS: The main purpose of reading BILL'S STORY is for **identification**. But, being alcoholics, we tend to look for the differences. The exercise in your assignment sheet was to mark what you could relate to as far as *drinking, thinking and feeling.*

READ: Page 1, paragraph 1   page 5, paragraph 3

Bill put together a business deal on the condition that he would not drink. He would have shared generously in the profits. But, that evening in a hotel room, one of the men passed a bottle of Applejack around. It went by Bill the first time and he said, "No thank you, I'm not drinking". The next time it came by, his mind told him that one little drink of Applejack wouldn't hurt. He took a drink and triggered the allergy and he couldn't stop, blowing the whole business deal. The importance in that statement is in the next paragraph: ***For the first time he could see what alcohol was doing to him. He could differentiate the true from the false.***

They call us alcoholics, "weak willed people". We are not weak willed people; the problem is we are "strong willed people". Our will is so strong we darned near killed ourselves drinking alcohol! We almost killed ourselves trying to find a way to drink and not get drunk. Weak willed people don't become alcoholic...the third time they vomit, they quit drinking. We "alkies", literally, kill ourselves trying to find a way to drink.

READ: Page 5, paragraph 4   page 9, paragraph 1

The friend that came to see Bill Wilson was Ebby Thatcher. Ebby and Bill were old school friends, they drank together on many occasions. Bill had heard that Ebby had gotten into a lot of trouble. Ebby came from a great family, but, his family had a lot of trouble with him. His father had passed away and had given Ebby his summer home. Ebby was supposed to be fixing it up. Ebby's family always kept Ebby "somewhere else". You know how a family will "always help" you if you "stay over there". They were trying to get rid of Ebby by keeping him up there in the little summer house.

Ebby was supposed to be painting it and fixing it up to live in. One time drunk, he set it on fire! Another time, again drunk, he was painting it and the pigeons crapped all over it, so he got his shotgun out and shot the pigeons off the roof, putting holes in the side of the house. Yet another time drunk, one day, he ran a car into a lady's house! Now, they had him up before the judge and they were going to put him into the "nut house". In those days, they didn't have treatment centers, so they put you in the state hospital. Bill hadn't heard about this. So, this is what Bill meant by ***"...recapturing the spirit of the other days".***

READ: Page 9, paragraph 2   page 9, paragraph 5

What Ebby told Bill was how Rowland Hazard and another guy appeared in court persuading the judge to suspend his commitment and to turn Ebby loose into their custody. They said, "We believe that we have found a way that Ebby can live without drinking." The judges then were not like they are today, they really didn't want to put us in nut houses and prisons back then…if they could avoid it…they did what they could. So, the judge turned Ebby loose into Rowland's care.

Rowland took Ebby home for a couple of weeks and then got him into the Oxford Groups. Next, he took him down to New York City, and there, Ebby went to work for Sam Shoemaker in the Bowery Mission. Ebby was attending the Oxford Group meetings and he heard about his friend Bill, so he went to see him. This, I believe, was the first Twelve-Step call on an alcoholic.

Ebby told Bill how these two guys had appeared in front of the judge, and how they took him to the Oxford Group meetings. There he learned that the **Solution to our problem** is a **Power greater than human power** and a vital **spiritual experience**.

For the first time, Bill understood the **problem** (as described by Dr. Silkworth) and now he could see the **solution** to the problem. Ebby brought to Bill, what later turned out to be, *Step Two*. Then he laid out for him a **practical program of action**. He said, "Bill, **if you will follow this program of action, you will find that Power greater than you and you won't have to drink**. That's what I've been doing and I've been sober for two months!"

Ebby laid out for Bill the **practical program of action**, which later turned out to be *Steps Three through Twelve*. Now we see that Bill has access to the first three Steps. We saw him take *Step One*, when **he admitted he was powerless**. There was no "Step One", when he admitted he was powerless. There was not a Step One written in those days, but we could see that he made that admission.
So, for the first time, Bill knew all three things…

6. **The PROBLEM** *step 1*
7. **The SOLUTION** *step 2*
8. **The PRACTICAL PROGRAM OF ACTION** *steps 3 -12*

READ: Page 9, paragraph 6   page 12, paragraph 4

Now we're going to find as we go through *The Big Book* that Bill, like so many writers, builds in your mind by the painting of pictures with the use of words. He's going to be talking all the way through the book about **a wonderful effective spiritual structure**.
Later on, he's going to tell us what that structure is, and says, **"…we are going to pass through it to freedom."** That last statement is his first reference to this.
He said, **"Upon a <u>foundation</u> of complete <u>willingness</u>, I might build what I saw in my friend"**. The *foundation of our recovery is based on <u>willingness</u>* and that really

comes through in Step One, where **we admit we are powerless over alcohol**. If we can make that admission 100%, then we can **begin to <u>believe</u> in the Power greater than ourselves**.

Until we can make the admission that alcohol is the power, it is, and always will be, the power greater than ourselves. Our real growth and spirituality will start with **Step One** and **<u>willingness</u>**, which is the **<u>foundation</u>**. Then later on, with **Step Two**, we are going to see where **<u>believing</u>** becomes the **<u>cornerstone</u>** of the **spiritual structure**.

Bill has now taken **Step One** and **Step Two**. No Steps were written in those days. But, we can see Bill doing those two things; the **admission of powerlessness** and the **coming to believe**.

READ: Page 12, paragraph 5   page 16, end of chapter

The Big Book was originated in textbook form as a Twelve-Step call to reach people that were not in Akron or New York so that anyone who picked up a copy of it could read and identify with the book. BILL'S STORY fits in exactly where it should in the standard textbook theory.

I can almost see Bill as he finishes up this chapter saying "I have described the vital **spiritual experience** and it's going to seem, to many of them, like some great happening way out there in the sky. It probably sounds a lot like religion and theology. Maybe I'd better get down to brass tacks and tell them exactly what took place in my life".

In the next chapter, "There is a Solution", Bill tells us exactly how this happened. Remember, in the beginning there was Bill and Ebby... that was the fellowship. Ebby brought to Bill the answer; the **Solution** to our **problem**.

Bill applied the Solution and recovered through a vital spiritual experience.
So, two things had to take place here:

   6. first, **the fellowship with Ebby**, then,
   7. the vital spiritual experience

As a result of this course of action, Bill got sober.

The next chapter explains exactly what these two things are all about.

BIG BOOK WORKSHOP HOMEWORK ASSIGNMENT

***NOTE: It is suggested that the homework be done soon after this workshop meeting and then reviewed with your sponsor before the next workshop meeting.**

5. Read **"STEP TWO"** in *The Twelve and Twelve* book – USE HIGHLIGHTER!!!
6. Read Chapter 2 **"THERE IS A SOLUTION"** in *The Big Book* (1st Time) -- USE HIGHLIGHTER!! (Just read and highlight the 1st time you read through the chapter.)
7. Read Chapter 2 **"THERE IS A SOLUTION"** in *The Big Book* (2nd Time). Answer the "Work Assignment Questions" below as you read the chapter the 2nd time.
8. Be prepared to discuss how you reacted to this chapter next week. Start writing what you can truly "manage" in your life. Write down your thoughts in your notebook as thoughts occur to you about whether you can or cannot manage life, and in particular, your life.

WORK ASSIGNMENT QUESTIONS
"THERE IS A SOLUTION"

Page 17

1. Is the fellowship, by itself, enough for you?

2. Do you, on your own and without help, have a way out?

Page 18

8. Have you come to believe that you suffer from an illness?

9. Did it engulf all whose lives touched you?

10. Did you see how you can reach another alcoholic?

Page 19

6. Is the elimination of your drinking enough or only a beginning?

7. If you go on just not drinking, will the problem(s) be taken care of?

Page 20

9. Does your life depend upon your constant thought of others and how you may help meet their needs?

10. Are you curious to discover how and why these people have recovered from a seemingly hopeless state of mind and body?

11. *The Big Book* answers the questions "What do I have to do?" Have you asked yourself that question? What is your answer?

12. When it comes to alcohol, can you "take it" or "leave it" alone?

WORK ASSIGNMENT QUESTIONS (Continued)
"THERE IS A SOLUTION"

Page 21

5) Did you have "the habit" bad enough that it gradually impaired you physically and mentally?

6) If given a good reason, can you give up alcohol entirely?

7) From your examination of yourself in the past weeks and your reading of *The Big Book*, are you a "real alcoholic"? *refer back to p. 21 & 34*
   If NOT, why not?
   If NOT, be prepared to discuss this during the workshop.

8) Did you at some stage of your drinking, lose control over the amount you drank once you started to drink?

9) Did you have control? Did you do absurd things? Were you a "Jekyll & Hyde"?

Note: The questions and observations on page 21 of *The Big Book* may help you in answering the question you have been writing about, having to do with your powerlessness over alcohol.

Page 22

5. Can you control the amount of alcohol you drink once you start drinking?

6. Does your experience abundantly confirm that once you put any alcohol into your body, something happens which makes it virtually impossible for you to stop?

7. Have you discovered your own truth? What are you? What separates you from alcohol?

Note: This section summarizes our common problem, which we have covered so far as to the admission of our powerlessness over alcohol (physically) after we take the first drink.

Page 23

2. Are these observations important to know and yet pointless if you never take the first drink?

3. Did this malady of the mind have a real hold on you, and were you baffled?

4. Have you suffered from the obsession that somehow, someday, you will beat the game?

WORK ASSIGNMENT QUESTIONS (Continued)
"THERE IS A SOLUTION"

2. Have you lost control? Do you believe you can assert your power of will to stay stopped?

Page 24

2. At a certain point in your drinking, did you pass into a state where the most powerful desire to stop drinking was of no avail?

3. Is it a fact that you have lost the power of choice when it comes to drinking?

4. Has your so-called "willpower" become practically nonexistent? Were you unable, at certain times, to bring into your consciousness with sufficient force, the memory of the suffering and humiliation of even a week or a month ago?

5. Are you without defense against the first drink?

6. When thoughts of the consequences of your drinking occurred, was "thinking it through" enough for you?

7. Have you said to yourself, "It won't hurt me this time"? Were there times you didn't think at all before taking that first drink?

8. Has this sort of thinking been fully established in you? Have you placed yourself beyond human aid?

Page 25

4. Do you believe the process requires self-searching, leveling of pride, and confession of shortcomings, for a successful consummation?

5. Do you believe that nothing less than a deep and effective spiritual experience will revolutionize your attitude toward life, your fellows, and God's Universe?

6. Do you believe there is a "middle of the road solution" for you?

7. Were you in a position where life was becoming impossible? Had you passed into the region from which there was no return through human aid?

8. Do you have any other alternatives than to either, a) Accept spiritual help, or b) Go on to the bitter end, blotting out the consciousness of your intolerable situation as best you can?

2. Do you honestly want to accept spiritual help and are you willing to make the effort?

3. Do you believe that with a profound knowledge of the inner workings of your mind, relapse is unthinkable?

4. In the mental sense (before the 1st drink), am I one of these people? Must I have this thing?

The identification with the first 8 pages of Bill's story is essential to the understanding of your own illness and to understand the part alcoholism has played in every affair throughout your entire lifetime. For, in step one, if you are not convinced that you are a "real" alcoholic, then you may not be wiling or able to go to the lengths that others have to recover from their alcoholism.

You don't know it yet, but you will suffer resistance from an internal source within your own thinking mind as you go through the step process, this thinking mind of yours will produce thoughts of a nature to disregard truths you're seeing before you and to disembark from the process altogether. It will work to slow down your momentum and lessen your desire.

It will only be your identification with the problem in the beginning that enables you to continue to forage through the steps, asides from God's grace which for as long as you are even just the slightest bit willing, will carry you through it all. If at any time or at any place along this journey, the one thing you mustn't skip or skimp upon would be gaining the full working knowledge about your alcoholism and its relationship within your life.

WEEK #3: Chapter 1— BILL'S STORY

(Last Week) we spent quite a bit of time talking about the **problem**, talking about **the <u>physical allergy</u> that ensures we can't safely drink,** talking about **the <u>obsession of the mind</u> that ensures that we can't keep from drinking** and the ultimate conclusion to that was:

> **If you can't safely drink without getting drunk, and**
> **if you can't keep from drinking, then**
> **you've become absolutely powerless over alcohol**

Most certainly **our lives had become unmanageable**, if not … we just keep on drinking and after a while it will be for sure.

(Tonight) …we're going to look at an example of a guy that had that problem. A good textbook never tells you anything that it doesn't back it up with more information. We are going to look at Bill's Story … Bill's Story is a classic example of an alcoholic who had the **<u>allergy</u>** and who had the **<u>obsession of the mind</u>**. Now we have to remember back in the 1930's, Bill learned very early on **the value of sharing your story with another alcoholic** when he went to see Dr. Bob, and immediately Dr. Bob could see his **<u>problem</u>** also. They went to see Bill Dobson and they shared their stories with Bill Dobson. Bill Dobson **could see his <u>problem</u> through their stories**, and they learned very early on that **it was necessary for one alcoholic to <u>identify</u> with another in order to be able to get their interest and get their attention**.

When the Big Book was first published they knew they wouldn't be able to sit down with the first person out here in California and share their story one on one. So the Big Book had to be complete enough to do that. So they said we'll put Bill's Story in here at the very beginning, and another alcoholic in reading Bill's Story will be able to identify with Bill. **If we can <u>identify</u> with Bill and see his alcoholism, see him make a recovery from that condition, we can begin to believe and we can begin to hope that we're enough like Bill Wilson… if he could recover from that condition then just maybe we could too.** Now a lot of you have said we have trouble identifying with Bill Wilson cause after all he was a night school lawyer and we were not, after all he was a New York City stock speculator and we were not, and a lot of the women say we can't identify with him because he's a man, and many people say well he was an older fellow and we couldn't identify there either. **But if we look for the way Bill thinks, and the way Bill acts and the way Bill drinks…if we're a real alcoholic there's not an alcoholic in this room that can't identify with Bill Wilson.** So as we go through Bill's Story… we'll look for:

9. Identification,
10. The progression of alcoholism
11. Bill drinking finally for the sickest reason of all, complete oblivion

Then we will look and see how Bill recovered from alcoholism and if we've identified with him, then we can begin to believe that if he could do it, just maybe we could it too.

<u>Identification:</u>

The Beginning of Believing…
The Beginning of Hope

WEEK #3: Chapter 1— BILL'S STORY

I too did not think I could identify with the "Bill Wilson" that I've seen pictures of… he was an old man, I thought. Turns out, **he was 43 years old when this book was written**, so a relatively young man. But as I began to study and read Bill's Story, I began to see that he was a very optimist person, hardworking, and had lots and lots of willpower. He was a self-made man who became very successful in his own right. Through Bill's story we're going to see:

1. **What he was like**
2. **How he learned that he was sick**
3. **How he affected a recovery**

The total story of Alcoholics Anonymous is contained in Bill Wilson's story.

Let's go to page one (1), "Bill's Story".

Big Book p. 1, par. 1

"War fever ran high in the New England town to which we new, young officers from Plattsburg were assigned, and we were flattered when the first citizens took us to their homes, making us feel heroic. Here was love, applause, war; moments sublime with intervals hilarious"

J & C Anybody ever have any moment's sublime with intervals hilarious? I have. I love the way Bill writes.

Big Book p. 1, par. 1, line 6

"I was part of life at last, and in the midst of the excitement I discovered liquor. I forgot the strong warnings and the prejudices of my people concerning drink. In time we sailed for "Over There." I was very lonely and again turned to alcohol."
We landed in England. I visited Winchester Cathedral. Much moved, I wandered outside. My attention was caught by a doggerel on an old tombstone:

> *"Here lies a Hampshire Grenadier Who caught his death*
> *Drinking cold small beer.*
>
> *A good soldier is ne'er forgot Whether he dieth by musket Or by pot."*

J & C Now when he says that about pot, he's not referring to this wacky weed. He's talking about a pot of beer, that's the way they used to drink it over in England at that time. He said

Big Book p. 1, par. 3

"Ominous warning which I failed to heed."
"Twenty-two, and a veteran of foreign wars, I went home at last. I fancied myself a leader, for had not the men of my battery given me a special token of appreciation? My talent for leadership, I imagined, could place me at the head of vast enterprises which I would manage with the utmost assurance. I took a night law course, and obtained employment as investigator for a surety company. The drive for success was on. I'd prove to the world I was important."

J & C I already identify with Bill Wilson. That seems to be one of the main characteristics behind every alcoholic I've ever known. **The great drive for success** was on; **I'll prove to the world that I'm important also**. It seems to be the driving force behind each one of us.

WEEK #3: Chapter 1— BILL'S STORY

Big Book p.2, par 1, line 4

"My work took me about Wall Street and little by little I became interested in the market. Many people lost money but some became very rich. Why not I? I studied economics and business as well as law. Potential alcoholic that I was, I nearly failed my law course. At one of the finals I was too drunk to think or write. Though my drinking was not yet continuous, it disturbed my wife."

J & C I can identify with Bill.

Big Book p.2, par. 1, line 11

"We had long talks when I would still her forebodings by telling her that men of genius conceived their best projects when drunk;"

J & C I have no trouble identifying with Bill Wilson.

Big Book p.2, par. 1, line 13

"that the most majestic constructions of philosophic thought were so derived."

J & C I can identify with Bill. …we make our living selling fast talk to slow thinking people, and Bill's trying to do some of that here, but we all know that Lois didn't buy that. He said

Big Book p.2, par. 2

"By the time I had completed the course, I knew the law was not for me. The inviting maelstrom of Wall Street had me in its grip. Business and financial leaders were my heroes. Out of this ally of drink and speculation, I commenced to forge the weapon that one day would turn in its flight like a boomerang and all but cut me to ribbons. Living modestly, my wife and I saved $1,000. It went into certain securities, then cheap and rather unpopular. I rightly imagined that they would some day have a great rise. I failed to persuade my broker friends to send me out looking over factories and managements, but my wife and I decided to go anyway. I had developed a theory that most people lost money in stocks through ignorance of markets. I discovered many more reasons later on."

J & C Now Bill is referring to a time back in the 1920's when the stock market was on a roll. Just about everybody that dealt with stocks was making money. All you had to do was buy them and hold unto them, let them go up in price, sell them, take your profits, buy some more. Everything was done on about a 10% margin; everything was pure speculation. Bill really became one of the first investment counselors on Wall Street. He began to say look, sooner or later this bubble is going to burst. Sooner or later we're going to have to start making our decisions based on fact rather than speculation. He went to the people who had the money and he said I don't have the money to do this but if you guys would back me financially, I'll leave New York City and I'll start visiting these companies. And I'll look at the plants and I'll talk to the employees and I'll examine the books wherever I can and I'll write up reports and send them back in here and we'll start making our decisions whether to buy or not based on fact. And they said, no, Bill, we don't need that kind of information. We're making about all the money we want to make anyhow. And you know how we alcoholics are, if we get a good idea, stubborn as hell, we're going to carry it out one way or another. He said the hell with them, I don't need them anyhow. I'll just go do this on my own.

Big Book p.2, par.3

"We gave up our positions and off we roared on a motorcycle, the sidecar stuffed with tent, blankets, a change of clothes, and three huge volumes of a financial reference service. Our friends thought a lunacy commission should be appointed. Perhaps they were right. I had had some success at speculation, so we had a little money, but we once worked on a farm for a month to avoid drawing on our small capital. That was the last honest manual labor on my part for many a day. We covered the whole eastern United States in a year. At the end of it, my reports to Wall Street procured me a position there and the use of a large expense account. The exercise of an option brought in more money, leaving us with a profit of several thousand dollars for that year."

WEEK #3: Chapter 1— BILL'S STORY

J & C Bill and Lois, traveling on the motorcycle, living in the tent, went up and down the eastern seaboard of the United States and he wrote up reports on approximately 100 of the largest companies in the eastern states sending them to New York City. The guys that had the money saw them and say oh yeah man this is great information and immediately they put Bill on the payroll, gave him a large expense account, the exercise in option made a good profit, for the first time in his life he's got something. He came from a little town called East Dorset, Vermont; he had never had anything before in his life. Here's how he feels

Big Book p.3, par.2
"For the next few years fortune threw money and applause my way. I had arrived."

J & C God how many of us have done the same kind of things Bill did.

Big Book p.3, par. 2,line 2
"My judgment and ideas were followed by many to the tune of paper millions. The great boom of the late twenties was seething and swelling. Drink was taking an important and exhilarating part in my life. There was loud talk in the jazz places uptown. Everyone spent in thousands and chattered in millions. Scoffers could scoff and be damned. I made a host of fair-weather friends."

J & C And here's Bill now back in New York City on top of the heap. He's making money for himself and a lot of other people. He's drinking also but drinking is not a problem right now it's a very exciting thing and Bill is really, really, really becoming a success at what he wanted to be. We also know though that **if he's alcoholic his drinking is going to get worse because it is a progressive thing**. Let's see where he goes now from the top of the heap. He said,

Big Book p.3, par. 3
"My drinking assumed more serious proportions, continuing all day and almost every night. The remonstrances of my friends terminated in a row and I became a lone wolf."

J & C How many of us have done the same thing. People began to say Bill, you're drinking too much. Bill, you're costing us money. Bill, why don't you cut back? Bill, why don't you quit**? And once again rather than even consider that Bill said, to hell with them I don't need them. He begins to operate on his own now.** I have no problem identifying with Bill Wilson.

Big Book p.3, par. 3, line 4
"There were many unhappy scenes in our sumptuous apartment. There had been no real infidelity, for loyalty to my wife, helped at times by extreme drunkenness, kept me out of those scrapes."

J & C Now I've always believed about everything Bill wrote, but I'm not sure about that. You see we have a book in A.A. called, As Bill Sees It, and in AlAnon they have a book called, "As Lois Remembers"… A whole lot different! They're not exactly the same either. Let's go over to page 4, 1st paragraph. Now here's old' Bill he's making lots of money, he's doing well, he's got lots of willpower, lots of hope for the future, hardworking, optimistic, a self made man. On page 4 it says,

Big Book p.4, par. 1
"Abruptly in October 1929 hell broke loose on the New York stock exchange. After one of those days of inferno, I wobbled from a hotel bar to a brokerage office. It was eight o'clock five hours after the market closed. The ticker still clattered. I was staring at an inch of the tape which bore the inscription XYZ-32. It had been 52 that morning. I was finished and so were many friends. The papers reported men jumping to death from the towers of High Finance. That disgusted me. I would not jump. I went back to the bar."

WEEK #3: Chapter 1— BILL'S STORY

J & C Bill had a solution to that, didn't he?

Big Book p.4, par. 1, line 11
> *"My friends had dropped several million since ten o'clock so what? Tomorrow was another day. As I drank, the old fierce determination to win came back."*

J & C How many of us have done the same thing. Just come out of the jailhouse, the divorce court, the hospital, or wherever, low, sad, depressed? Stop off in the bar have a couple of drinks and as the alcohol courses through our veins we say, we'll show them. By God they're not going to treat us that way. And we're off and we're running again, **that old fierce determination to be somebody to show them.**

Big Book p.4, par. 2
> *"Next morning I telephoned a friend in Montreal. He had plenty of money left and thought I had better go to Canada."*

J & C Now Bill was a drunk, he wasn't stupid; he knew where the money was so he went to Canada.

Big Book p.4, par. 2, line 3
> *"By the following spring we were living in our accustomed style. I felt like Napoleon returning from Elba. No St. Helena for me! But drinking caught up with me again and my generous friend had to let me go. This time we stayed broke."*

J & C Now **we see our drinking progressing** to the point where we can no longer even hold a job.

Big Book p.4, par.3
> *"We went to live with my wife's parents. I found a job; then lost it as the result of a brawl with a taxi driver. Mercifully, no one could guess that I was to have no real employment for five years, or hardly draw a sober breath. My wife began to work in a department store, coming home exhausted to find me drunk. I became an unwelcome hanger-on at brokerage places."*

J & C Where he used to be the fair-haired boy, where he used to make lots of money for lots of people, he goes in there now and they say, Bill, we'd rather you didn't come in here today. Your about half drunk and you don't look good and your smelling bad, you're embarrassing us in front of our customers, please move right on down the street. Certainly, **certainly we can see the progression of alcoholism. We've gone from excitement to now then we've gone to the point where it controls us completely**, no longer hold a job, **nobody wants us around anymore**. It starts to get worse,

Big Book p.5, par.1
> *"Liquor ceased to be a luxury; it became a necessity."*

J & C Now we're drinking for an entirely different reason. **We're drinking now because we absolutely have to drink in order to live. No fun left anymore, no excitement, drinking in order to be able to live.**

WEEK #3: Chapter 1— BILL'S STORY

Big Book p.5, par. 1, line 2

"'Bathtub' gin, two bottles a day, and often three, got to be routine. Sometimes a small deal would net a few hundred dollars, and I would pay my bills at the bars and delicatessens. This went on endlessly, and I began to waken very early in the morning shaking violently. A tumbler full of gin followed by half a dozen bottles of beer would be required if I were to eat any breakfast. Nevertheless, I still thought I could control the situation, and there were periods of sobriety which renewed my wife's hope."

J & C Remember last night Dr. Silkworth said **we really cannot differentiate the true from the false. To us what we're doing is normal**. We see that Bill's life is going to hell in a hand basket already. Bill can't see that. He thinks that he **can still control the situation.** Let's see were he goes on control. Things were real bad in Bill's life but it says,

Big Book p.5, par. 2-3

"Gradually things got worse. The house was taken over by the mortgage holder, my mother-in-law died, my wife and father-in-law became ill. Then I got a promising business opportunity. Stocks were at the low point of 1932, and I had somehow formed a group to buy. I was to share generously in the profits. Then I went on a prodigious bender, and that chance vanished."

J & C This is a story within itself. The people that had the money knew how good Bill was at putting these deals together. They came to Bill and said "Bill we've got a proposition for you. We've got an opportunity to not only to make money for us, but to make money for you. If you can stay sober we'd like for you to handle this thing." And Bill said, "Don't you worry about that drinking. I'm through with that drinking! You'll not have to worry about that." Bill worked for a matter of months putting this deal together and a few days before it was to be successfully completely, one night they are all sitting around in the hotel room talking about this and that. Somebody passed around a bottle of Applejack. This was during the days of prohibition. It came to Bill, and he said, "No thank you, I'm not drinking anymore". After a while it came back to him, and the guy next to him said, "Bill, you don't understand what this is...this is the finest Applejack in the world. It is called 'Jersey Lightening'...you better have a drink." Bill's mind said, "Hmmm, I've never tasted any 'Jersey Lightening'". Bill gave it no more thought than that... he reached out, grabbed the bottle, took a drink, triggered the allergy, couldn't sober up and blew the whole deal. Now the importance in it lies with the next statement. He said,

Big Book p.5, par. 4

"I woke up. This had to be stopped. I saw I could not take so much as one drink. I was through forever. Before then, I had written lots of sweet promises, but my wife happily observed that this time I meant business. And so I did."

J & C For the first time Bill could differentiate the truth from the false. For the first time he could truly see what alcohol was doing to him. **And he did just like all the rest of us, he trotted out his willpower and he said, "Sick him Will".** We're through with that drinking... we'll never drink as long as we live." Now they try to tell us we are weak willed people...don't you believe that! We are strong willed people! Weak willed people do not become alcoholics; first time they vomit they quit drinking. An alcoholic knows there's got to be some way to drink without puking; we damn near kill ourselves! You know? We got lots of willpower. You see Bill doesn't know what we learned (last week). **Anytime there's a battle going on between the willpower and the obsession of the mind, the obsession of the mind is stronger than willpower and it always wins**, that's how strong it is. Let's see what happened to him on willpower. He said,

Big Book p.5, par. 5

"Shortly afterward I came home drunk. There had been no fight. Where had been my high resolve? I simply didn't know. It hadn't even come to mind. Someone had pushed a drink my way, and I had taken it. Was I crazy?"

WEEK #3: Chapter 1— BILL'S STORY

J & C You see if his willpower's not working then he begins to question his sanity. Am I crazy is that it?

Big Book p.5, par. 5, line 5

"I began to wonder, for such an appalling lack of perspective seemed near being just that. Renewing my resolve, I tried again. Some time passed, and confidence began to be replaced by cocksureness. I could laugh at the gin mills. Now I had what it takes! One day I walked into a cafe to telephone. In no time I was beating on the bar asking myself how it happened. As the whisky rose to my head I told myself I would manage better next time, but I might as well get good and drunk then. And I did."

J & C Anybody in here identify with Bill Wilson?

Big Book p.6, par. 1

"The remorse, horror and hopelessness of the next morning are unforgettable. The courage to do battle was not there. My brain raced uncontrollably and there was a terrible sense of impending calamity. I hardly dared cross the street, lest I collapse and be run down by an early morning truck, for it was scarcely daylight. An all night place supplied me with a dozen glasses of ale. My writhing nerves were stilled at last. A morning paper told me the market had gone to hell again. Well, so had I. The market would recover, but I wouldn't. That was a hard thought. Should I kill myself? No not now. Then a mental fog settled down. Gin would fix that. So two bottles, and oblivion."

J & C See Bill questioned, **he used his willpower and that didn't work, he begin to question his sanity and that didn't work, and then he began to contemplate suicide**, and then he was drinking for the sickest effect of all total oblivion. And that's where we find Bill at this time. He said,

Big Book p.6, par. 2

"The mind and body are marvelous mechanisms, for mine endured this agony two more years. Sometimes I stole from my wife's slender purse when the morning terror and madness were on me. Again I swayed dizzily before an open window, or the medicine cabinet where there was poison, cursing myself for a weakling. There were flights from city to country and back, as my wife and I sought escape. Then came the night when the physical and mental torture was so hellish I feared I would burst through my window, sash and all. Somehow I managed to drag my mattress to a lower floor, lest I suddenly leap. A doctor came with a heavy sedative. Next day found me drinking both gin and sedative. This combination soon landed me on the rocks. People feared for my sanity. So did I. I could eat little or nothing when drinking, and I was forty pounds under weight."

J & C Here we find Bill drinking for oblivion, not eating very often. I can identify with Bill. He's dying of malnutrition, and I can identify with Bill because when I was drinking those last years of my drinking occasionally I'd eat a bologna sandwich cause I knew you were supposed to eat something rather than just drink and that's what Bill was doing at this time, dying of malnutrition.

Big Book p. 7, par. 1

"My brother-in-law is a physician, and through his kindness and that of my mother I was placed in a nationally-known hospital for the mental and physical rehabilitation of alcoholics."

J & C This is the Towns Hospital in New York City and this is the summer of 1933.

Big Book p. 7, par. 1, line 4
"Under the so-called belladonna treatment my brain cleared."

** Belladonna was a drug that they used to fool the body into thinking it had alcohol in it, it was used for withdrawal purposes. It's what they use Valium for today.

WEEK #3: Chapter 1— BILL'S STORY

Big Book p. 7, par. 1, line 5
"Hydrotherapy and mild exercise helped much.

J & C Hydrotherapy is water treatment; we saw some of that in a treatment center in Australia back in the 1980's. They would put the alcoholic on a gurney, roll him into the shower room and they had showerheads all the way around the shower room alternating hot and cold water. Be in there for about thirty minutes. Doesn't cure alcoholism, but it makes a clean drunk out of you I'll guarantee you that. Those guys would come out of there and their skin all wrinkled up and shriveled up. He said,

Big Book p. 7, par. 1, line 6
"Best of all, I met a kind doctor who explained that though certainly selfish and foolish, I had been seriously ill, bodily and mentally."

J & C Now this is Dr. Silkworth. Silky sat down with him and explained his ideas about the **physical allergy and the obsession of the mind**. And here's the effect it had on Bill. He said,

Big Book p. 7, par. 2
"It relieved me somewhat to learn that in alcoholics the will is amazingly weakened when it comes to combating liquor, though if often remains strong in other respects. My incredible behavior in the face of a desperate desire to stop was explained. Understanding myself now, I fared forth in high hope. For three or four months the goose hung high. I went to town regularly and even made a little money. Surely this was the answer self- knowledge."

J & C For the first time Bill understood his problem.

He knew it <u>was not</u> willpower.
He knew it <u>was not</u> moral character and sin.

He knew it <u>was</u> **a physical allergy coupled with the obsession of the mind,** and that's what **made him absolutely powerless.**

And he said, "Now that I know what's wrong with me I'll not have to drink any longer."
Let's see where he goes from here.

The information we learned last (week) about the Doctor's Opinion and the illness of alcoholism is very, very important information, but you know it's just information. **It will not solve alcoholism, just because we know what the problem is**…as Bill found out.

Big Book p. 7, par 3
"But it was not, for the frightful day came when I drank once more. The curve of my declining moral and bodily health fell off like a ski-jump. After a time I returned to the hospital."

J & C Now this is the summer of 1934. A year later Bill, goes back into "The Towns" for the second time.

Big Book p. 7, par 3, line 4
"This was the finish, the curtain, it seemed to me. My weary and despairing wife was informed that it would all end with heart failure during delirium tremens, or I would develop a wet brain, perhaps within a year. We would soon have to give me over to the undertaker of the asylum."

WEEK #3: Chapter 1— BILL'S STORY

J & C Bill was lying in the hospital room there all sick, he overheard Lois and Dr. Silkworth talking. She said "Dr. Silkworth is there any hope for him?" And he said, "No I don't believe so Lois, we're going to have to give him over to the undertaker or the asylum, 'cause there's no solution for Bill." And Bill said,

Big Book p. 7, par. 4

"They did not need to tell me. I knew, and almost welcomed the idea. It was a devastating blow to my pride. I, who had thought so well of myself and my abilities, of my capacity to surmount obstacles, was cornered at last. Now I was to plunge into the dark, joining that endless procession of sots who had gone on before. I thought of my poor wife. There had been much happiness after all. What would I not give to make amends? But that was over now."

J & C Bill was a very hardworking, optimistic individual and now we see Bill, he is hopeless, he is without hope. But we all know you can't live long without hope, you've got to have hope, but Bill is hopeless at the moment. Now let's look at this next statement very carefully. He said,

Big Book p. 8, par. 1

"No words can tell of the loneliness and despair I found in that bitter morass of self-pity. Quicksand stretched around me in all directions. I had met my match. I had been overwhelmed. Alcohol was my master."

J & C I've never seen a better description of Step 1. (There was) no Step 1 written in those days, but surely this is where Bill took it (from). He admitted completed defeat. Alcohol had whipped him in a fair fight. **He was completely powerless over alcohol**. Now if that should happen to you and me today, chances are we would say… "I guess I'd better go to AA". But Bill didn't have any AA to go to. He's in the best facility he knows. So, even though he's admitted his powerlessness… even though he's taken what we know as Step 1… the only thing he can do is leave that hospital and try to stay sober on his own.

Big Book p. 8, par. 2

"Trembling, I stepped from the hospital a broken man. Fear sobered me for a bit. Then came the insidious insanity of that first drink, and on Armistice Day 1934, I was off again. Everyone became resigned to the certainty that I would have to be shut up somewhere, or would stumble along to a miserable end. How dark it is before the dawn! In reality that was the beginning of my last debauch. I was soon to be catapulted into what I like to call the fourth dimension of existence. I was to know happiness, peace, and usefulness, in a way of life that is incredibly more wonderful as time passes. Near the end of that bleak November, I sat drinking in my kitchen."

J & C And I imagine it was a pretty bleak November. He started drinking on November the 11th, triggered the allergy, couldn't stop, and has been drunk now for about 3 weeks.

Big Book p. 8, par. 3, line 2

"With a certain satisfaction I reflected there was enough gin concealed about the house to carry me through that night and the next day. My wife was at work. I wondered whether I dared hide a full bottle of gin near the head of our bed. I would need it before daylight. My musing was interrupted by the telephone. The cheery voice of an old school friend asked if he might come over."

J & C Now this was Ebby Thatcher. Bill and Ebby had gone to school together when they were younger, did lots of drinking together. Bill knew about Ebby and he knew how Ebby drank. And Ebby said *"he was sober"*. And if you'll notice that's in squiggly writing *(italics)*; squiggly writing in the Big Book is very important. This really amazed Bill…<u>Ebby is sober</u>. He said,

WEEK #3: Chapter 1— BILL'S STORY

Big Book p. 9, line 1

"It was years since I could remember his coming to New York in that condition. I was amazed. Rumor had it that he had been committed for alcoholic insanity."

J & C The last Bill had heard about Ebby was that Ebby was going to be committed to the State Insane Asylum in the State of Vermont for alcoholic insanity. That's what they used to do with people like us before we had the treatment centers. They would haul us in front of a judge and the judge would commit us to the state insane asylum for alcoholic insanity for an undetermined period of time. Till you got well; you would stay there until you got well. That's the last Bill heard about Ebby. He said,

Big Book p. 9, line 4

"I wondered how he had escaped."

J & C Bill was amazed that Ebby was out of this treatment center, err insane asylum, excuse me...
Same thing.... They've renamed everything (these days). They talk about dysfunctional families today; well mine was just crazy as hell. But Ebby came from a very prominent family in Albany, New York. In fact his father was the Mayor of Albany... a very prominent family.

Ebby's drinking was embarrassing the family, so they called Ebby in one day and said "Ebby you're embarrassing the family with your drinking and we would like for you to just basically get out of town and go on over there to Vermont and stay at the old summer place and we'll be over there this summer. While you're there... you might as well sober up... and if you get sober... you might as well make yourself useful and paint and fix up the old summer place because we'll be using it." So Ebby went out, got out of town and went over to Vermont to begin to fix up the old summer place... painting and fixing it up.

One day he finished painting this wall and he looked at it and he was admiring his work and he noticed that some pigeons were doing some things on the side of his wall that he didn't like (bird droppings all over the wall). So he went in the house, got his shotgun, and began to shoot at the pigeons, blowing holes in the side of the wall. Well the neighbors they didn't like that at all, so they called the police and had him arrested. They took him before the judge and they were going to commit him for alcoholic insanity. But Ebby got real lucky; two fellows interceded on his behalf. One guy's name was Rowland Hazard and the other was Cebra Graves. They asked the judge if he might release Ebby to their care because they were going to the Oxford Group.

They felt if they took Ebby to the Oxford Group meetings and if he would apply the tenets of the Oxford Group to his life, maybe he too could stay sober as they had. Well Ebby began to go to the Oxford Group meetings and he began to stay sober and a couple of months later he goes to New York to the Calvary Mission which was the headquarters of the Oxford Group at that time. He began to stay there in that mission and after a while he remembered his friend Bill... he said "I think I'll go over and talk to Bill, maybe I can help Bill stay sober as these two fellows have helped me." Now Bill didn't know any of this... Bill said, "I wondered how he had escaped."

Big Book p. 9, line 5

"Of course he would have dinner, and then I could drink openly with him. Unmindful of his welfare, I thought only of recapturing the spirit of other days. There was that time we had chartered an airplane to complete a jag! His coming was an oasis in this dreary desert of futility. The very thing an oasis! Drinkers are like that.
The door opened and he stood there, fresh-skinned and glowing. There was something about his eyes. He was inexplicably different. What had happened?
I pushed a drink across the table. He refused it. Disappointed but curious, I wondered what had got into the fellow. He wasn't himself.
"Come, what's all this about? I queried.
He looked straight at me. Simply, but smilingly, he said, "I've got religion."

WEEK #3: Chapter 1— BILL'S STORY

J & C Now I'm damn glad that didn't happen in my kitchen. I have no idea what I would have done. But here's what Bill did. He said:

Big Book p. 9, par. 5-6

"I was aghast. So that was it - last summer an alcoholic crackpot; now, I suspected, a little cracked about religion. He had that starry-eyed look. Yes, the old boy was on fire all right. But bless his heart, let him rant! Besides, my gin would last longer than his preaching.

But he did no ranting. In a matter of fact way he told how two men had appeared in court, persuading the judge to suspend his commitment. They had told of a simple religious idea and a practical program of action.

That was two months ago and the result was self-evident. It worked!"

...a simple religious idea = Step 2
...a practical program of action = Steps 3 – 12

J & C So now then Bill knows all three things. He got the **problem** from Dr. Silkworth, he got the **Solution**, referred to here as "**a simple religious idea**" from Ebby and he got the **practical program of action** from Ebby; so now he knows all three things. But Bill is also just like so many of us; he did not like this simple religious idea. Now Bill's thoughts and his ideas about God and about religion, etc. were enough that it made him resent what Ebby had brought to him. He said,

Big Book p. 9, par. 7

"He had come to pass his experience along to me if I cared to have it. I was shocked, but interested. Certainly I was interested. I had to be, for I was hopeless.

He talked for hours. Childhood memories rose before me. I could almost hear the sound of the preacher's voice as I sat, on still Sundays, way over there on the hillside; there was that proffered temperance pledge I never signed; my grandfather's good natured contempt of some church fold and their doings; his insistence that the spheres really had their music; but his denial of the preacher's right to tell him how he must listen;"

J & C Now Bill's grandfather Grandpa Griffith raised him from twelve years on. And Grandpa Griffith believed in some power greater than human power but he wouldn't let anybody tell him how he had to believe in it. His grandpa had a great problem with the world's religions; he passed that along to Bill.

Big Book p. 10, par 1, line 9

"...his fearlessness as he spoke of these things just before he died; these recollections welled up from the past. They made me swallow hard.
That war-time day in old Winchester Cathedral came back again."

J & C Bill's having a problem now with this religious idea that Ebby's talking about. We've seen him take Step 1. In the next couple of pages we're going to see him take Step 2. Let's see how he came to be able to accept this religious idea. Now Bill's already took Step 1, so now he's between Steps 1 and 2, he hasn't taken Step 2 yet. He begins to ponder these things. He said,

Big Book p. 10, par. 3

"I had always believed in a Power greater that myself. I had often pondered these things. I was not an atheist. Few people really are, for that means blind faith in the strange proposition that this universe originated in a cipher and aimlessly rushes nowhere. My intellectual heroes, the chemists, the astronomers, even the evolutionist, suggested vast laws and forces at work. Despite contrary indications, I had little doubt that a might purpose and rhythm underlay all. How could there be so much of precise and immutable law, and no intelligence? I simply had to believe in a Spirit of the Universe, who knew neither time nor limitation. But that was as far as I had gone."

WEEK #3: Chapter 1— BILL'S STORY

J & C Now here's where I really begin to identify with Bill Wilson.

Big Book p. 10, par. 4

"With ministers, and the world's religions, I parted right there. When they talked of a God personal to me, who was love, superhuman strength and direction, I became irritated and my mind snapped shut against such a theory. To Christ I conceded the certainty of a great man, not too closely followed by those who claimed Him. His moral teaching most excellent. For myself, I had adopted those parts which seemed convenient and not too difficult; the rest I disregarded."

J & C Anybody in here identify with Bill Wilson, huh? You betcha. We can see that Bill's having a terrible time with this religious idea. Now let's go down to the middle paragraph.

Big Book p. 11, par. 3

"But my friend sat before me, and he made the pointblank declaration that God had done for him what he could not do for himself. His human will had failed. Doctors had pronounced him incurable. Society was about to lock him up. Like myself, he had admitted complete defeat. Then he had, in effect, been raised from the dead, suddenly taken from the scrap heap to a level of life better than the best he had ever known!
Had this power originated in him? Obviously it had not. There had been no more power in him than there was in me at that minute; and this was none at all."

J & C **This is why the identification process is so important**. Bill knew about Ebby. He knew how Ebby drank. And he knew that **if Ebby had been sober two months, some power greater than Ebby had to be working in Ebby's life.**

Whether Bill likes it or not, **is absolutely beside the point**; Ebby is living *proof* of it.

That's what you and I offer to the newcomer. When we sit there, talking to the newcomer, we are living *proof* that **some power greater than human power is working in our lives**... Whether the newcomer likes it or not **is beside the point**...We are the *proof* of it. [handwritten: do you believe that I believe it?] Ebby was the *proof* for Bill.

Now I'd liked to have been there that day, sitting in a corner watching them. Bill's about two-thirds drunk...Ebby has come out of the Oxford Groups, who were a group of people practicing first century Christianity to the best of their ability. The terms they used were highly religious in nature. Ebby is on fire and he's talking about God, and Bill doesn't like it at all. They're sitting there arguing with each other about who God is and what He is... Bill said "Don't give me that religious crap! Oh yeah, I believe in the Great Mind, The Spirit of Nature, but don't give me that other kind of stuff!" Ebby's trying to "put it on" old Bill... they're arguing back and forth, back and forth, back and forth. Let's go over to page 12, first paragraph. He said,

Big Book p. 12, par. 1

"Despite the living example of my friend there remained in me the vestiges of my old prejudice. The word God still aroused a certain antipathy. When the thought was expressed that there might be a God personal to me this feeling was intensified. I didn't like the idea. I could go for such conceptions as Creative intelligence, Universal Mind or Spirit of Nature but I resisted the thought of a Czar of the Heavens, however loving His sway might be. I have since talked with scores of men who felt the same way."

J & C In other words Bill was saying there's got to be a harder way to do this, what you're saying is too simple. Now I guess Ebby finally, finally got tired of this deal. Let's look at the next statement very carefully. If you notice it's in squiggly writing.

WEEK #3: Chapter 1— BILL'S STORY

Big Book p. 12, par. 2
"My friend suggested what then seemed a novel idea. He said, "Why don't you choose your own conception of God?"

J & C In other words, he said, Bill what are we arguing about? What difference does it make what we call Him. ***Why don't you choose your own conception of God?***
We're no longer dealing with religion now; we're (now) dealing with spirituality. You see, religion says, this is the way you have to believe. Spirituality says it really doesn't make any difference how you believe, the only question is… **are you willing to believe?** So we're through with religion, now we're talking about spirituality. And here's the effect that it had on Bill.

Big Book p. 12, par. 3
"That statement hit me hard. It melted the icy intellectual mountain in whose shadow I had lived and shivered many years. I stood in the sunlight at last."

J & C It took all arguments away from him. He couldn't argue with that statement.

Big Book p. 12, par. 4
"It was only a matter of being willing to believe in a Power greater than myself. Nothing more was required of me to make my beginning. I saw that growth could start from that point. Upon a foundation of complete willingness I might build what I saw in my friend. Would I have it? Of course I would!"

J & C Surely, this is when Bill took Step 2. (There was) no Step 2 written in those days…but here's where **he came to believe in a Power greater than himself**, based on Ebby's simple little statement, ***"Why don't you choose your own conception of God?"***

That statement has opened the door for countless millions of we alcoholics who were having trouble with religion… and I think **the reason it really works is we're allowed here to have our own conception of God**. You know, as I look back in my lifetime, I realize I've never had any problem with my own conception of anything! Let me believe the way I want to and I'm ready to go! Bill is now taking a Step 2. Isn't that something? (Bill was taking a Step 2) when he made the statement, **"I saw that growth could start from that point. Upon a foundation of complete willingness I might build what I saw in my friend. Would I have it? Of course I would!"**

This is Bill's first reference to a wonderfully effective spiritual structure…he's going to start painting a picture, in our minds, using words. Eventually he'll tell us what the structure is, and show us where we'll pass through it to freedom. His first reference to it is…**"Upon a foundation of complete willingness I might build what I saw in my friend."**

The <u>foundation</u> of this structure is <u>willingness</u>. That came from **<u>Step 1</u>**. When we could see **what we were doing would no longer work**…**<u>we became willing to change</u>**. Later on we're going to see where **<u>Believing</u>… <u>Step 2</u>… is the <u>cornerstone</u> of that structure**. And eventually he'll tell us exactly what it is. (It's) a beautiful way to teach…painting pictures in our mind using words.

**If we are willing, and if we believe,
then we have already started on the road to recovery**

Bill has now taken Steps 1 and 2. Immediately Ebby starts taking him to Oxford Group meetings, but remember…**Bill is still drinking.** He triggered the allergy on November 11… he can't stop.

WEEK #3: Chapter 1— BILL'S STORY

J & C On about December 10th, 1934, probably, Bill was put back in the hospital for the third (3rd) time for withdrawal from alcohol by Doctor Silkworth. Ebby comes to visit with him,

>   11.   They begin to apply the little Oxford Group's **program of action**, and
>   12.   Bill had his **spiritual experience**. (After Steps 3-12)

Let's look on page 13. Let's see if we can't see the last 10 steps of Alcoholics Anonymous. He's taken (Steps) one (1) & two (2)… let's see if we can't see the last ten (10). He said,

Big Book p.13, par.2
>   *"At the hospital I was separated from alcohol for the last time. Treatment seemed wise, for I showed signs of delirium tremens.*
>   *There I humbly offered myself to God, as I then I understood Him, to do with me as He would. I placed myself unreservedly under His care and direction. I admitted for the first time that of myself I was nothing; that without Him I was lost."*

J & C **The first (1st) tenet, that the Oxford Group had, was SURRENDER.** Now Bill, later on when he wrote the steps, he realized that no alcoholic would like the word surrender…so he changed their (the oxford Group's) 1st Step into our (AA's) 3rd where, **"We made a decision to turn our will and life over to the Care of God as we Understand Him"**. We see him there, taking the first Oxford Group tenet, which turned out to be our **Step 3.** He's now taken 1, 2 and 3. He said,

Big Book p.13, par. 3
>   *"I ruthlessly faced my sins…"*

J & C I ruthlessly faced my sins. **Their second (2nd) tenet was EXAMINE YOUR SINS.** And Bill knew that no good alcoholic's going to do that, so he changed that into **"Made a searching and fearless moral inventory of ourselves."** He's taking **Step 4** there.

Big Book p.13, par. 3
>   *"…and became willing to have my new-found Friend take them away, root and branch. I have not had a drink since."*

J & C **"…** became willing to have my new-found <u>Friend</u> take them away, root and branch". You'll notice <u>Friend</u> is capitalized. This is one of the words Bill uses for God. And that little statement "… became willing to have my new-found Friend take them away, root and branch", later became **Steps 6 and 7. We became willing to have God remove these things** and **Humbly asked Him to do so.** There we're dealing with six (6) and seven (7).

Big Book p.13, par. 4
>   *"My schoolmate visited me, and I fully acquainted him with my problems and deficiencies."*

J & C He's taking what we know today as **Step 5**, there in the Towns Hospital with Ebby.

Big Book p.13, par. 4
>   *"We made a list of people I had hurt or toward whom I felt resentment. I expressed my entire willingness to approach these individuals, admitting my wrong. Never was I to be critical of them. I was to right all such matters to the utmost of my ability."*

WEEK #3: Chapter 1— BILL'S STORY

J & C They had an Oxford Group **tenet** called **RESTITUION**. And Bill knew that no self-respecting alcoholic is going to do restitution, so he took that and made two Steps out of it, **Steps 8 and 9**,
where **we made a list and became willing**, and then, **made amends**. There he's dealing with eight (8) and nine (9).

Big Book p.13, par. 5
"I was to test my thinking by the new God-consciousness within. Common sense would thus become uncommon sense."

J & C That statement later became <u>Step 10</u> where **we continue to take personal inventory and when we were wrong promptly admitted it.**

Big Book p.13, par. 5
"I was to sit quietly when in doubt, asking only for direction and strength to meet my problems as He would have me. Never was I to pray for myself, except as my requests bore on my usefulness to others. Then only might I expect to receive. But that would be in great measure."

J & C And there we see all the elements of <u>Step 11</u>, where **"we sought through prayer and meditation to improve our conscious contact with God."**

Big Book p.13, par. 6
"My friend promised when these things were done I would enter upon a new relationship with my Creator; that I would have the elements of a way of living which answered all my problems."

J & C It's got to be the first part of <u>Step 12</u>. **"Having had a spiritual awakening as the result of these steps..."**

So we see Bill, in the Towns Hospital, applying the Oxford Group tenets which later he made into the last ten steps of Alcoholics Anonymous. This is why he was able to say in "How It Works",
"These are the steps we took which are suggested as a program of recovery..."
Bill took them in the Towns Hospital with the help of Ebby. Now let's see what happened to him.

Big Book p.13, par. 6
"Belief in the power of God, plus enough willingness, honesty and humility to establish and maintain the new order of things, were the essential requirements. Simple, but not easy; a price had to be paid. It meant destruction of self-centeredness. I must turn in all things to the Father of Light who presides over us all."

J & C Poor old alcoholics have to give up the two (2) most important things in our lives...the first thing is our alcohol and the second thing is our self-centeredness. Very difficult to do...very difficult but very simple

Big Book p.14, par. 3
"These were revolutionary and drastic proposals, but the moment I fully accepted them, the effect was electric. There was a sense of victory, followed by such a peace and serenity as I had never know. There was utter confidence. I felt lifted up, as though the great clean wind of a mountain top blew through and through. God comes to most men gradually, but His impact on me was sudden and profound. For a moment I was alarmed, and called my friend, the doctor, to ask if I were still sane. He listened in wonder as I talked."

J & C You know Bill overhead Lois and Dr. Silkworth talking so he'd thought he gone crazy. He thought he'd check it out with Dr. Silkworth to see if he had gone crazy. Finally he shared with the doctor his experience.

WEEK #3: Chapter 1— BILL'S STORY

Big Book p.14, par. 5

"Finally he shook his head saying, "Something has happened to you I don't understand. But you had better hang on to it. Anything is better than the way you were." The good doctor now sees many men who have such experiences. He knows that they are real."

J & C Now we don't know what happened to Bill that day, we were not there to see that. But we know this was probably about December the 14th of 1934. We do know that Bill didn't die until January of 1971. We do know that it was never necessary for him to take another drink from this day until the day that he died. Something profound took place in his life that day.

Bill always said, 'I had a vital spiritual experience as the result of these steps, during which old ideas were cast aside and replaced with a new set of ideas, and I was able to live the rest of my live without drinking.'

Now here's a guy that went in the hospital, selfish and self-centered to the extreme, always doing what he wanted to do whenever he wanted to do it. That was his attitude when he went in there. Let's look at his attitude now that he's had the **spiritual experience**

Big Book p.14, par. 6

"While I lay in the hospital the thought came that there were thousands of hopeless alcoholics who might be glad to have what had been so freely given me. Perhaps I could help some of them. They in turn might work with others."

J & C Bill had that gigantic **spiritual experience** and then he immediately began to think of how he can give it to other people. Something profound happened with Bill. He said.

Big Book p.14, par 7

"My friend had emphasized the absolute necessity of demonstrating these principles in all my affairs. Particularly was it imperative to work with others as he had worked with me. Faith without works was dead, he said. And how appallingly true for the alcoholic! For if an alcoholic failed to perfect and enlarge his spiritual life through work and self-sacrifice for others, he could not survive the certain trials and low spots ahead. If he did not work, he would surely drink again, and if he drank, he would surely die. Then faith would be dead indeed. With us it is just like that."

J & C This time you'll notice it's a small 'f'…he's referring to Ebby now. Thank God Bill knew that and accepted that fact 'cause when he was in Akron, about to get drunk, he remember how back in New York City, even though **he'd never helped anybody else, that he, himself, had felt better**. That's why he got hold of Dr. Bob, to try to help Dr. Bob. **Not necessarily to sober up Bob, but to keep Bill from getting drunk**. Thank God it kept him from getting drunk, and Bob sobered up and from there we have the fellowship of Alcoholics Anonymous.

Faith without works is dead.
(Chapter 6, Into Action, p. 76 & 88)

And you know, **just about anybody I see drink today, that's been in A.A. for any period of time, usually they have quit working with other people.** And when they quit working with other people: **1) They start thinking about self only; and 2) after awhile, all the old problems come back; and 3) they end up getting drunk all over again!**

Always, working with others will help us when nothing else will.

Big Book p.15, par. 2

"My wife and I abandoned ourselves with enthusiasm to the idea of helping other alcoholics to a solution of their problems. It was fortunate, for my old business associates remained skeptical for a year and a half, during which I found little work. I was not too well at the time, and was plagued by waves of self-pity and resentment. This sometimes nearly drove me back to drink, but I soon found that when all other measure failed, work with another alcoholic would save the day. Many times I have gone to my old hospital in despair. On talking to a man there, I would be amazingly lifted up and set on my feet. It is a design for living that works in rough going."

J & C We took a design for living that works in rough going and turned it into a non-drinking society I'm afraid. This is a design for living.

The work is really, really hard, but the pay is really, really good too.

We've managed to stay sober, isn't that something? Now if we are a brand new alcoholic out here in California, no fellowship around us, the first contact we've ever had is this book called Alcoholics Anonymous, and we have:

8. Read THE DOCTOR'S OPINION, we've been able to **see what our problem is**
9. Read BILL'S STORY, we've been **able to identify with another alcoholic**
10. Saw Bill go from **drinking for fun** to **drinking because of absolute necessity** and going finally, to the sickest of all reasons, **drinking to achieve complete oblivion.**
11. Saw him **recover from that condition**

Surely, we can say to ourselves…

We are enough like this guy… that if he can recover, just maybe we could recover too!

•The Beginning of Belief;
•The Beginning of Hope.

WEEK FOUR: CHAPTER TWO – THERE IS A SOLUTION

READ: Page 17, paragraph 1   page 17, paragraph 2

The fellowship of Alcoholics Anonymous is a great thing. There is power in people who are supporting each other and the AA fellowship is a very strong support group. It's therapeutic to be among others who have recovered from the same problem. But, we think that fellowship alone would never have held us together in the way we are now joined. This is a very important warning in *The Big Book*.

Early on, people in this program didn't have a lot of problems with the fellowship like we have today. The earlier people didn't have much fellowship at all. There were only a few small groups when *The Big Book* was written; one in New York, a small number in Cleveland, and Akron, Ohio, and a few other groups scattered around here and there. So you see, they could not go to 90 meetings in 90 days. **They had to work the real program directly out of *The Big Book*.**

Today we have a much larger AA fellowship. You could just go around "fellowshipping" and never work the program suggested in *The Big Book*. You can just live off the fellowship but you can't get and stay sober from the fellowship alone because **the vital spiritual experience comes from the action outlined in the first 164 pages of *The Big Book***. The fellowship alone will not change your life. Some people say "Go to 90 meetings in 90 days and you'll get sober". Well, you may get DRY from alcohol, but you don't recover from the **"DIS–EASE"**. You can no more get sober, than you can become a parent by going to 90 PTA meetings for 90 days. **You have to take some steps**.

READ: Page 17, paragraph 3

Here, Bill is saying, **"fellowship is not enough"**. He said, **"The tremendous fact for every one of us is that we have discovered a common solution"**. The *common problem* is a great bond, but he said the real thing is this ***common solution***. *The Big Book* carries the great message of the **common solution**. Later on it is revealed that **the common <u>solution</u> to alcoholism is a vital <u>spiritual experience</u>**.

We determined from the first part of *The Big Book* that we are powerless. In this part of the book, he writes the prescription. The prescription is **<u>Power</u>**, and Bill tells us the power of the fellowship and the power of the common solution will overcome any person's powerlessness over alcohol.

Anyone can get sober, but the real questions are: *"How do you stay sober?"*, *"How do you change?"*, *"How do you learn to live in such a manner that you are able to stay sober in the future?"*

Bill warns us, that even though the fellowship is one of the powerful elements in the cement that binds us together, that alone is not enough. The great fact is that we need both elements for recovery, the same two things Bill needed to have in order to recover.

4. The <u>fellowship</u> (Bill had with Ebby)
5. The <u>practical program of action</u>, which led him to the vital **spiritual** <u>experience</u>.

This is the real <u>SOLUTION</u> to the disease of alcoholism.

READ: Page 18, paragraph 1   page 23, paragraph 2

There is no way that I can trigger my allergy, produce the **phenomenon of craving**, end up drunk, sick and in trouble if I don't take the first drink. That makes good sense to me.

"Therefore, the main problem of the alcoholic is centered in the mind rather than in the body." The fact that I'm allergic to alcohol is important for me to understand, but the real problem centers in the mind rather than the body. **All action is born in thought!** There is no way that I can drink unless my mind tells me that it's OK to take a drink.

"There is the obsession that somehow, someday, we will beat the game." Here is the word **"obsession"** now entering into the picture. The great obsession of every alcoholic is to drink like normal people. This is the great lie that we believe that someday, somehow, we are going to be able to beat the game. We actually believe a lie and based on the lie, we make a decision to take a drink. We take the drink and that triggers the allergy and then we can't stop.
          The real problem centers in the mind rather than the body.

READ: Page 23, paragraph 3   page 25, top of page

"We are without defense against the first drink." If we could only remember what a drink does to us… if only we could remember the jail houses, the divorce courts, the hospitals, the humiliations, the pain and sufferings of the last drunk… **we wouldn't take a drink. But we can't remember with sufficient force to keep us from taking the first drink.** The mind will give us some excuse to take it. **"There is a complete failure of the kind of defense that keeps us from putting our hand on a hot stove."**
Alcohol is like a hot stove… it has burned us over and over again. We are strangely insane when it comes to alcohol.

If we have "**placed ourselves beyond human aid**", then the AA fellowship alone will not bring about recovery from the disease of alcoholism because the fellowship is made up of a bunch of human beings who are just as powerless as I am. Recovery will have to come through something other than human power.

READ Page 25, paragraph 1 "There is a Solution"   page 25, paragraph 2

READ: Page 567, Appendix II – "Spiritual Experience"

I've learned a couple of things by reading this appendix. My concept of a **Spiritual Experience** is not at all what I had when I first read this book. This is an entirely different concept. I've learned that it doesn't make any difference whether it is a **Spiritual Experience** or a **Spiritual Awakening**, either one can occur. One is slow and one is fast, but the end result will be **I've tapped an unsuspected inner resource** of strength, which I identify as **"a Power greater than human power"**…or…**"God as I understand Him"**. This is a key statement that we need, because later on we are going to look at this **unsuspected inner resource** of strength.

The one key word in the entire appendix is **"CHANGE"**. Bill is the kind of writer that repeats himself over and over. A good writer uses different words to repeat himself. Notice on p.567, he uses the word **"change"** in many different ways. In the 1st paragraph he talked about a **"personality *change* sufficient to bring about recovery"**. In the 2nd paragraph he again said **"personality *changes*… in the nature of sudden and spectacular upheavals."** An "upheaval" is a "change". In the 3rd paragraph he talks about **"revolutionary *changes*"** To "revolutionize" is to "change something entirely". Here he also talks about **"an immediate and overwhelming God-consciousness"**. To overwhelm something is to change it, **"a vast *change* in feeling and outlook"**. In the 4th paragraph, first sentence, he talks about **"transformations"**. To "transform" is to "change". In the middle of this paragraph he talks about **"profound alterations"**. To "alter" is also to "change". **So the key word in this vital spiritual experience is to *CHANGE* our personality.**

When we get to AA we are usually **restless, irritable, and discontented**. We come in filled with **shame, fear, guilt, and remorse**. That is our personality when we enter AA. If we want to stay sober, we need to find a new way to live. We are going to have to **change** our personality, and become peaceful, happy, serene, useful, and helpful human beings. The **fellowship** alone will not bring this **change** in us without the **practical program of action** that is outlined in the first 164 pages of *The Big Book*. It's the combination of both that brings about the vital **spiritual experience**.

We are told in *The Big Book* there are **TWO POWERS**. One is the **fellowship** (which supports us) the other is in the common solution which is the **practical program of action** (which changes us), and which will give us the vital **spiritual experience**. We need both powers in order to recover. It is doubtful that any of us are going to recover without the fellowship. But we also doubt if any of us will recover without the vital spiritual experience.

READ: Page 25, paragraph 3   page 26, top of page

The only two alternatives we have are: 1) **To go on to the bitter end, blotting out the consciousness of our intolerable situation as best we can**, or 2) **Accept spiritual help**.

A good textbook never tells you something without giving you a good example of it. "The Doctor's Opinion" was followed by "Bills Story", wherein lies the perfect example of alcoholism. He has now told us of the need for the vital **spiritual experience**. On page 26, we see an example of a fellow who had this vital spiritual experience and where the idea came from; his name was Rowland Hazard. He was the man that went to the judge and got Ebby Thatcher released to his custody.

REFER TO CHART/DIAGRAM: "What Is the Solution?" page 31

READ: Page 26, paragraph 1   page 27, paragraph 4

Dr. Carl Jung, a celebrated psychiatrist, gave Rowland the solution, a vital **spiritual experience**. Rowland came back to New York and got involved in the Oxford Group program. By using their Steps and their program of action, he was able to find his power and recover.

Now we can see where the Steps came from. The First Step came from Dr. Silkworth, a non-alcoholic. The Second Step came from Dr. Carl Jung, another non-alcoholic. Rowland Hazard got in the Oxford Group, a group of non-alcoholics. The strange thing is how God used all these non-alcoholic people to put this program together. Bill was the key figure that put all these ideas into our program of action, but Bill did not create any of these Steps. Bill's mind was used by God as a vessel to put all these ideas together, to bring us the program we know today.

READ: Page 27, paragraph 4   page 29, paragraph 1

"Further on, clear-cut directions are given showing how we recovered." We have previously seen these words **precisely**, **specifically**, and now we see the words **clear-cut**. This does not sound like *"cafeteria-style"* to us. It doesn't sound like you take what you want and leave the rest. They are telling us exactly what they had to do in order to recover from the disease of alcoholism. The things we have learned up to this point are the things they had to learn in order to recover, i.e. *obtain sobriety*.

READ: Page 29, paragraph 2 to the end of page

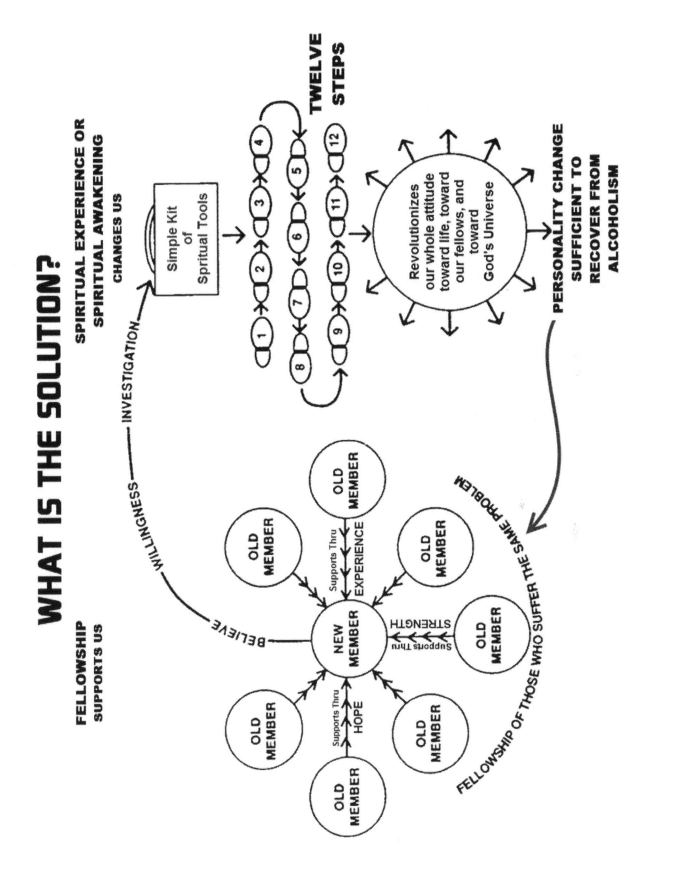

WHAT IS THE SOLUTION?

SPIRITUAL EXPERIENCE OR
SPIRITUAL AWAKENING
CHANGES US

FELLOWSHIP
SUPPORTS US

TWELVE STEPS

Simple Kit of Spritual Tools

INVESTIGATION — WILLINGNESS — BELIEVE

Revolutionizes our whole attitude toward life, toward our fellows, and toward God's Universe

PERSONALITY CHANGE SUFFICIENT TO RECOVER FROM ALCOHOLISM

OLD MEMBER

NEW MEMBER

Supports Thru EXPERIENCE

Supports Thru STRENGTH

Supports Thru HOPE

FELLOWSHIP OF THOSE WHO SUFFER THE SAME PROBLEM

55

BIG BOOK WORKSHOP HOMEWORK ASSIGNMENT

***NOTE: It is suggested that the homework be done soon after the workshop meeting and then reviewed with your sponsor before the next workshop meeting.**

6. Read **"STEP TWO"** in the *Twelve and Twelve book* – USE HIGHLIGHTER!
7. Read Chapter 3 **"More About Alcoholism"** in the "Big Book" (1st time) – USE HIGHLIGHTER! (Just read and highlight the 1st time you read through the chapter.)
8. Read Chapter 3 **"More About Alcoholism"** in the "Big Book" (2nd time). Answer the "Work Assignment Questions" below as you read the chapter for the 2nd time.
9. Does your writing in your book list those things you attempted to do to control your use of alcohol and your failures? Be prepared to discuss how it applies in your life.

WORK ASSIGNMENT QUESTIONS
"MORE ABOUT ALCOHOLISM"

Page 30

9. Have you been unwilling to admit you are a real alcoholic? Are you bodily and mentally different?

10. Has your drinking career been characterized by countless vain attempts to prove you can drink like other people?

11. Have you suffered from the obsession that somehow, someday, you can control and enjoy your drinking?

12. Was the persistence of this illusion astonishing? Did you pursue it into the gates of insanity or death?

13. Have you learned that you have to fully concede to your innermost self that you are alcoholic? Is this the first step in recovery?

14. Do you believe the delusion that you are like other people or presently may be has to be smashed?

15. Do you believe that you will ever recover control? Did you at times feel you were regaining control but were such intervals usually brief and inevitably followed by still less control which led in time to pitiful and incomprehensible demoralization?

16. Are you convinced you were in the grip of a progressive illness and over any considerable period of time you got worse and never better?

WORK ASSIGNMENT QUESTIONS (Continued)
"MORE ABOUT ALCOHOLISM"

Page 31

13. Does there appear to be any kind of treatment which will make you like other people?

14. Do you believe there is such a thing as making a normal drinker out of an alcoholic?

15. By every form of self-deception and experimentation, have you tried to prove yourself an exception to the rule, therefore non-alcoholic?

16. Have you tried long enough and hard enough to drink like other people? What are some of the methods you have tried?

Page 32

12. To get a full knowledge of your condition (if there were no other way to find out) would you be willing to consider the idea of diagnosing yourself and trying some controlled drinking? Trying to drink and stopping abruptly; trying it more than once?

13. Do you believe that a long period of sobriety and self-discipline would qualify you to drink like other people?

14. Do you believe that by gathering all your forces, you could stop altogether?

Page 33

13. Do you believe that to stop drinking, there must be no reservations of any kind, or any lurking notion that someday you will be immune to alcohol?

14. Can you stay stopped on your own willpower?

Page 34

10) Do you desire to stop altogether and can you do that on a non-spiritual basis? Have you lost the power to choose whether you will drink or not drink?

11) No matter how great the necessity or wish, can you leave it alone (stay stopped)?

Page 35

8. Do you believe that the crux of your problem is the mental state, which would precede a relapse into drinking?

9. Do you believe that if you fail to increase your spiritual life, you will drink again?

33

WORK ASSIGNMENT QUESTIONS (Continued)
"MORE ABOUT ALCOHOLISM"

Page 37

5. During your drinking, did your sound thinking fail to hold you in check and an insane idea won out?

Page 38

3. However intelligent you may have been in other respects, where alcohol was involved, were you strangely insane?

Page 39

1. Do you believe you could stay stopped on the basis of self-knowledge alone?

Page 42

9. Do you have an alcoholic mind and do you believe that the time and place will come that you will drink again?

10. Do you believe this problem has you hopelessly defeated? Has this process snuffed out the last flicker of conviction that you could do the job yourself?

11. Do you believe that you will have to throw several lifelong conceptions out the window to go through with the program of action?

12. Have you discovered that spiritual principals will solve all your problems?

Page 43

9. Is there any doubt in your mind that you are 100% hopeless apart from divine help and is there any other solution?

10. Do you believe that at certain times you will have no effective mental defense against the first drink and neither you nor any other human being can provide that defense? Must your defense come from a Higher Power?

WEEK FIVE: CHAPTER THREE - MORE ABOUT ALCOHOLISM

Bill said, "Even though I've told them of the need for spirituality, they still are not going to want it. They probably have the same aversions to spirituality and religion as I had. I should explain to them a little more about the disease of alcoholism in order to convince them of the need for the vital spiritual experience."

In this chapter, "More About Alcoholism", Bill shows us why we are going to need to have a spiritual awakening if we are going to exist. In this chapter he talks about one thing and one thing only, **the insanity of alcoholism**.

READ: Page 30, paragraph 1   page 30, paragraph 2

Many of us in A.A. have been very confused about this word 'insanity'. Others of us said, "I don't have any trouble with the word insanity because I remember all the crazy stupid things I did while drinking!" Those crazy stupid things we did while we were drinking are not caused by insanity, they are caused by alcohol. Alcohol is a sedative drug, which lowers our inhibitions and allows us to do stupid, crazy things.

Insanity deals with the inability to see the truth. It has nothing to do with being crazy. If you are a crazy person that means you lost most of your brains. Insanity is entirely different than crazy. It deals with the ability to see the truth about a subject or not see it. In the dictionary, the word sane means, "a whole mind." If you are sane, your mind is whole and you can see the truth. If you are insane, your mind is less than whole. At certain times you can't see the truth about something. It does not mean you are all gone, it just means that you are not quite all here. And when it comes to alcohol, at times we are not quite all here.

We seem to be unable to see the truth. We believe a lie about alcohol. If you believe a lie, your mind is less than whole and you have a degree of insanity. That's all we're referring to when we talk about illusion and delusion. They all mean believing a lie.

The rest of this chapter is devoted to examples, which show us the "believing of a lie" and shows us the state of the mind just prior to taking the first drink. Now remember that just prior to taking the first drink, the mind is stone cold sober. Let's look at the mind, alcohol free, just prior to the first drink.

READ: Page 30, paragraph 3   page 33, paragraph 1

It takes some of us many times of trying it one more time to come to the realization that:

"Once an Alcoholic, Always an Alcoholic"

"We are like men who have lost there legs; we can never regrow new ones."

READ: Page 33, paragraph 2   READ AFTER: page 37, paragraph 1

How can such lack of proportion or the ability to think straight be called anything other than plain insanity? This kind of thinking about alcohol has been a characteristic in every single one of us.

READ: Page 37, paragraph 2   page 42, top paragraph

Can you see that in those strange mental blank spots (insanity), that willpower and self-knowledge will not keep you from taking that first drink?

READ: Page 42, paragraph 2   page 43, bottom of page

Now Bill has convinced me in this chapter that if I don't have that vital spiritual awakening there is no way I will stay sober because my insanity will always lead me back to thinking I can take that first drink.

Now we are faced with the idea that we are going to need a vital spiritual experience. Having come from a religion that taught me hellfire and brimstone, well, this put me in a terrible spot. Thank God, Bill came from the same place. Knowing a spiritual awakening is vital to our recovery, he wrote for us another chapter, "We Agnostics."

I think "Chapter Four – We Agnostics" is the greatest piece of spiritual information I have ever read. A.A. gives me two things, 1) It gives me the concept of "God as I understand Him", and 2) Chapter Four gives me a new understanding of God. It is in Chapter Four that my God changed from hellfire and brimstone to a kind and loving God. Chapter Four lets me make that leap from what God used to be, to a God of my understanding that I can use in my life to have that vital spiritual experience.

The <u>Sickness</u> is Unrecognizable
Within Ourselves, by Ourselves...

We suffer from a spiritual blindness, a disease of perception, which prevents us from seeing the very illness we need to recover from. To assume that you can fix, that which you cannot determine, is the very brand of insanity that we suffer from. Herein lies the reason we need to grant spiritual concent to another human being to help guide us on this journey. We cannot do this alone, for if we try, our delusional natures will lie to us and at best we could only see partial truths which have always failed us.

©2016 Aron Schwartz

I'm going to have to make a decision soon. I am at the "turning point". I will have to decide to continue drinking till I die or live on a spiritual basis. Based on my own knowledge I cannot make that decision. Thank God for Chapter Four!

BIG BOOK WORKSHOP HOMEWORK ASSIGNMENT

***NOTE: It is suggested that the homework be done soon after the workshop meeting and then reviewed with your sponsor before the next workshop meeting.

10. Read Chapter Four "We Agnostics" in *The Big Book* (1st time) – USE HIGHLIGHTER! (Just read and highlight the 1st time you read through the chapter.)

11. Read Chapter Four "We Agnostics" in *The Big Book* (2nd time). Answer the "Work Assignment Questions" below when you read the chapter the 2nd time.

12. By now you should have completed writing most of your memories about why you are powerless over alcohol and why your life is unmanageable. If you are having
difficulty with these problems, discuss this with your sponsor.

WORK ASSIGNMENT QUESTIONS
"WE AGNOSTICS"

PAGE 44
13. Does a spiritual experience seem impossible? Do you feel as though you are an atheist? Are you an agnostic?

14. Have you had to face the fact that you must find a spiritual basis of life or else?

PAGE 45
17. Would a mere code of morals or a better philosophy of life be sufficient to overcome your alcoholism?

18. Is lack of power your dilemma?

19. Do you believe the main object of this book is to enable you to find a Power greater than yourself that will solve your problem?

PAGE 46
17. When God is mentioned, do you have honest doubt and prejudice?

18. Have you been able to lay aside prejudice and express a willingness to believe in a power greater than yourself?

19. Do you believe your own conception, however inadequate, is sufficient to make an approach and to effect a contact with God? (provided you take other simple steps)

20. Do you believe the realm of the spirit is broad, roomy, and all-inclusive?

WORK ASSIGNMENT QUESTIONS (Continued)
"WE AGNOSTICS"

PAGE 47

15. Do you believe this is all you need to commence spiritual growth and to effect your first conscious relationship with God (first half of the Second Step)?

16. Do you now believe or are you even willing to believe, that there is a power greater than yourself? Do you believe that upon this simple cornerstone a wonderfully effective spiritual structure can be built?

17. Do you believe you cannot make use of spiritual principles unless you accept many things on faith which seem difficult to believe? Do you believe there is a process from simple belief to faith?

PAGE 48

15. Have you found yourself handicapped by obstinacy, sensitivity, and unreasonable prejudice, and has even casual reference to spiritual things made you bristle with antagonism? Do you believe this thinking has to be abandoned?

16. Faced with alcoholic destruction (Step One), have you become as open minded on spiritual matters as you tried to be on other questions? In this respect was alcohol a great persuader? Did it finally beat you into a state of reasonableness?

PAGE 49

12) In the past, have you chosen to believe that your human intelligence was the last word; the alpha and the omega, the beginning and the end of all? Was that vain of you?

PAGE 50

10. Have you ever given the spiritual side of life a fair hearing?

11. Do you believe you need to gain access to and believe in a Power greater than yourself? Do you believe that this Power, in your case, can accomplish the miraculous, the humanly impossible?

12. Do you believe you will have to whole-heartedly meet a few simple requirements to have a revolutionary change in your way of living and thinking?

PAGE 51

6. Leaving aside the drink question, do you see the underlying reasons why you were making "heavy-going" of life (lack of Power)?

WORK ASSIGNMENT QUESTIONS (Continued)
"WE AGNOSTICS"

4. In the realm of the spirit, has your mind been fettered by superstition, tradition and all sorts of fixed ideas?

PAGE 52

13. Do you need to ask yourself why you should apply to your human problems (the unmanageability of your Life) the same readiness to change your point of view?

14. Did you stop doubting the power of God when you saw others solve their problems by a simple reliance upon God?

15. In the past, have you stuck to the idea that self-sufficiency will solve your problem?

PAGE 53

11. Do you believe it is more sane and logical to believe than not to believe?

12. Faced with the First Step and crushed by a self-imposed crisis that you cannot postpone or evade, do you believe you have to fearlessly face the proposition that either God is everything or else He is nothing? That God either is or He isn't? What is your choice to be (second half of Step Two)?

13. Having arrived at this point, are you squarely confronted with the question of faith? Can you duck the issue? Have you already walked far over the bridge of reason toward the desired shore of faith?

14. Have you been faithful to the God of reason in one way or another? If so, have you discovered that faith has been involved all the time?

PAGE 54

5. Can you still say the whole thing is nothing; created out of nothing; meaning nothing?

6. Have you seen that reason isn't everything?

PAGE 55

3. Have you been fooling yourself?

4. Do you believe, deep down within every man, woman and child is the fundamental idea of God?

5. Have you seen that faith in some type of God is a part of your make-up, just as much as the feeling you have for a friend?

2. Do you believe He is as much a fact as you are?

3. Do you believe you will find the Great Reality deep down within?

4. Do you believe in the last analysis, it is ONLY there (deep down within) that God can be found?

5. Has the testimony of these people helped to sweep away prejudice?

6. Enabled you to think honestly?

7. Encouraged you to search diligently within yourself?

8. Do you believe with this attitude you cannot fail and that the consciousness of your belief is sure to come to you?

9. Do you believe as you draw near to God, that He will disclose Himself to you?

NOTES:

(Use this space to make any notes that you've accumulated throughout this workshop)

WEEK #5 – MORE ABOUT ALCOHOLISM - Leader Notes

{OPTIONAL REVIEW OF LAST WEEK}
Last week we looked at little picture "What is the Solution?" On the left-hand side of the picture we saw the fellowship, which supports us. We saw where the older members through the sharing of their experience, strength and hope with the newcomer, provides enough support for the newcomer to be able to stay sober for a period of time. By the way, it's a two way street. As we older members support the new member we draw strength from that too. There is great strength in the fellowship. It would be almost impossible to be in AA today for very long and not begin to believe that there is some Power greater than human power working, for when you hear countless hundreds of people saying: "It's only by the grace of God"; or "because of God as I understand Him"; or "because of the Power greater than I am I haven't found it necessary to take a drink".

You can hardly hear that over and over and over and not begin to believe there is some Power working within this thing. The instant the newcomer begins to believe that, it opens their mind, and they become willing to investigate. And upon investigation we find that simple "kit of spiritual tools" that is laid at our feet, the 12 Steps of Alcoholics Anonymous. As we work and apply those steps in our lives we undergo a personality change sufficient to recover from alcoholism. We find a Power greater than human power. When that happens to us, we then have become older members of Alcoholics Anonymous. Now we can go back to the left-hand side of the sheet and we can help support the next newcomer and help them work their program so they can have a spiritual experience also.

The Big Book plainly states that you can not give something away that you haven't got. Now somewhere down the line when they quit working the program out of the book, then in self-defense they starting measuring success by, how long have you been sober rather than by the quality of that sobriety. In the beginning everybody was expected to work the program, have a spiritual experience. If they didn't want to do that they were told you might as well leave here because we can't help you if you don't to that. So our older membership was based on quality of sobriety rather than quantity of sobriety.

Now today, you see all kinds of people in AA. You see some that have been in here maybe 6 months. They've got a good sponsor. They got immediately into the program. They have worked the steps, they have had a spiritual awakening, and they're always laughing, cutting up, having fun, always helping AA and doing what they can for other alcoholics. They are a delight to behold and you just love to be around them. Only sober 6 months. You've got others that have been in the 6-8-10 years. Treated it like a cafeteria. Took some but left what they didn't want. Now they're better than they used to be, but, you never know what kind of shape they're going to be in when you run into them. One day they're up, the next day they're down. They're kind of like a yo-yo going back and forth. Then you see some people that have been in here 15-16-18-20 years. Never worked a step and damn proud of it. And they're the ones that say, "By God, if you want what we've got, you better be willing to go to any damn lengths to get it". Now some of those guys feel so bad you'd like to buy them a drink. You know they would feel better with a drink! So we are NOT talking about quantity of sobriety here. We're talking about quality of sobriety.

WEEK #5 – MORE ABOUT ALCOHOLISM - Leader Notes

{BEGIN WEEK #4 READING}

Only those that have had the spiritual experience can help another have a spiritual experience. You simply can't give away something you don't have. I can imagine Bill running all this through his mind. And he probably says to himself: "They're not going to like this idea of a spiritual experience any more than I did." You remember he had an aversion to these things. He and Ebby argued about this for a long time. And I think Bill says "I need to tell them just exactly what's going to happen to them if they don't have this spiritual experience." So he writes another chapter and he called it 'MORE ABOUT ALCOHOLISM", and in this chapter he talks about one thing and one thing only. He talks about the insanity of alcoholism.

You know, Step 2 says, "We came to believe that a power greater that ourselves could restore us to sanity." Well if we've got to be restored to sanity, that indicates we must be insane. Many alcoholics are highly offended when you bring this up. They say "Oh don't tell me I'm insane. Sure, I do some pretty crazy, stupid things when drinking but when I'm sober I'm much like normal people." Other alcoholics say "Well I don't have any trouble with this insanity idea because I remember the crazy, stupid things I did while drinking." In either case they are referring to the stupid things we do while drunk. NO, that's not insanity. The stupid things we do while drunk are caused by a mind that is filled with alcohol which lowers the inhibitions, and if your mind is filled with something that lowers your inhibitions, look out! You are going to do some pretty crazy stupid things all right. That's why they give all that free booze away at casinos! That's not caused by insanity, that's caused by alcohol itself. In order for us to understand this, we finally had to go back to the dictionary again and to look up the word 'sanity', and it's defined in the dictionary as:

Sanity - wholeness of mind or completeness of mind

If your mind is whole, if your mind is complete, that means you can see the truth about everything around you and you will normally then make decisions based on truth and life turns out to be pretty good. An insane mind is one that is less than whole. A mind that is less than whole cannot always see the truth about everything around it. Sometimes the insane mind makes a decision based upon a lie and then life becomes pretty lousy. To be insane does not mean you're crazy. If you're crazy that means you've lost more than half your marbles, and you have got to be locked up somewhere to protect you and society from you. That's craziness. But insanity is just less than whole.

I think one of the best ways I know to illustrate it is to imagine a pie and set it here in front of us. Let's cut that pie into ten pieces. You come along and I give you a piece of pie. My pie is now "less than whole" but I've still got 90% of it. Somebody else comes along and I give them a piece of pie. My pie is now even more, "less than whole", but I still have 80% of it. Insanity does not mean you are all gone. It just means your not quite all here.

When it comes to alcohol, from time to time, it seems as though we are not quite all here… we can't always see the truth about alcohol… we make a decision based upon a lie, then we run into the truth and life becomes an absolute living hell. So let's look within the mind of we alcoholics just before we take the first drink… Stone cold sober…
Can we or can we not see the truth?

If we can see the truth, we're sane.
If we can't, we're insane.

WEEK #5 – MORE ABOUT ALCOHOLISM - Leader Notes

In 'Chapter 3 – More About Alcoholism', Bill is going to show us this by a series of examples. He's going to give us 'the man of 30', he's going to look at 'Jim', he's going to look at the 'jaywalker' and he's going to look at 'Fred'. With each example, we are going to look into their mind to see if we can or cannot see the truth about alcohol.

Chapter 3 is called 'More About Alcoholism'. It could just as easily be called 'More <u>Truth</u> About Alcoholism'. I've heard all my life, if you know the truth, the truth will set you free. Therefore if you're not free, it's because you don't know the truth. This chapter should give me more truth so I can base my life upon truth rather than upon things that are not true.

[Read: Page 30, Paragraph 1   Page 30, Paragraph 2]

In these two paragraphs Bill has used four different words that all mean the same thing. He said, "The idea that somehow, someday he will control and enjoy his drinking is the great <u>obsession</u> of every abnormal drinker." Now we know an obsession is an idea that is so strong it can make you believe something that's not true. It can make you believe a lie.

"The persistence of this <u>illusion</u> is astonishing." We know what an illusionist is. An illusionist is a magician. And they can stand in front of you and with slight of hand and a few props they can make you believe something that is not true. So an illusion also means to believe something that is not true or to believe a lie.

"Many pursue it into the gates of <u>insanity</u> or death." Insanity is to believe something that is not true. In the next paragraph he said, "The <u>delusion</u> that we are like other people, or presently may be, has to be smashed." Delusion means the same thing. If you've deluded yourself, it means you've come to believe something that is not true.

So you may see Bill using any one of four terms: Obsession; Illusion; Insanity; Delusion. All four mean exactly the same thing: "to believe something that is not true"; or "to believe a lie".

READ: Page 30, Paragraph 3   Page 33, Paragraph 1

Now we know the truth to be this:

"Once an alcoholic, always an alcoholic"

We've never seen one single case where one of us was able to go back to successful drinking… to believe anything different than that is to believe something that is not true, or to believe a lie. This guy believed that after 25 years of sobriety he could now drink like normal people. Now based upon that belief he took a drink, triggered the allergy, couldn't stop…four years later he's dead. Now is his real problem the fact that he has a physical allergy to alcohol or a form of insanity that tells him it's OK to drink alcohol after 25 years of sobriety?

The real problem is centered in our mind telling us we can drink, rather than in our body, that ensures that we can't drink.

[Read: page 33, paragraph 2   page 35, paragraph 1]
{-- JIM --}
{Leader Comment: Now we're going to look in old Jim's mind just before he gets drunk and we're going to see whether he is sane or insane. Continue reading…}

WEEK #5 – MORE ABOUT ALCOHOLISM - Leader Notes

[Page 35, paragraph 2   p 37, Paragraph 2]

In this story we get to look at Jim's mind just before he gets drunk and we can see the switch from sane to insane thinking. Jim is a typical alcoholic, isn't he? They told him about Step 1… the physical allergy, the obsession of the mind, the powerless condition. They told him about Step 2… that a Power greater than ourselves could restore us to sanity. A little later on the Big Book it says, Step 3 is just a beginning. So apparently Jim took steps 1, 2 and 3 and immediately things started to get better for him. But Jim failed to enlarge his spiritual life. The book is going to tell us that the only way we enlarge on Step 3, is steps 4-5-6-7-8-9-10-11 and 12 … Jim didn't do Steps 4-12. Jim only did Steps 1, 2 and 3. (The A.A. waltz)

Jim got drunk six times in a row. Each time they went over there and worked with him, carefully reviewing what had happened. (You get drunk six times in a row today and they probably won't have anything to do with you.) He got drunk again. They said, "My God Jim this is seven times in a row! Let's don't go through this any more. You sit down here and you tell us exactly how this has happened." On page 36 we see where Jim was sane and then we see where he was insane.

We read this book for years before we saw this. "I came to work on Tuesday morning." Where was he all day Monday? We alcoholics are bad about Mondays. I think any of us that had to be a salesman for a concern we once owned, would probably be a little irritated by having to work at the place we once owned. That's normal sane thinking. Then the boss probably said "Hey Jim, by the way, where were you all day yesterday anyhow?" Not too serious but just enough to irritate him. A little restless, a little irritable a little discontented. What's more normal than if you're a car salesman, you want to get away from the shop for a while, drive out in the country, see somebody that we already know that we're trying to sell a car to. That would be normal sane thinking for an alcoholic car salesman. It's certainly normal, if you're hungry, to stop at a roadside place to get a sandwich.

The fact that there is a bar there is beside the point. We have no intention of drinking. We're hungry… we're going to get a sandwich… normal sane thinking for an alcoholic car salesman. We're not going in there to drink. We've eaten there many times during the months we were sober. We're going to go in there, get a sandwich and maybe sell a car while we're in there… normal sane thinking for an alcoholic car salesman. It is normal then to sit down at a table to order a sandwich and a glass of milk… normal sane thinking for an alcoholic car salesman. Now if you're hungry enough there's nothing wrong with two sandwiches and two glasses of milk. That would be normal sane thinking for an alcoholic car salesman… two sandwiches… two glasses of milk. Now comes the squiggly writing. That's italic.

Big Book p. 36, par 2 "Suddenly the thought crossed my mind that if I were to put an ounce of whiskey in my milk it couldn't hurt me on a full stomach."

This is absolute insanity! For this guy to believe that he can take whisky, mix it with milk and take it on a full stomach and it won't hurt him. Now based on that insane idea, he makes a decision and takes some action. We take the first drink…Now we've got it inside of ourselves…The physical allergy takes over….Now we can't stop. If you were looking for a definition of insanity that would be it right there. How can the lack of proportion of the ability to think straight be called anything else? Now is Jim's real problem the fact that he has physical allergy to alcohol OR that he has a form of insanity that tells him it's OK to drink alcohol mixed with milk on a full stomach?

The real problem is centered in the mind telling us we can drink, rather than the body, that ensures that we cannot.

WEEK #5 – MORE ABOUT ALCOHOLISM - Leader Notes

{-- JAYWALKER --}

Bill's next example is the "jaywalker". Now I don't understand this guy at all. But I can see him out here on the interstate, waiting for a truck or bus to come down through there. He jumps out in front of it, spins around two or three times to how close it can come to him without actually hitting him. For some reason he gets a thrill out of it. Don't understand him but I can see him doing it.

[READ: Page 37, paragraph 3   page 39, paragraph 1]

I think that's so appropriate today. You know, because of awareness, education and the justice system, many people are getting to AA before they have to lose everything. Now you might see them come in here still married and still have job. They may even still have a car, but I bet they lost their drivers license! When we start talking to those people about insanity they say "Hey, don't tell me I'm crazy! I haven't lost anything! I've got my job. I've got my blah blah blah". NO... we're not talking about that at all. We are talking about one thing and one thing only:
Can we or can we not see the truth about alcohol?
                    If we can we are sane, if we can't then we are insane.

Now for the low bottom drunk like Jim, it's probably easier for him to see his insanity because he lost everything that he had. For a high bottom drunk that hasn't lost a lot of stuff, sometimes it's a little more difficult for them to see it. But I will tell you this, whether you are low bottom or high bottom, if you get drunk, you're going to get drunk the same way by <u>believing something</u> <u>that is not true</u>.

[Read P 39, Paragraph 2   Page 43, to the end of chapter]
{-- FRED --}

Fred is the opposite of Jim. Fred is high bottom. Fred never lost anything. Jim didn't feel too good the day he got drunk. Fred is on top of the world the day he gets drunk, yet he got drunk the same way. He believed a lie. Let's look at Fred's state of mind again: Big Book p. 40 "I was much impressed with what you fellows said about alcoholism, but I frankly did not believe it would be possible for me to drink again.

I somewhat appreciated your ideas about the subtle insanity which precedes the first drink, but I was confident it could not happen to me after what I had learned. I reasoned I was not so far advanced as most of you fellows, that I had been usually successful in licking my other personal problems, that I would therefore be successful where you men failed. I felt I had every right to be self-confident, that it would be only a matter of exercising my will power and keeping on guard. In this frame of mind, I went about my business and for a time all was well. I had no trouble refusing drinks, and began to wonder if I had not been making too hard work of a simple matter."

<u>We think Fred began to get drunk right here.</u> He began to say "Ah this staying sober is easy... nothing to this!" Now is Fred's real problem the fact that he has a physical allergy to alcohol or that he has a form of insanity that tells him it's OK to have a couple of cocktails with dinner?
The real problem is centered in the mind telling us we can drink, rather than in the body, that ensures we can not.

WEEK #5 – MORE ABOUT ALCOHOLISM - Leader Notes

You know Rowland had the same idea that self-knowledge would fix it. Even Bill had the idea that self-knowledge would fix it and here Fred had the idea that self-knowledge would fix it. Bill is trying to show us that they ALL had the <u>obsession of the mind</u>. Bill just took us through all these examples to say:

Big Book p. 43, par 3 "Once more: the alcoholic at certain times has no effective mental defence against the first drink. Except in a few rare cases, neither he nor any other human being can provide such a defense. His defense must come from a Higher Power."

That's it… that IS the solution
>You can't heal a sick mind with a sick mind.
>>Self-knowledge won't cut it, the more we try to think our way out it, the deeper into it we get. It must come from a Higher Power… our defense must come from a Higher Power.

Notice he didn't say "the practicing alcoholic" or "the drinking alcoholic". He just said the alcoholic. Now what that means to me today is that I have no effective mental defense against the first drink. Left on my own resources, invariably I'm going to go right back to drinking again, without the aid of a Power greater than human power.

Now if you're the kind of alcoholic that I am, and if you were raised in a similar church setting that I was, by the end of Chapter 3 you are now faced with a huge dilemma. Bill has convinced me in Chapter 3, without the aid of a Power greater than me, I'm going back to drinking. But I also felt that even though that was true, it wouldn't be possible for me to get the aid of a Power greater than I am. What I remember hearing about God when I was growing up and in church was hellfire and brimstone and that I was going to hell for lying and cheating and stealing and drinking whiskey and committing adultery. By the time I got to AA I had being doing that for many years. I felt that if God had anything to do with me it wouldn't be anything good. It would certainly be something bad.

I remember so clearly when I separated from God. My church gave me the rules. They said if you do this, this and this you'll be OK. If you do that, that and that you're going to hell. Now I didn't have any trouble with the rules at all, until one day it seemed to me that they looked me straight in the eye and said "To think about doing it is just as bad as doing it". And I said, "Oh crap! I've had it now!" Because I'd been thinking about doing it for a long time! I thought to myself "If you are going to hell for thinking about it, then you might as well just go ahead and do it". So I did. But I didn't go to hell immediately, and in my mind I said "They have been lying to me all along! This is a conspiracy to keep me from having any fun! From this day on I do not intend to pay any attention to what they have to say. I don't have any intention of following God's rules, their rules or anybody else's rules. From this day on I'm going to do it my way. I'm going to do whatever I want whenever I want and if they don't like it, so be it." Now when I got to AA, I had that same attitude. When I first walked into AA I had that same spiritual knowledge of God. No wonder we have trouble with this God thing when we get to AA. Anybody else ever have those kinds of feelings about God and people?

I think Bill recognized this. I think he said, "Sooner or later I'm going to have to ask these people to make a decision about God". And I think he said in his mind that "They are not going to be able to make that decision based upon old ideas." That's what I had when I got here, old ideas. And I think he said, "I believe I need to give them some new information about God". Where they might be able to discard some old ideas, pick up some new ideas, and then they'll be able to make a decision about this God thing.

WEEK #5 – MORE ABOUT ALCOHOLISM - Leader Notes

To help us with this dilemma, Bill wrote another chapter in the Big Book called, "We Agnostics", which I think is one of the greatest pieces of spiritual information I've ever read in my life. As I read that chapter and studied it, I could see where some of my old ideas, old prejudices about God and religion, were wrong.

When I could see where my old ideas were wrong then I could discard them, and I could accept some new ideas about God and then I could make a decision. Not based on hellfire and brimstone but based on a God of justice… there was no way could I have ever made the decision about God until I tossed aside my old prejudices about God and accepted some new ideas. Thank God for Chapter 4. Let's look at just a little bit of it just before leave tonight.

Dr. Carl Jung told Rowland Hazard about ideas, emotions and attitudes. That's what we're going to be looking at now. Ideas, emotions and attitudes, which were the guiding force of the lives of these people, are suddenly cast to one side. Most certainly the ideas, emotions and attitudes that I had toward God were that of a child. I couldn't accept it then, I couldn't accept it later, I couldn't accept it when I got here and I can't accept it today because I need new ideas and emotions and attitudes about this. I needed new information.

Chapter 4 – We Agnostics… lets break down the title so we can understand it better… just the word "agnostic" means something to me. The root of the word "nostic" means "knowledge", the first part "ag" means "without", put the "ag" in front of it and you get "agnostic" or "without knowledge". Therefore, "We Agnostics" means "Those of us who are without knowledge." That was me alright, and the knowledge that I did have was not good. Bill had the same experiences that we did.

When Ebby presented him with the solution he was aghast at that solution. Some of us are aghast at that solution also. Bill said "When they talked of a God personal to me my mind became irritated and my mind snapped shut against such theories." And certainly that's the way many of us reacted. Later on in the Big Book it tells us that "…when the spiritual malady is overcome we straighten out mentally and physically." Hmmm, "…the spiritual malady…"

The understanding of "God of my understanding"

When that is straightened out, we will straighten out mentally and physically.
The next chapter, We Agnostics, is an attempt to help must see that for all
of our thinking, we had been wrong about the idea of faith and that maybe
we should think about giving it a try….

WEEK SIX: Chapter 4 – WE AGNOSTICS

READ: Page 44, paragraph 1   page 44, paragraph 3

In the first paragraph, Bill asks us two questions:

15. **When you honestly want to, is it true you cannot quit entirely?**   (That is the **obsession**.)
16. **When drinking, do you have little control over the amount you take?**   (That is the **allergy**.)

If your honest answer to either or both of these questions is "yes" then you are probably alcoholic. We need not ask ourselves anything more than those two questions to determine whether or not we are alcoholic.

Some people tend to over complicate things. Our fellowship today has taken **two simple questions** and first expanded them to **ten questions**, then **twenty questions** and finally turned it into a **pamphlet**, which has **forty-four questions**! Thank God, Ebby didn't have the forty-four questions when he went into Bill's kitchen. Imagine Bill sitting there drunk…he has been drinking for three weeks straight. Now imagine if Ebby had asked, "Bill, has alcohol been bothering your reputation?" Hell, he hadn't had a reputation in years! Or if Ebby had asked, "Has alcohol been interfering with your sex life?" He hadn't had any of that in years either. One of the forty-four questions asks, "Do you drink alone?" Well think about it…If I'm buying, the answer is "yes"… and if you're buying, then "no".

We had an old friend that used to live in Tyler, Texas. His name was Wino Joe. I've always felt sorry for everybody in AA that didn't get to meet Wino Joe. He was a real character. He's dead now, but Wino Joe had made up his own list to ask yourself to see if you're alcoholic. The first question on his list was "Has the roof of your mouth ever been sunburned while drinking?" He said, "If it has, you're probably alcoholic." I think the second question was, "Have you ever been arrested for drunk driving from the back seat of somebody else's car?" The third one I loved was, "Have you ever been arrested for public drunkenness while in jail?" He had a big list of them.

We only need the two questions Bill gave us. I use them all the time. People come to me and ask, "Do you think I might be alcoholic?" I say, "I have no idea. Let me ask you a couple of questions. Have you been able to quit drinking entirely left on your own resources?" If they are a real alcoholic, they have to say "no". Then I ask, "Do you have any control over the amount you take after you've started drinking?" If they are a real alcoholic, they've got to say "no", and then I say, "Well you're probably an alcoholic". That's about as simple as you can make it. Now, if that is your case too, you may be suffering from an illness which only a **spiritual experience** can conquer.

We are a very unique people. We are the few people in the world that have an illness of the mind and the body that can only be overcome by a spiritual experience. We realize that we are the only people in the world that have an illness that is a terminal illness and we can come out of it in better shape than when we went into it.

The third paragraph has two words that need to be defined: "**Atheist**" and "**Agnostic**"

    ATHEIST - **One who says God does not exist.** If a person really believes that, there is no power on earth for him greater than human power. The only power that he can depend upon is his own mind. He can't really trust other people. Since there is no God, he must run his own show, effect his own destiny, and make his own decisions. **Are you an atheist?**

AGNOSTIC - **One who believes God exists, but because you cannot prove it, he acts as though God does not exist.** He runs his own show, effects his own decisions, stands on his own two feet, and rules his destiny. In other words, he acts exactly like the atheist does, yet he believes that God exists. **Are you an agnostic?**

For either case, **atheist** or **agnostic**, we are going to have to find some way to have this **spiritual experience**, and to use this Power greater than human power. For many of us that seems to be an impossible task. Let's see how we make that transition: "How do I get from that state to the state of being a true Believer?" A true believer is one who believes in God and acts as if he does: He doesn't stand on his own two feet, doesn't run his own show, and doesn't rule his own destiny. He turns to God for help and gets the guidance and the strength and the Power he needs. He believes that God does exist. Even the atheist will admit that there is such a thing as evolution and if evolution isn't evidence of some Power greater than human power, I don't know what is. I think most of us are agnostics when we get to A.A. We believe in God, but we don't turn to God for help and direction. We run our own show. And we get the <u>same results</u> as the atheist.

READ: Page 44, paragraph 4   page 45, paragraph 2

I've never met an alcoholic yet who didn't have a **code of morals** or a **philosophy for life**. We know what we should do and we know what we shouldn't do. We know how we should live and we know how we shouldn't live. But our problem is **because of our alcoholism, we are unable to live up to those codes, those philosophies and those morals**.

"Lack of power that was our dilemma." You know if we weren't powerless we wouldn't be here would we? It goes on to say *"Its main objective is to enable you to find a Power greater than yourself which will solve your problem."* It doesn't say which will help **you** solve it. It says the main objective is to <u>enable</u> you to find the Power greater than yourself and then **that Power will solve the problem**. Interestingly enough, from this point on we are through talking about alcohol. From page 45 on, we will talk about one thing and one thing only. **How we can find this Power?** And if we can find the **Power**, then **the Power will solve the problem**.

We know that for every one of us the main problem is a lack of Power. We were driven here under the lash of alcoholism. We came here because **we are powerless over alcohol**. If we're powerless, **we lack the power**, and **then the obvious answer is Power**, and **the question is, whether you're atheist or agnostic or not, how do you find the Power?** Surely we're not true believers because if we were, we would have had the Power before we came to A.A. However, we can get this Power and apply it in our lives in order to overcome our disease. Now, **if we're atheist or agnostic, maybe we can change to a true believer and find that Power and then that Power will solve our problem.** The rest of the chapter is devoted to how do you find that Power. The whole rest of the book is devoted to that one subject. It is a very simple procedure and it starts over on page 47.

READ: Page 45, paragraph 3   page 47, paragraph 2

So the wonderfully effective <u>spiritual structure</u> we're building is the <u>spiritual experience</u> or the <u>spiritual awakening</u>. The <u>foundation</u> of that structure was <u>Step One</u>, which is <u>willingness</u>. Bill also tells us the **<u>cornerstone</u>** of that structure is **<u>Step Two</u>; <u>believing</u>**. Bill tells us that the cornerstone is to believe or to be willing to believe that there is Power greater that human power. This is the beginning. Bill calls this the "cornerstone". Remember, when we took Step One that was **<u>willingness</u>** to change. Once you see that you're powerless over alcohol and your life has become unmanageable and that this isn't going to work, then you become willing to change.

That's the "foundation". Once the foundation is laid, on that foundation we lay a cornerstone. After you become willing to change, then you have to believe you can change. Step Two is the "cornerstone". All we have to do to start off in this program is to **believe** or **become willing to believe**. So we have two parts of the wonderfully effective spiritual structure in place if we can say "yes, we believe" or "yes, we are willing to believe". Notice the asterisk at the bottom of the page. Please be sure to read Appendix II about the "Spiritual Experience". This is the third time we have been referred to Appendix II Spiritual Experience; the wonderfully effective **spiritual structure** is this vital **spiritual experience**. We are going to see as we progress through the steps that we are building that spiritual experience, or that spiritual structure. We have already put two of the stones in place, so we are already building the structure as we are going through the book, chapter by chapter.

READ: Page 47, paragraph 3   page 48, top paragraph

All you have to do to start out is to believe. **Believing** comes before you do something and **Faith** comes after you believe and then take action. Today, how can you not believe that there must be some Power working within this fellowship of Alcoholics Anonymous? When you first come in here, you don't know that to be true, but you can believe it. And if you **stay** with us long enough and **work the program** and **have a spiritual experience**, then you'll know it; and that is **Faith**. But, *faith without works is dead*.

READ: Page 48, paragraph 1   page 51, paragraph 1

The reason we have everything we've got today is because it's been developed within the last century. Students of Ancient History tell us that the intellect of men in those days was equal to the best of today. I used to think we invented this stuff because we were smarter. But we really aren't. People who lived thousands of years ago were just as smart as we are today. Yet in ancient times, material progress was painfully slow. Very little of this stuff was developed years ago. Thousands of years ago, even 500 years ago, you were not allowed to believe differently.

You couldn't believe anything different because of superstition, tradition, and fixed ideas. These kept you from believing differently and you couldn't change anything. It's only in the last 100 years that our minds have been freed in the realm of the material to believe differently. The reason we went to the moon is because somebody believed we could do that. This is the same reason why we have microwaves, cars, and television.

I think the story of Columbus is one of the greatest examples of what you can do when you are willing to change your belief. Some 500 years ago most of what they called the "civilized world" was situated around the shores of the Mediterranean Sea and the western shores of Europe.
They had found a place called the East Indies. In the East Indies you could get gold, silk, and spices; lots of goody goodies. But it took literally years get to the East Indies. They were trying to find a new trade route to the East Indies. Somebody asked "Is there any possibility that we can sail a ship there?"

The answer was, "No dummy! Don't you know you can only sail as far as the northeast end of the Mediterranean Sea, and then you have to go by land?" Camelback, horseback, foot-back, however they traveled…that trip took years complete. "Well what would happen if we sailed in the other direction?" And they said, "Well idiot, don't you know if you sail that way you're going to fall off the edge of the earth!" In those days everyone thought the world was flat and if you sailed out there too far to the west you would sail off the edge of the earth.

I don't know why they believed that, but I assume it was because some people who sailed out there, didn't come back, and they just thought they had sailed off the edge. Wouldn't it be great if the world was flat? We could take all of this environmental junk and trash out of here and go push it overboard off the edge and be done with it all!

Now here's Columbus, and we believe that Columbus had to be an alcoholic because if you're going to believe differently than the entire world and everybody in it and you're going to stand there and express that belief; you are going to have to be tougher than hell to do it! Many times if you express a belief different than what everybody else believes they would burn you at the stake or hang you from a tree, or cut your head off or something.

But Columbus was tough enough and bullheaded enough to be able to stand there and say, "I believe that the world is round: I do not believe it's flat". Then he made one of the most drunken statements the world has ever heard, he said, "I believe we can get to the East by sailing west." Now if that isn't drunk thinking I don't know what is! Many of his mannerisms indicated Columbus was an alcoholic:

When he left he didn't know where he was going.
When he got there he didn't know where he was.
When he got back he didn't even know where he had been.
But what really made him an alcoholic was a woman financed the whole trip for him; twice!

Columbus followed a formula; a little formula that the world has always known and used:
To change anything at all, there are certain things that have to take place.

The first thing you have to do in order to change anything is to be <u>willing</u> to change. *Circumstances* are what make us willing. Trying to find the new trade route to the East Indies is what made Columbus willing to change. **The second thing you have to do to change anything is to <u>believe</u> you can.** Columbus said, "I believe that the world is round, not flat, and I believe you can get to the East by sailing west." But his belief wasn't enough because he was still standing on the shore of the ocean the day he expressed that belief. Some days, weeks, months, years later he did **the third thing, he <u>made a decision</u>**. He said "By golly I'm going to go find out whether this thing is round or flat. Can you really get to the East by sailing west?" But his decision wasn't enough either, because he was still standing on the shore of the ocean the day he made that decision. Some days, weeks, months, years later he did **the fourth thing you have to do, he started <u>taking action</u>**.

The first thing Columbus did is he went to the King of Portugal to get the money. But the King of Portugal being a very astute businessman said, "There's no way I'm going to let you have this money because you'll sail out there and sail right off the edge of this sucker and I'll lose it all". He didn't give up and then went to see the Queen of Spain. Columbus sweet-talked her and promised that he would bring back gold, silk, spices, and the 'goody goodies' of life. She gave him the money.

He bought three ships, hired crew members and loaded those ships with provisions for the trip. Then they set sail and began to go east by sailing west…sailing west, day, after day, after day. Now we don't know for sure, but we have a suspicion that on that first trip he hired a special sailor and put him on the bow of the lead ship at night with a lantern and whispered in his ear, "I believe this thing is round, but if you see the edge of this damn thing you holler so we can get turned around in time!"

Now, after sailing due west for several days, they got results. They found land on the other side, which was the result of the action that they had taken. Columbus thought it was the East Indies. It wasn't; it was the West Indies, but he had proven to himself that the world is not flat, it is round, and you won't sail off the edge of it. He turned around and went back to Europe, right back to the Queen of Spain, and she asked, "Columbus, where's the gold, silk and spices you promised you would bring me?" He said, "Sweetheart I'm sorry but I didn't find any. Tell you what I'll do; if you will refinance me I'll go back. Trust me honey. Please? This time I'll find it!" She re-financed him and he got some more ships, more provisions, more crew members and began to go east by sailing west with one big difference; the second trip he didn't hire the lookout and put him on the bow of the lead ship at night. **This time he went back on faith; he went back on knowledge. The first time he went on belief.**

You can't start with faith. The only things you can do are:

- **start with belief** (Step Two)
- **make the decision** (Step Three)
- **take the action** (Steps Four through Eleven)
- **get the results and then you will have faith**

I would love to sit here and tell you today that the Twelve Steps of Alcoholics Anonymous are brand new and that the world has never seen anything like them before, but if I did, I would be telling you a lie. Because the Twelve Steps are based on the same identical formula that Columbus and any other human being has ever used to change anything.

The first thing we have to do in order to recover from alcoholism is to be <u>willing to change</u>, and that's what **Step One** gives us; the **<u>willingness</u>**. As soon as we can see that what we are doing is no longer going to work, then we become willing to change. The second thing we have to do is to **believe we can;** that's **Step Two.** But that belief will do us no good unless we **make a decision about it;** that's **Step Three.** However, that decision will do us no good unless we **take the action**, and those are **Steps Four, Five, Six, Seven, Eight, Nine, Ten, and Eleven.** The result of the actions are that **we too will get results**, just as it says in the first part of Step Twelve; "Having had a spiritual awakening, **as the result of these steps..." we now have faith. We now have knowledge. We no longer just believe**.

You see, I don't just believe that God will restore me to sanity; having worked the Steps, I *know* He will, because He has done so (first part of Step Twelve).

Those of us who have been restored to sanity and now have faith; can now help:
The next newcomer come to **believe** (Step Two)
They can make a **decision** (Step Three)
We take them by the hand and walk with them through the **action steps** (Steps Four through Eleven)
Then they will get **results**, have a spiritual awakening, and they will know (first part of Step Twelve)
Then they can go help the next newcomer come to **believe** (second part of Step Twelve)

There is only one thing we can't do for the newcomer: **<u>We cannot make them willing</u>** (Step One). That's a job they have to work on themselves.

How does an alcoholic become willing to change?

Very simple...drink lots of alcohol! I hear people come to AA and they say "I've been working on Step One for three years in AA" and I say, "No you haven't!" **You don't work on Step One (willingness) in AA. You work on Step One out there... and when you have drunk enough, when you just can't stand it any longer, then you become willing to change.** Then we can begin to help you by helping you come to believe, decide, act, and have a spiritual awakening.

It's the same formula that the world has always used to change the status of anything. Now if,

... I know I need the Power
I know the beginning of the finding of the Power is just to believe
I know the procedure (formula) to follow to find the Power

I only need to know one more thing: Where am I going to find that Power?

READ: Page 51, paragraph 2   page 55, Top of page

Again, we see another illustration of the **power of believing** and how this **power is used**. There are other illustrations throughout the book. Bill talks about electricity. Electricity is a power greater than us. We can harness it. We know how to generate electricity, but we don't know that much about it. They say it's a force of undetermined origin. We don't really know where electricity comes from or where it begins.

 I think this is like the Power we receive from God. Like great powers and all the powers in our universe, we don't know where they exist. But, *we don't have to know about them to use them*. Bill talks about the Wright brothers. How can a bicycle mechanic **believe** he can build an airplane? But they did believe. The Wright brothers went out and they believed, and they made a decision, and they took the thing out and a lot of times they crashed, but **they didn't stop**. If you fail, if you believe and you make a decision and you fail, it's real simple: All you have to do is change what you believe. **Change** your decision and you'll finally get it right. And that's what they did and finally they got the thing to fly.

We are the only ones that can allow limitations in our lives. **Whatever we believe, we become**. So be careful if you believe some bad stuff. You had better watch it because it's going to be a part of your life. If we want to **change bad beliefs to good beliefs**, we will have to **change our minds** and begin **to believe differently**. This is what we read in the **"Spiritual Experience"** on page 567.

I think this little story about the Wright brothers was put in here to show us, that most of us were Agnostics. Since most of us believed in God, but couldn't prove it we had to take a chance. That little story shows us that proof is not always right. I found in my life that any Power greater than human power can't really be proven one way or another. Only **the results of our actions will prove it**. God is the same way: I don't have to understand God and you don't have to prove it to me to be able to find the Power. Now, if **I know I need the Power, I know the beginning is the belief**, and if **I know the formula** to find it, the only thing left I have to know is where that power is. My book is complete - it gives me everything I need to have. On page 55, it tells me where to find that **Power**.

READ: Page 55 paragraph 1   page 57, to the end of Chapter 4

I think *The Big Book* is telling me that **God dwells within me**. I think today that every man, woman, and child on the face of the earth has some form of knowledge inside themselves, and that form of knowledge seems to be able to tell us what we should do and what we should not do. It seems to be able to tell us the difference between right and wrong. It seems to be able to tell us how we should and should not live. What most of us have done in our chase for money, power, prestige and sex, is we have disregarded that knowledge, pushed it inside ourselves and obscured it.

But now, we begin to operate on a **conscious knowledge of the mind to satisfy our wants, needs, and desires**. I think some people want to call that knowledge "common sense." Others might want to refer to it as a conscience and surely some would call it the soul. Still others call it innate intelligence. I don't really feel it makes much difference what we call it as long as we recognize the fact that it is there. I've had evidence of this in my life and you have too. Sometimes I was getting ready to do something and some voice from somewhere would say to me, "I don't think you ought to do that", and I wouldn't pay any attention to it. I'd go right ahead and do it. And I'd just get into a hell-of-a shape. And then that same voice would say, "See, I told you not to do it." It's been a part of me all my life.

"Have you ever gazed up at the stars at night and wondered to yourself; who could have made all of this? Have you ever looked inside of a medical text book and realized how intricate the mechanical workings of the human body were; and how complex and synergistic everything down to the smallest atoms was; each having a purpose within itself and within the greater whole. Have you ever thought to yourself that no human could've made this, that there must be something at work here, so incredibly powerful, intelligent and miraculous to have been able to create such complex synergism throughout all of the world natural world, not to mention the universes'.?"

Remember, in the Appendix II it talked about tapping into an unsuspected inner resource of strength that we might want to identify with a Power greater than ourselves or God as we understand Him. If God dwells within me, and I believe He does, then **He dwells within you**. It also means we can have a personal God. I don't have to worry anymore whether it's hellfire, damnation or brimstone. If He dwells within me, then He's my own personal God. This has given me **a completely new concept of God, as I understand Him**.

It has changed my understanding of God from hellfire and brimstone to an entirely different kind of God. It has given me a simple little procedure that if I will follow it, I will be able to find that Power and I don't have to know anything - all I have to do is believe, and decide, and act. Then I'll get results. Then I can go back and help the next person "come to believe". I don't believe we could make our decision without this chapter. Most spiritual things you read will try to prove God to you. This chapter doesn't do that. It gives you a procedure that if you will follow it, God will prove Himself as the results of what you get from following this procedure.

This is some of the greatest information I have ever learned:
> **I can have my own personal God**
> **He dwells within me**
> **My knowledge comes from and through Him**
> **I will be able to find that Power!**

Am I ready to make a decision? You bet! When He was the God of justice, when He was hellfire and brimstone, I wasn't ready to make that decision. But throughout this chapter my concept of God has changed entirely. I'm beginning to believe He just might be a kind and loving God, and just maybe He will start doing some good things for me, not hellfire and brimstone. Now I am ready to make a decision. I don't think it is by accident that the very next chapter is titled 'How It Works'. Now Bill sits down and he writes the chapter 'How it Works' which contains some of the best spiritual information the world has ever seen…a little formula…a set of proposals…

Bill called them, the Twelve Steps of Alcoholics Anonymous.

THE BIG BOOK WORKSHOP HOMEWORK ASSIGNMENT

***NOTE: It is suggested that the homework be done soon after the workshop meeting and then reviewed with your sponsor before the next workshop meeting.**

13. In your notebook write what you can believe about a Power greater than yourself. On another page write what you cannot believe about God. As you go forward from this point, it will be those things that you believe or which fit your conception of God that you will be using. You can be comforted in knowing that "our own conception, however inadequate, was sufficient to make the approach and to effect a contact with Him." (*The Big Book,* page 46)

14. Read Chapter 5, **"How It Works"** (p58 - p63) in *The Big Book* (1st Time) – USE HIGHLIGHTER (Just read and highlight the 1st time you read through the chapter.)

15. Read Chapter 5, **"How It Works"** (p58 - p63) in the "*The Big Book*" (2nd Time).
    Answer the "Work Assignment Questions" below as you read the chapter for the 2nd time. **4)**
Be prepared to discuss the material in Chapter 5, page 58 to 63 (i.e. through the part that concludes Step Three)

WORK ASSIGNMENT QUESTIONS: "HOW IT WORKS"

PAGE 60
7. Do you question whether you are capable of being honest with yourself?
    (If you do have questions you're not capable of being honest with yourself, yet.)

NOTE: *The state of mind you are asked to have when you start the steps is: honesty, fearlessness, thoroughness and a willingness to go to any length.*

5. What do half measures avail us?

6. Are you convinced that a life run on self-will can hardly be a success?

7. Can you see the effects of self-centeredness in your life?

8. Have you been self-centered? (*List examples of your self-centeredness in your notebook.*)

PAGE 62
16. Did you know that you could not reduce self-centeredness by wishing or trying your own will power?

17. Are you willing to make the decisions set forth at the bottom of page 62?

PAGE 63
Take note of the promises that follow as the result of taking of Step Three (described at the top of page 63)

1. Are you willing to take this step?

WEEK #6 – WE AGNOSTICS
Joe and Charlie Transcript

Dr. Carl Jung told Rowland Hazard about ideas, emotions and attitudes. That's what we're going to be looking at now. Ideas, emotions and attitudes, which were the guiding force of the lives of these people, are suddenly cast to one side. Most certainly the ideas, emotions and attitudes that I had toward God were that of a child. I couldn't accept it then, I couldn't accept it later, I couldn't accept it when I got here and I can't accept it today because I need new ideas and emotions and attitudes about this. I needed new information.

"We Agnostics"... lets break down the title so we can understand it better... just the word "agnostic" means something to me. The root of the word **"nostic"** means **"knowledge"**, the first part **"ag"** means **"without"**, put the "**ag**" in front you get **"agnostic"** or **"without knowledge"**. Therefore, **"We Agnostics"** means **"Those of us who are without knowledge**."

That's me alright, and the knowledge that I did have wasn't good. Bill had the same experiences that we did. When Ebby presented him with the solution he was aghast. Some of us are aghast at the solution also. Bill said **"When they talked of a God personal to me my mind became irritated and my mind snapped shut against such theories."** And certainly that's the way many of us reacted. Later on in the Big Book it tells us that **"...when the spiritual malady is overcome we straighten out mentally and physically."** Hmmm, "...the spiritual malady..."

The understanding of, "God of my understanding"

When that is straightened out we will straighten out mentally and physically. The chapter "We Agnostics", is an attempt to do that. 'Father' Bill Wilson said... (some of you know "Father Bill" said this to us many, many times, and I love it) he said that this chapter is not put here to teach me that there is any particular type of religion or type of God. Bill said this chapter is simply put here so that I might read, question and wonder... to get some ideas, emotions and attitudes... some new ones.... and **to open up my mind to the point that God might prove to me there is a God**. Now with that understanding, this chapter makes more sense to me and becomes extremely valuable in my life.

[READ: Page 44, Paragraph 1   Page 44, Paragraph 3]

Let's look closer at the first paragraph: *"In the preceding chapters, you have learned something of alcoholism. We hope we have made clear the distinction between the alcoholic and the non-alcoholic. If, when you honestly want to, you find you cannot quit entirely,* (Because of the obsession) *or if, when drinking, you have little control over the amount you take,* (Because of the allergy) *you are probably alcoholic."*

Isn't that simple? But, people like to expand on things. They took the 2 questions out of the Big Book and some years later they made a little pamphlet that had 10 questions in it. But that wasn't enough; they made another one that had 20 questions in it. I think we're up to 44 questions today. Thank God that Ebby didn't have the 44 questions with him when he walked into Bill's kitchen. He would have said "Bill, has alcohol been bothering your reputation?" Bill hadn't had a reputation in years. Then he would have said, "Bill, has alcohol been interfering with your sex life". If he was anything like I was he wouldn't have had any of that in a long time either. One of the 44 questions asks "Do you drink alone?" Well think about it... If I'm buying, the answer is "yes"... and if you're buying, then "no".

WEEK #6 – WE AGNOSTICS
Joe and Charlie Transcript

We had an old friend that used to live in Tyler, Texas. His name was Wino Joe. I've always felt sorry for everybody in AA that didn't get to meet Wino Joe. He was a real character. He's dead now. But Wino Joe had made up his own list to ask yourself to see if you're alcoholic. The first question on his list was "Has the roof of your mouth ever been sunburned while drinking?" He said, "If it has, you're probably alcoholic." I think the second question was "Have you ever been arrested for drunk driving from the back seat of somebody else's car?" The third one I loved was "Have you ever been arrested for public drunkenness while in jail?" He had a big list of them.

We only need the two questions Bill gave us. I use them all the time. People come to me and ask "Do you think I might be alcoholic?" I say, "I have no idea. Let me ask you a couple of questions. Have you been able to quit drinking entirely left on your own resources?" If they are a real alcoholic, they've have to so "no". Then I ask, "Do you have any control over the amount you take after you've started drinking?" If they are a real alcoholic, they've got to so "no", and then I say, "Well you're probably an alcoholic". That's about as simple as you can make it. Now, if that is your case too, you may be suffering from an illness which only a spiritual experience can conquer.

You know we are very unique people. We number amongst few people in the world today who suffer from a two-fold illness that can only be overcome by a spiritual experience; who have a terminal illness that we can come out of in better shape then we were when we went into it, if we can have this spiritual experience. We are unique people.

Now let's look at the second paragraph again: *"To one who feels he is an atheist or agnostic such an experience seems impossible, but to continue as he is means disaster, especially if he is an alcoholic of the hopeless variety. To be doomed to an alcoholic death* (Step 1) *or to live on a spiritual basis* (Step 2) *are not*

I had to stop right here, and ask:

What is my belief as far as this 'God thing' is concerned?

Today we find there is only one of three ways that you can believe as far as God is concerned:

One way is to be an <u>atheist</u>. Now an atheist says, "There is no God". Therefore they have no power greater than human power to turn to. The atheist would have to stand on their own two feet and run their own show.

The second way is to be an <u>agnostic</u>. So I had to go to the dictionary and look that word up, and like we said the word **agnostic means without knowledge.** An agnostic believes that there is a God, but since we have never tried to use Gods power in our life, we ran our own show, we stood on our own two feet... we have never received God's Power... so we don't <u>know</u> that God exists. Agnostics believe in some kind of God but don't really know whether that's true or not. I think that most of us are agnostic when we get here. Most of us get here with some belief in a God, but we have never turned to that God and we've been running our own show and standing on our own two feet and doing our own thing. Even though we believed in God, we acted as if we did not believe in Him. **An agnostic is one without knowledge of God, just belief.**

The third way is the <u>true believer</u>. A true believer is one that knows that God exists... doesn't just believe it... knows it. A true believer is one who has experienced God's Power in their life and God has given them what they need to have a successful life.

WEEK #6 – WE AGNOSTICS
Joe and Charlie Transcript

I don't think any of us get here as a true believer, because if we knew God and experienced God's Power, then we wouldn't have to come to AA to solve our problem. Most of us come here as agnostics. Whether we are atheist or agnostic, the question becomes: **How do you get from that stage, to the stage of one who is a true believer that can receive God's Power in our life?**

[READ: Page 44, Paragraph 4   Page 45, Paragraph 2]

You know if

"Lack of power that was our dilemma."

we? It goes on to say *"Its main object is to enable you to find a Power greater than yourself which will solve your problem."* It doesn't say which will enable you to solve it… or will help you solve it. It says the main object is to enable you to find the Power greater than yourself and then that Power will solve the problem. …Interestingly enough from page 45 on in the Big Book of Alcoholics Anonymous we don't talk about alcohol anymore. We're through with that. We talk about one thing and one thing only, whether you are atheist or agnostic, if you are powerless, **how do you find that Power?**

[READ: Page 45, Paragraph 3   Page 47, Paragraph 3]

"Much to our relief, we discovered we did not need to consider another's conception of God. Our own conception, however inadequate, was sufficient to make the approach and to effect a contact with Him." My sponsor, at the time, noticed that I had a real problem with this idea about God and he asked me about it. I said "I'm having a hard time trying to understand." He suggested I do something that helped him and maybe it would help me. He said "Why don't you go home tonight and write down on a piece of paper what you would like God to be, put aside all that stuff that you think that you know, and just write down on a piece of paper what you would like God to be." So I went home that night and I wrote down some things… things I'm not going to tell you… because it's up to you what you would like God to be. I wrote down some things that I wanted God to be and I showed them to my sponsor and he looked at them and he said "That's good, you can begin with that." You see, I didn't know you could do that!

Growing up I was told I had to believe as they did, that you had to have faith in what they had faith in otherwise you were going to hell. But my sponsor gave me permission and I needed that permission to sit down and to say that I would like God to be these things. When I showed him what I wrote on that paper, he said "That's good. You can start with that and you can begin with that." So that's exactly what I did. Here is where we can cast aside the first old idea. The old idea that I had was that you had to believe as they believed. They had me convinced that if you didn't believe as they believed there is no way that you're going to get anything good when it comes to God. So I was very pleased to find out that I can cast aside that old idea and I can have my own conception of God. And like we said earlier, I find I have never had any problem with my own conception of anything. This let me start believing in God. Now I've got an entirely different idea. An old idea cast aside replaced with a new idea. I can begin right here. You see all I had to quit doing was saying "no, there is not", and start seeking… saying "YES"… "Maybe"… I started seeking. I asked my sponsor, "You mean I need to find God?" And my sponsor said "God is not lost." It didn't take me long to figure out who was lost. He said "It's just like the book says, **it's in the seeking. It's not in the finding**." All I had to do was seek. That's all this book is asking me to do in this chapter. It is asking me to seek with an open mind and to wonder and to think and eventually God will disclose himself to me; and that's exactly what happened.

WEEK #5 – WE AGNOSTICS
Joe and Charlie Transcript

I was taught as a kid growing up, that the way to God was a very narrow path, that if you strayed off either side of this narrow path you were going to get in to a hell of a shape. I was taught that God was very, very exclusive and that only those that believed, as they believed, would be able to make any contact with God. Those were old ideas. Now my book says: *"We found that God does not make too hard terms with those who seek Him. To us, the Realm of Spirit is broad, roomy, all inclusive; never exclusive or forbidding to those who earnestly seek."*

Old ideas cast aside replaced with some new ideas… we begin to find this Power greater than human power by changing old ideas to new ideas. Bill tells us more on page 47: *"When, therefore, we speak to you of God, we mean your own conception of God. This applies, too, to other spiritual expressions which you find in this book. Do not let any prejudice you may have against spiritual terms deter you* Prejudice is nothing more than old ideas. Do not let any old ideas you may have against spiritual terms deter you from honestly asking yourself what they mean to you. *"At the start, this was all we needed to commence spiritual growth, to effect our first conscious relation with God as we understood Him. Afterward, we found ourselves accepting many things which then seemed entirely out of reach. That was growth, but if we wished to grow we had to begin somewhere. So we used our own conception, however limited it was."*
I needed a beginning place and that's where I started.

Now Bill tells us, *"We needed to ask ourselves but one short question. --"Do I now believe,"* (the agnostic has always believed in some kind of God) *"...or am I even willing to believe..."* (the atheist can become willing to believe that there is some kind of God) *"...that there is a Power greater than myself? As soon as a man can say that he does believe…"* (the agnostic) *"...or is willing to believe..."* (the atheist) *"…we emphatically assure him that he is on his way. It has been repeatedly proven among us that upon this simple cornerstone a wonderfully effective spiritual structure can be built.*"*

In this paragraph Bill makes real sure that we understand what is meant by those terms. He says, "It has been repeatedly proven among us that upon this simple cornerstone a wonderfully effective spiritual structure can be built.*" **So the wonderfully effective spiritual structure we're building is the spiritual experience or the spiritual awakening.**

He tells us that the cornerstone is to believe or to be willing to believe that there is power greater that human power. **The <u>foundation</u> of that structure was <u>Step One</u>, which is <u>willingness</u>**. He also tells us **the <u>cornerstone</u> of that structure is <u>Step Two</u>, <u>believing</u>**. So we have two parts of the wonderfully effective spiritual structure in place, if we can say "yes, we believe" or "yes, we are willing to believe".

"That was great news to us, for we had assumed we could not make use of spiritual principles unless we accepted many things on faith which seemed difficult to believe."

That has always been one of my great problems with this 'God thing'. Faith indicates surety. Faith indicates knowledge. Faith indicates after the fact information. One of my problems has always been when the minister would say, "All you have to do is have faith and everything will be alright". Well I never could have faith because I had no knowledge of God. I didn't know for sure that God would do anything for me. The best I can possibly do is to start with belief, and there is a big difference between belief and faith.

WEEK #6– WE AGNOSTICS
Joe and Charlie Transcript

over there to John, he'll do you a good job and he'll charge you a reasonable price." Well I don't know whether that's true or not. The best I can do with that information is if I believe it strong enough that I'll take my car over to John. Sure enough he does a good job and he charges me a reasonable price. When I leave there **I know** that he will do that. When I went there **I believed** that he would do that. Now six months later I have trouble with my car again but this time I don't ask you or anybody else where to take it. I take it right back to John. This time I took my car to John on faith… took it on knowledge.

You can't start with faith; you can only start with belief. That's all we have to do. We have to believe or we become willing to believe that there is a Power greater than we are and we're on the road to spiritual recovery. We don't have to know anything. Thank God Step Two says *we came to believe that a power greater than ourselves could restore us to sanity*. Didn't say we came to know. Didn't say we had faith in that, we *just came to believe*. I came to believe based upon what I'd read in the book and that you told me that there is a Power greater than I am that can restore me to sanity. I didn't know that, I just believed that. If the first thing I have to do, to find this Power, is just believe, or be willing to believe, then the next thing I need, is to know what procedure do I follow in order to find that Power?

[READ: Page 47, Paragraph 4   Page 51, Paragraph1]

I used to wonder why today we have cell phones, TVs, cars and airplanes and why people100, 200 or 500 years ago didn't have or invent those things. I thought we were just smarter than they were. But I've come to find out that they had the same intellect as we do. Intellect means the capacity to learn. They had the same capacity to learn as we do, but the thing that kept them in 'the dark ages', so to speak, was **superstition, tradition and all sorts of fixed ideas.**

In the Northeast United States some 225 years ago or so, people came here for religious freedom. They wanted to practice their religion as they understood it, and as long as you agreed with their religion and you practiced your religion somewhat like they did you were OK. But if you had any thoughts or ideas that were different and you expressed those openly and it didn't agree with what they thought they would burn you at the stake as a witch. So if you had any different ideas you certainly didn't express them, you kept them to yourself. **Superstition, tradition and all sorts of fixed ideas kept people from growing**. I think we as a country have gotten over that today, and our minds now are open to many, many things.

I think his story of Columbus is one of the greatest examples of what you can do when you are willing to change your belief. Some 500 years ago most of what they call the 'civilized world' was situated around the shores of the Mediterranean Sea and the western shores of Europe. They had found a place called the East Indies. In the East Indies you could get gold, silk, and spices; lots of goody goodies. But it took literally years get to the East Indies. They were trying to find a new trade route to the East Indies. Somebody asked "Is there any possibility that we can sail a ship there?" The answer was, "No dummy! Don't you know you can only sail as far as the northeast end of the Mediterranean Sea, and then you have to go by land"; Camelback, horseback, foot-back, however they traveled… that trip took years complete. "Well what would happen if we sailed in the other direction?" And they said, "Well idiot, don't you know if you sail that way you're going to fall off the edge of the earth!"

WEEK #6 – WE AGNOSTICS
Joe and Charlie Transcript

In those days everyone thought the world was flat and if you sailed out there too far to the west you would sail off the edge of the earth. I don't know why they believed that, but I assume it was because some people sailed out there, didn't come back, and they just thought they had sailed off the edge. Wouldn't it be great if the world was flat? We could take all this environmental junk and trash out there and go push it overboard off the edge and be done with it!

Now here's Columbus, and we believe that Columbus had to be an alcoholic because if you're going to believe differently than the entire world and everybody in it and you're going to stand there and express that belief, you are going to have to be tougher than hell to do it! Many times if you express a belief different than what everybody else believes they would burn you at the stake or hang you from a tree, or cut your head off or something. But Columbus was tough enough and bullheaded enough to be able to stand there and say, "I believe that the world is round; I do not believe it's flat". Then he made one of the most drunken statements the world has ever heard, he said, "I believe we can get east by sailing west." Now if that isn't drunk thinking I don't know what is!

Many of his mannerisms indicated Columbus was an alcoholic:
- When he left he didn't know where he was going.
- When he got there he didn't know where he was.
- When he got back he didn't even know where he had been.

But what really made him an alcoholic was a woman financed the whole trip for him! Twice!

Columbus followed a formula; a little formula that the world has always known and used. To change anything at all, there are certain things that have to take place.

The first thing you have to do in order to change anything is to be <u>willing</u> to change. Circumstances are what make us willing. Trying to find the new trade route to the East Indies is what made Columbus willing to change. **The second thing you have to do to change anything is to <u>believe</u> you can.** Columbus said, "I believe that the world is round, not flat, and I believe you can get East by sailing West." But his belief wasn't enough because he was still standing on the shore of the ocean the day he expressed that belief. Some days, weeks, months, years later he did **the third thing, he <u>made a decision</u>.** He said "By golly I'm going to go find out whether this thing is round or flat. Can you really get east by sailing west?" But his decision wasn't enough either, because he was still standing on the shore of the ocean the day he made that decision. Some days, weeks, months, years later he did **the fourth thing you have to do, he started <u>taking action</u>.**

The first thing Columbus did is he went to the King of Portugal to get the money. But the King of Portugal being a very astute businessman said, "There's no way I'm going to let you have this money because you'll sail out there and sail right off the edge of this sucker and I'll lose it all". He didn't give up and then went to see the Queen of Spain. Columbus sweet-talked her and promised that he would bring back gold, silk, spices and the 'goody goodies' of life. She gave him the money. He bought three ships, hired crew members and loaded those ships with provisions for the trip. Then they set sail and began to go east by sailing west… sailing west, day, after day, after day. Now we don't know for sure, but we have a suspicion that on that first trip he hired a special sailor and put him on the bow of the lead ship at night with a lantern and whispered in his ear, "I believe this thing is round, but if you see the edge of this damn thing you holler so we can get turned around in time!"

WEEK #6 – WE AGNOSTICS
Joe and Charlie Transcript

Now, after sailing due west for several days, they got results. They found land on the other side, which was the result of the action that they had taken. Columbus thought it was the East Indies, it wasn't, it was the West Indies, but he had proven to himself that the world is not flat, it is round, and you won't sail off the edge of it. He turned around and went back to Europe, right back to the Queen of Spain, and she asked "Columbus, where's the gold, silk and spices you promised you would bring me?" He said, "Sweetheart I'm sorry but I didn't find any. Tell you what I'll do; if you will refinance me I'll go back. Trust me honey. Please? This time I'll find it!" She re-financed him and he got some more ships, more provisions, more crew members and began to go east by sailing west with one big difference; the second trip he didn't hire the lookout and put him on the bow of the lead ship at night. **This time he went back on faith; he went back on knowledge. The first time he went on belief.**

You can't start with faith. The only thing you can do is:
start with belief   **(Step 2)**
make the decision   **(Step 3)**
take the action   **(Steps 4-11)**
get the results and then you will have faith

I would love to sit here and tell you today that the Twelve Steps of Alcoholics Anonymous are brand new and that the world has never seen anything like them before, but if I did, I would be telling you a lie. Because, the 12 Steps are based on the same identical formula that Columbus and any other human being has ever used to change anything.

The first thing we have to do in order to recover from alcoholism is to be <u>willing to change</u>, and that's what **Step 1** gives us; the <u>**willingness**</u>. As soon as we can see that what we are doing is no longer going to work, then we become willing to change. The second thing we have to do is to **<u>believe</u> we can;** that's **Step 2.** But that belief will do us no good unless we **<u>make a decision</u> about it;** that's **Step 3.** However, that decision will do us no good unless we **<u>take the action</u>**, and that's **Steps 4, 5, 6, 7, 8, 9, 10 and 11.** The result of the action is **we too will get results**, just as it says in the first part of Step 12; "Having had a spiritual awakening, **as the result of these steps..."** We now have faith. We now have knowledge. We no longer just believe.

You see I don't just believe that God will restore me to sanity; having worked the Steps, I know He will, because He has done so (1st part of Step 12).

Those of us who have been restored to sanity and now have faith; we can go back and help:
The next newcomer come to **believe** (Step 2)
They can make a **decision** (Step 3)
We take them by the hand and walk with them through the **action steps** (Steps 4-11)
Then they will get **results**, have a spiritual awakening, and they will know (1st part Step 12)
Then they can go help the next newcomer come to **believe** (2nd part Step 12)

There is only one thing we can't do for the newcomer: It's a job they have to work on themselves.

We cannot make them willing. (Step 1)

WEEK #6 – WE AGNOSTICS
Joe and Charlie Transcript

How does an alcoholic become willing to change?

Very simple… drink lots of alcohol! I hear people come to AA and they say "I've been working on Step 1 for three years in AA" and I say "No you haven't!" **You don't work on Step 1 (willingness) in AA. You work on Step 1 out there… and when you have drunk enough; when you just can't stand it any longer; then you become willing to change.** Then we can begin to help you by helping you come to believe, decide, act and have a spiritual awakening; it's the same formula that the world has always used to change the status of anything. Now if:

I know I need the Power

I know the beginning of the finding of the Power is just to believe
I know the procedure (formula) to follow to find the Power

I only need to know one more thing… Where am I going to find that Power?

[READ: Page 51, Paragraph 2   Page 57, End of Chapter]

I think we get here just as confused about 'where God IS', as we were ever confused about anything else. As a kid growing up, somewhere I got a picture in my mind. Now I don't know whether I dreamed it or saw it, but in my mind when I thought about God, he was a tall elderly gentleman; He stood on a cloud up in the sky and had long flowing white robes, long white hair, a golden halo around his head, and sunrays shooting out of that halo, and a big stick in his right hand. I am not sure whether I saw that or whether I dreamed it, but one of the reasons I thought God was there is because every time the minister talked about God he always pointed up there so I knew he had to be up there somewhere.

What really confused me was I noticed every time the minister wanted to talk to God, he always looked down. The minister pointed up as if to show me where God was, but then looked down when talking to God... no wonder I was confused as a kid about where God is! So I looked and I looked and I looked and I looked, and I never could find God because I never did know where He was. **It took the Big Book of Alcoholics Anonymous to tell me just exactly where I'm going to find Him.**

Many years ago I was sponsoring this young man and one morning he told me a story that really helped me a lot; this is the story he told me: There were three wise men in the east and they took from man the crown of life, the one thing that would make us the happiest. They took it away with them. They said, "Now that we took it away from them, what are we going to do with it?" One of them said "Here's what we will do, we will take it to the highest mountain on the face of the earth and we'll hide it up there, and they'll never be able to find it."

The other two said "Yeah, but you know how they are, they'll hunt and they'll search and they'll eventually find it." The third one said "Ok, I'll tell you what, we'll take it to the deepest crevice of the deepest ocean and hide it there and they'll never think about looking for it there." The other two said again, "Sure, but you know how they are, they'll hunt and they'll search and they'll eventually find it." Finally the third one said, "Hmmm… OK… Here's what we'll do, we'll hide it within man himself, and he'll never think of looking for it there!"

WEEK #6 – WE AGNOSTICS
Joe and Charlie Transcript

A God of your own understanding is sure to come to you with an open mind.

It seems as though all human beings are born with some basic knowledge, deep down inside themselves, probably lying at a subconscious level. That basic knowledge seems to be able to tell us what we should do and what we shouldn't do. It seems to be able to tell us how we should live and how we shouldn't live. I'm sure a lot of people would like to refer to that as just plain old common sense.

I think others might want to call it innate intelligence. Some might want to call it the conscious. Others might want to call it the soul. I don't think it makes any difference what we call it, as long as we **recognize the fact that it's there**. If you're anything like I am, as far back as I can remember I have always been aware of that knowledge.

There used to be times that I would be getting ready to do something, and some voice somewhere from within me would say, "I don't believe you ought to be doing this." And I wouldn't pay a bit of attention to it, and I'd go right ahead and do it and I'd get in one hell of a mess. And that same little voice would say see, "I told you not to do it in the first place". Now if that's true, and if that is God, then what that means to me today is:

If God dwells within me, then I've got my own personal God.

If he dwells within me, then he's my own personal God and He and I can come together in very simple and understandable terms.

This is some of the greatest information I have ever learned:
I can have my own personal God that dwells within me. My knowledge comes from Him and through Him I will be able to find that Power!

Am I ready to make a decision? You bet! When He was the God of justice, when He was hellfire and brimstone, I wasn't ready to make that decision. But throughout this chapter my concept of God has changed entirely. I'm beginning to believe He just might be a kind and loving God, and just maybe He will start doing some good things for me, not hellfire and brimstone.

Now I am ready to make a decision. I don't think it is by accident that the very next chapter is titled 'How It Works'. Now Bill sits down and he writes the chapter 'How it Works' which contains some of the best spiritual information the world has every seen… a little formula… a set of proposals…

Bill called them, the Twelve Steps of Alcoholics Anonymous.

WEEK SEVEN: Chapter 5 – HOW IT WORKS (Step Three)

Now as we have completed the **Chapter to the Agnostics**, we have laid the **foundation** and have established the first Two Steps.

Keeping in mind the problems Bill was having with the first forty people, writing the book was quite a task. Bill was writing the book in Hank's office in New Jersey and his secretary Ruth Hock would type these chapters out as Bill stood behind her. As these chapters were finished they were sent to the Akron and New York groups. The groups would go over each chapter and every word. This was a real task and we really don't know all they went through to get this book written. Ruth said that she had typed this manuscript forty-four times before it was finally printed!

Bill had completed the first four chapters and felt the groundwork had been laid. He felt it was now time for the main purpose of the book, to show alcoholics how to recover. Prior to writing this chapter he was having trouble. He prayed for guidance and then laid down. After a few minutes he picked up his pad and pencil and began to write. He said that it seemed as though his pencil had a mind of its own. Within thirty minutes he had written "How it Works" and the Twelve Steps. He really didn't know how many Steps he needed as he started. He had the Six Steps from the Oxford Group. He knew the Steps needed expanding in order to close the loopholes the drunks would jump through. When he finished, he numbered them. He noticed there were Twelve Steps and equated this with the twelve Apostles.

He had just finished the Steps when Howard, a New York member, stopped by to see him. Bill had a newcomer with him. They took a look at the Steps and neither one of them liked them. Both of them started giving Bill hell about the Steps. You know how alcoholics are, **they don't like change**. They had six steps in the Oxford Group and didn't care for him doubling the Steps. How would you feel if you went to a meeting and all of a sudden you had twenty-four steps? There were a lot of discussions and arguments in the groups. This crisis was probably only one of many in writing *The Big Book*. The writing of the book stopped and they went through a great dilemma. Some changes were made and they were able to go on with the book. Now we are going to read what Bill wrote that night as it appears in the Original Manuscript.

(From the Original Manuscript)

Chapter Five
HOW IT WORKS

Rarely have we seen a person fail who has thoroughly followed our **directions**. Those who do not recover are people who cannot or will not completely give themselves to this simple program. Usually men and women who are constitutionally incapable of being honest with themselves. There are such unfortunates. They are not at fault; they seem to have been born that way. They are naturally incapable of grasping and developing a way of life which demands rigorous honesty. Their chances are less than average. There are those, too, who suffer from grave emotional and mental disorders, but many of them do recover if they have the capacity to be honest.

Our stories disclose in a general way what we used to be like, what happened, and what we are like now. If you have decided you want what we have and are willing to go to any length to get it - then you are ready to **follow directions**.

At some of these **you** may balk. **You** may think **you** can find an easier, softer way. **We doubt if you can**. With all the earnestness at our command, we beg of you to be fearless and thorough from the very start. Some of us have tried to hold on to our old ideas and the result was nil until we let go absolutely.

Remember that **you** are dealing with alcohol - cunning, baffling, powerful! **Without help it is too much for you**. But there is one who has all Power - that one is God. **You must find him now**!

Half measures will avail **you** nothing. **You** stand at the turning point. **Throw yourself under His** protection and care with complete abandon.

Now we think you can take it! Here are the steps we took, which are suggested as **your** program of recovery:

1. Admitted we were powerless over alcohol - that our lives had become unmanageable.
2. Came to believe that a Power greater than ourselves could restore us to sanity.
3. Made a decision to turn our will and our lives over to the care **and direction** of God as we understood Him.
4. Made a searching and fearless moral inventory of ourselves.
5. Admitted to God, to ourselves, and to another human being the exact nature of our wrongs.
6. Were entirely willing that God remove all these defects of character.
7. Humbly, **on our knees,** asked him to remove our shortcomings - **holding nothing back**.
8. Made a list of all persons we had harmed, and became willing to make **complete** amends to them all.
9. Made direct amends to such people wherever possible, except when to do so would injure them or others.
10. Continued to take personal inventory and when we were wrong promptly admitted it.
11. Sought through prayer and meditation to improve our contact with God, praying only for the knowledge of His will for us and the power to carry that out.
12. Having had a spiritual **experience** as a result of **this course of action**, we tried to carry this message to **others, especially** alcoholics, and to practice these principles in all our affairs.

You may exclaim, "What an order, I can't go through with it." Do not be discouraged. No one among us has been able to maintain anything like perfect adherence to these principles. We are not saints. The point is that we are willing to grow along spiritual lines. The principles we have set down are guides to progress. We claim spiritual progress rather than spiritual perfection.

Our description of the alcoholic, the chapter to the agnostic, and our personal adventures before and after, **have been designed to sell you** three pertinent ideas:

1 That **you** are alcoholic and cannot manage **your own life**.
2 That probably no human power **can relieve your** alcoholism.
3 That God **can and will**.

If you are not convinced on these vital issues, you ought to re-read the book to this point or else throw it away!

We think in the **final statement**, Bill makes it clear what he has been trying to convey to us. He has been using the Doctor's Opinion and the first four chapters to sell us three pertinent ideas. Those three pertinent ideas are contained in Steps One and Two. So, if you are not convinced, you should read the book again or throw it away.

The very next thing he is going to start us on is Step Three. If you don't have Steps One and Two you can't do Step Three. Before the book was written, they would go out to the hospital, jails, or wherever, and by sharing of their stories they would convince him that he was alcoholic also. Through talking about the **disease**, the **physical allergy** and the **obsession of the mind**, they could help him see his **problem** and take Step One. Then they would ask if they could come back in a day or two.

They would return and begin talking about **Spirituality**, telling him how they had found it necessary to find a **Power Greater than human power**, and how they **apply it in their lives in order to recover**. They would help this alcoholic that had already identified with them, to be able to take what we know today as Step Two. Then they would take him to the Oxford Group meeting. They invited him to the meeting and would tell them that they had been talking with him and are **convinced** that he knows he is an alcoholic and that he **believes that God can restore him to sanity**, so we want to **sponsor him into the group**. That is what sponsorship was back then. The group would then vote on whether or not to take him into the group. After he was voted into the group, two or three of them would take him upstairs in Dr. Bob's house. **They would get down on their knees and he would make his surrender**, which we know today as Step Three.

So, if you are sold on Steps One and Two, you are now ready to take Step Three. From Step Three on, the book tells us with every Step, why you need to take it, how to take it and what the results will be. It does not do that with Steps One and Two because **they are not Working Steps**. Steps One and Two are **Conclusions of the Mind** that we draw based upon the information presented to us in the Doctor's Opinion and the first four chapters.

I think it is also clear, that Bill meant for these Steps to be a set of **individual directions** for the individuals to recover because he kept saying you, you, you. He did not call them **suggestions**, Bill called them **directions**. The rest of the fellowship immediately was upset when they saw this. Changing from 6 steps to 12 steps was bad enough, but what they really didn't like was the word 'directions'. They said, "Bill, you can't give an alcoholic direction. If you try, he won't do a damned thing!" Another bunch thought it wasn't strict enough. They argued back and forth. They said, "Instead of saying 'you' and 'you had to'; let's say 'we' and 'we had to'." Bill didn't want to change anything but the group insisted because it was their book, not his.

Finally, Bill realized he was going to have to accommodate their wishes. With the suggestion of a non-alcoholic psychiatrist they made some changes; they decided to drop 'directions' and make it 'suggestions' and quit saying you, you, you and say we, we, we and quit saying 'must', and use 'ought'. People would probably use the book a little more. Also as a compromise between the fundamental Christians and the Atheists, they decided on 'God as we understand him'.

Now, Bill is a real alcoholic, and alcohol is **cunning, baffling and powerful**. He said, "OK, I will agree to your changes, but I'm going to make a deal with you right now. I'm tired of fighting over this book. I'm not going to fight with you anymore. If I am to finish the book, you will have to let me be the final authority from here on out." They didn't want to write it either, so, they agreed to let Bill be the final authority from then on. What Bill knew that they didn't, was that he was going to put the word 'directions' back in the book, just two pages later. The rest of the way through the book he's used the words 'you' and 'must' also. This is the story of "How It Works", as it is written today.

READ: Page 60, paragraph 3   page 60, paragraph 4 "motives are good."

There are three words in Step Three that need to be defined. If we can understand them as the writer understood them, then it makes Step Three easy.

1. **Decision** - The word decision implies there is going to be further action.
2. **Will** - My will is nothing more than my mind; the power of choosing my actions or my thoughts.
3. **Life** - My life is nothing more than my actions. What I am today is the sum total of all the actions I have taken throughout my lifetime.

One of the problems many of us have in Step Three is that if we take Step Three, we will turn our will and our lives over to the care of God as we understand Him. But the Step said we make (made) a decision to do that. If we could turn it over in Step Three, we wouldn't need the rest of the Steps. If we make a decision to do something we are going to need to take certain action. The Action needed is Steps Four through Nine. All action is born in thought! If the thinking is right then the actions are right and usually the life is okay. If the thinking is lousy, the actions are lousy and life goes to hell in a hand-basket.

READ: Page 60, "Most people"   page 62, paragraph 3

"This concept was the keystone of the new and triumphant arch through which we passed to freedom." Again, we can see he is adding to the spiritual structure. In Step One, willingness was the foundation. In Step Two, believing was the cornerstone, and we didn't even know what we were building. Now here in Step Three, he tells us we are building an arch through which we passed to freedom. Step Three is the keystone in this arch. So we gain another stone in the structure. The keystone is the supporting stone at the top of the arch. It is the stone that holds the arch together. *(See diagram on p.53.)*

READ: Page 63, paragraph 1

We thought well before taking this Step, making sure we were ready; that we could at last abandon ourselves utterly to Him. This was only a beginning. Though if honestly and humbly made, an effect, sometimes a very great one, was felt at once.

LEADER: Review the chart "Road to Decision" on page 54 of the workshop handout.

WE ARE NOW READY TO TAKE STEP Three: Many groups take this step together and recite the prayer that is set forth on page 63 at this time.

> *"God, I offer myself to Thee - to build with me and to do with me as Thou wilt. Relieve me of the bondage of self, that I may better do Thy will. Take away my difficulties, that victory over them may bear witness to those I would help of Thy power, Thy love, and Thy Way of life. May I do Thy will, always!"*

BIG BOOK WORKSHOP HOMEWORK ASSIGNMENT

1. Continue reading page 63, paragraph 4, through the end of the chapter. Read and be prepared to discuss Step One of the Inventory Guide. You should be prepared to start your Step Four next week.

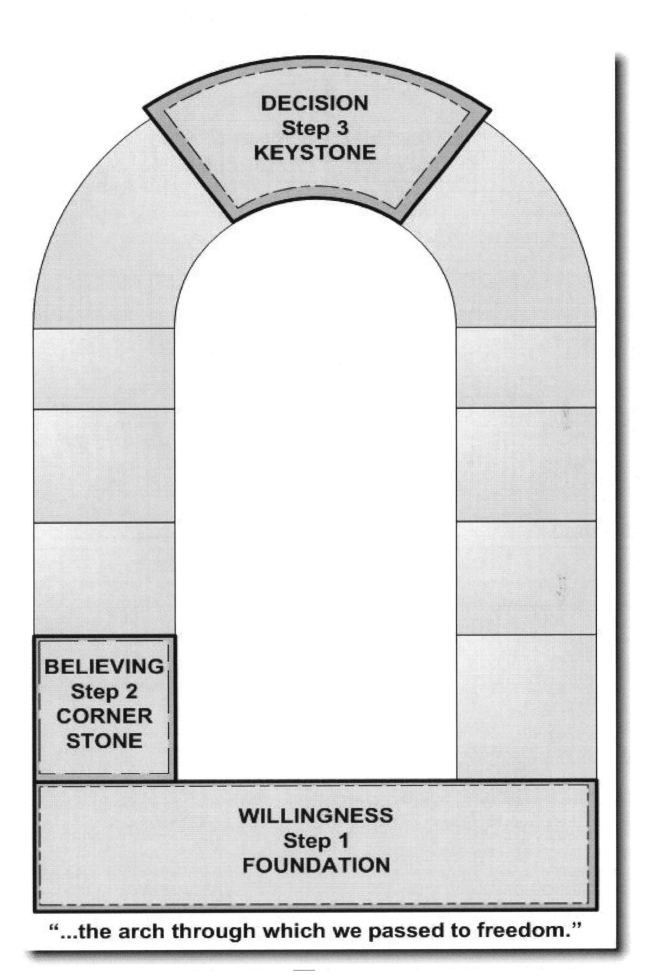

DECISION
Step 3
KEYSTONE

BELIEVING
Step 2
CORNER
STONE

WILLINGNESS
Step 1
FOUNDATION

"...the arch through which we passed to freedom."

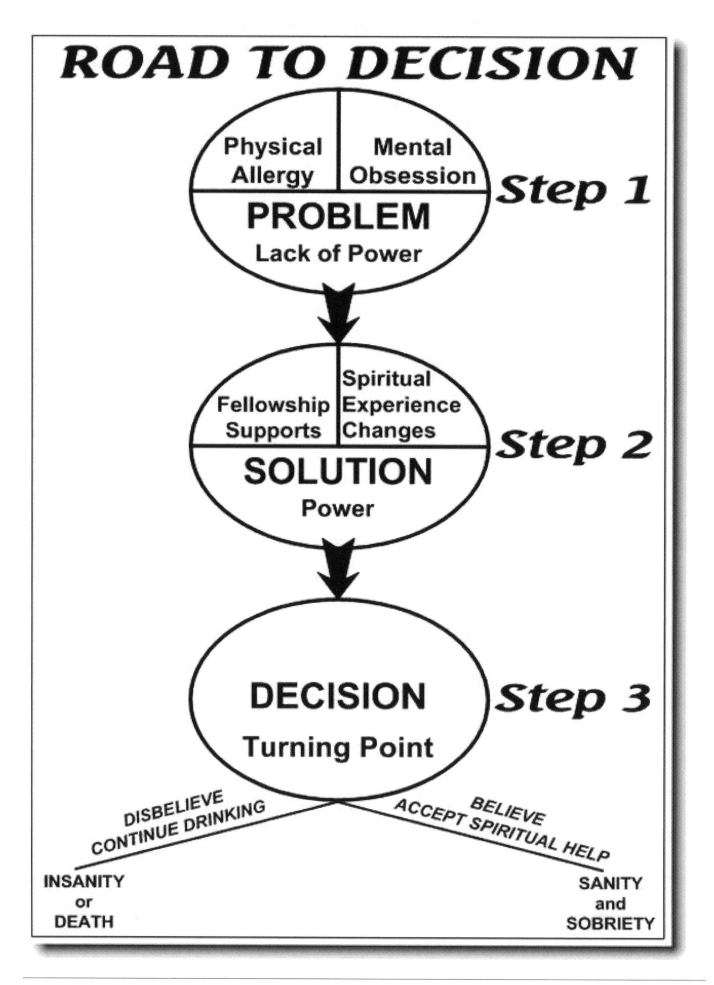

ROAD TO DECISION

Physical Allergy | Mental Obsession

PROBLEM

Lack of Power

Step 1

Fellowship Supports | Spiritual Experience Changes

SOLUTION

Power

Step 2

DECISION

Turning Point

Step 3

DISBELIEVE CONTINUE DRINKING

BELIEVE ACCEPT SPIRITUAL HELP

INSANITY or DEATH

SANITY and SOBRIETY

WEEK #7 – How It Works *(Step 3)*
Joe and Charlie Transcript

You know back on page 45 it said the main object of this book was to enable me to find a power greater than myself which would solve my problem. And Bill's going to sit down here now and he's going to right some of the best spiritual information the worlds every seen a little formula, or proposals he called them, the Twelve Steps of Alcoholics Anonymous. I can just see Bill with the problem that he has. You know we've got Protestants in AA and we've got Catholics in AA, we've got Jewish people in AA, we got a sprinkling of Muslims in AA, we got some Buddhists come into AA at that time and how are you going to write a set of steps or proposals that's not going to offend these people, quite a chore for a guy like Bill or anybody, to tell you the truth. The Oxford Groups were coming from 1st Century Christianity, they had those 4 absolutes and they were really, really strong. They wouldn't give you any slack at all. They were more interested in the letter of the law rather than the spirit of the law. Bill was interested in the spirit of these things rather than in the letter of them, that's why it's a spiritual program. So Bill had one gigantic problem here try to write these steps in order to in such a manner they wouldn't offend anybody. And he accomplished that through the Twelve Steps of Alcoholics Anonymous

These 4 absolutes that the Oxford Group said you had to practice were ***absolute love, absolute purity, absolute honesty, and absolute unselfishness***. These alcoholics were having a hell of a time being absolute anything except absolute drunks you know. They said Bill we need to get rid of that kind of stuff. Also they had made their own little steps, six of them which came from the Oxford Group tenets. But Bill could see loopholes in these steps that the alcoholic mind was slipping through and he knew they were going to have to have more strength, and he knew they were going to have to be expanded, but he didn't know how far. In trying to satisfy that bunch, in trying to satisfy the people from all different religions, and trying to satisfy those that didn't want God in here, Bill had a terrible time with it. By that time, AA had divided into, you might say, three factions.

In Akron where Dr. Bob was they didn't have any problem with God. Dr. Bob was a highly religious man, he used the Bible and he insisted that everybody he worked with use it too. God was no problem there.

But the New York City people were an entirely different breed of cat. They really didn't want anything to do with God if they could avoid it. They would have preferred a book dealing with the mind rather than spirituality, PERIOD. There was finally a third faction that said, let's talk about God, but let's not talk about him too much, let's come down somewhere in the middle of this thing. So Bill's trying to satisfy them all, and he said he tried, and he tried, and he tried and he tried to get started on Chapter 5. This is going to be the directions on how to recover. Bill said "I simply can't do it!" He said "One night while in bed leaning with a pillow behind his back against the headboard, pad and pencil in hand trying to start Chapter 5, I finally just gave up. I put down the pad and the pencil and I prayed and asked God for help and direction and then I meditated for maybe 10 or 15 minutes.

After a while I reached over and picked up the pad and the pencil and it felt as if the pencil had a mind of its own as it raced across the pages." In less than 30 minutes Bill had written 'How It Works'; One of the greatest pieces of spiritual information the world has ever seen. After he had written it he went back and numbered these proposals and he found out there were twelve (12), and he hadn't set out to write twelve (12). He went back and numbered them to be sure and there were twelve (12) alright. Now almost immediately after having done that somebody knocked on the door. One of the guys in the New York City group had one of his sponsees with him; they knew that Bill stayed up late working on the book anyhow so they had

WEEK #7 – How It Works *(Step 3)*
Joe and Charlie Transcript

come by to see Bill on their way home. Bill could hardly wait to show the work to this old older member. "Look, look, look, at the new 12 steps!" The older member said "What in the hell is this! We only had Ten Commandments and now you've got twelve. Six has been sufficient for everything up till now. I don't like it at all!" The fight was on. They fought and fought until Lois finally came in and gave them a cup of coffee and settled them down. Then Bill presented 'How It Works' to the other members and that's when the crap really hit the fan. They began to say to Bill, "This sounds too much like the Oxford Group absolutes. You're going to have to get some of that stuff out of there. Bill you're trying to give directions to people and you don't have the right to tell anybody what they have to do!" And Bill this, and Bill that, and Bill this and Bill that. And they almost destroyed not only the book project, but the little fellowship in its entirety. Can you imagine what kind of fight you would have if you left here today and went back to your group and you had 12 steps when you left but now you had 24? There would be a little fightin' going on don't you think? That's what Bill was up to

Let's read 'How It Works', which most of you have probably heard before, from the original manuscript. As we read through, I think you'll be able to see the differences between what Bill wrote that night and what the fellowship forced him to change in order to have what we have today. Let's go through it for just a moment and see the differences.

Chapter 5 - Original Manuscript

"Rarely have we seen a person fail who has thoroughly followed our **DIRECTIONS** *(path)*. Those who do not recover are people who cannot or will not completely give themselves to this simple program, usually men and women who are constitutionally incapable of being honest with themselves. There are such unfortunates. They are not at fault; they seem to have been born that way. They are naturally incapable of grasping and developing a **WAY OF LIFE** *(manner of living)*, which demands rigorous honestly. Their chances are less than average. There are those, too, who suffer from grave emotional and mental disorders, but many of them do recover if they have the capacity to be honest.

Our stories disclose in a general way what we used to be like, what happened, and what we are like now. If you have decided you want what we have and are willing to go to any length to get it-- then you are ready to **FOLLOW DIRECTIONS** *(take certain steps)*. At some of these **YOU MAY BALK** *(we balked)*. **YOU MAY THINK YOU CAN** *(we thought we could)* find an easier, softer way. But **WE DOUBT IF YOU CAN** *(we could not)*. With all the earnestness at our command, we beg of you to be fearless and thorough from the very start. Some of us have tried to hold on to our old ideas and the result was nil until we let go absolutely.

Remember that **YOU ARE DEALING** *(we deal)* with alcohol--cunning, baffling, powerful! Without help it is too much for **YOU** *(us)*. But there is One who has all power--that One is God. **YOU MUST** *(may you)* find Him now.

Half measures **WILL AVAIL YOU** *(availed us)* nothing. **YOU STAND** *(we stood)* at the turning point. **THROW YOURSELF UNDER** *(We asked)* his protection and care with complete abandon. **NOW WE THINK YOU CAN TAKE IT.**

WEEK #7 – How It Works *(Step 3)*
Joe and Charlie Transcript

Here are the steps we took, which are suggested as **YOUR** *(a)* program of recovery:

1. We admitted we were powerless over alcohol--that our lives had become unmanageable
2. Came to believe that a Power greater than ourselves could restore us to sanity.
3. Made a decision to turn our will and our lives over to the care **AND <u>DIRECTION</u>** of God, as we understood Him.
4. Made a searching and fearless moral inventory of ourselves.
5. Admitted to God, to ourselves, and to another human being the exact nature of our wrongs.
6. Were entirely **WILLING THAT** *(ready to have)* God remove all these defects of character.
7. Humbly **ON OUR KNEES** asked Him to remove our shortcomings- **HOLDING NOTHING BACK**.
8. Made a list of all persons we had harmed, and became willing to make **<u>COMPLETE</u>** amends to them all.
9. Made direct amends to such people wherever possible, except when to do so would injure them or others.
10. Continued to take personal inventory and when we were wrong promptly admitted it.
11. Sought though prayer and meditation to improve our *(conscious)* contact with God *(as we understood him)*, praying only for knowledge of His will for us and the power to carry that out.
12. Having had a spiritual **EXPERIENCE** *(awakening)* as the result of this **COURSE OF ACTION** *(these steps),* we tried to carry this message to **OTHERS, ESPECIALLY** alcoholics, and to practice these principles in all our affairs

NOW YOU MAY EXCLAIM *(many of us exclaimed)* "What an order! I can't go through with it." Do not be discouraged. No one among us has been able to maintain anything like perfect adherence to these principles. We are not saints. The point is, that we are willing to grow along spiritual lines. The principles we have set down are guides to progress. We claim spiritual progress rather than spiritual perfection.

Our description of the alcoholic {that's The Doctor's Opinion, Bill's Story, Ch. 2, Ch. 3} the chapter to the agnostic {Chapter 4} and our personal adventures before and after {Bill's Story, and those in the back of the book} **HAVE BEEN DESIGNED TO SELL YOU** *(make clear)* three pertinent ideas:
   A. That **YOU ARE** *(we were)* alcoholic and **CAN NOT** *(could not)* manage **YOUR** *(our)* own **LIFE** *(lives)* {Step One}
   B. That probably no human power **CAN RELIEVE YOUR** *(could have relieved our)* alcoholism. {Step Two}
   C. That God **CAN AND WILL** *(could and would if He were sought)* {The rest of Step Two}

IF YOU ARE NOT CONVINCED ON THESE VITAL ISSUES, YOU OUGHT TO RE-READ THE BOOK TO THIS POINT, OR ELSE THROW IT AWAY.

You could see that Bill's intention was not **suggestions**; he was going to give us **real directions** on how to work the Steps and when to work the Steps. He's giving us precise, specific, clear-cut directions on how to do that and he was very adamant about that. But the crap hit the fan and they demanded he make some changes in this original "How It Works". The chapter 'How It Works' that we have in the book today includes the changes that were forced upon Bill. So Bill made a little compromise. He said "I will make these changes but from now on I will complete the rest of this book or else you can do." Well they didn't want to write the rest of the book; they wanted Bill to continue to do that, so they agreed to continue to let Bill write the rest of the book without much interference on their part

I can just see old Bill when he wrote this and gave it to them and they begin to fight and argue over it and they begin to tell him he's going to have to change it. Remember Bill's stubborn and bullheaded just like the rest of us. And he said "No, I'm not going to change this" and they said, "Well Bill you are, don't you remember it's not your book it's our book. That's the deal we made to begin with." He said "That doesn't make any difference. I'm not going to change this part of the book." And they said, "Well you are going to change it." And he said "what you guys don't realize is these aren't my words anyhow, these are Gods words. They came after prayer and meditation." And they said, "We don't give a damn whose words they are, it's our book, and you're going to change it."

Finally Bill realized that if he didn't compromise, they would destroy this project and maybe the whole fellowship. There was a non-alcoholic psychologist around in those days and he made some suggestions. He said, "why don't you change it from directions to suggestions, you'll still get your meaning across and probably more people would accept it. Where you're saying you, you, you," he said, "don't do that; don't tell them what they have to do, change that to we. Say this is what we had to do. You'll get your message across and more people will probably accept it."

And he said, "Where you're saying must, must, change that to ought, ought and it will be more acceptable." Bill very reluctantly made those changes. Now today we don't know if they hadn't made the changes, if they'd left it like it was originally maybe instead of two million worldwide (1988), we'd have 10 million. But also if they hadn't made the changes instead of 2 million worldwide we might only have ten thousand. Who knows? Nobody knows. We just know this is the history behind this particular part of the book.

Bill was cunning, baffling and powerful also. He said "Okay, I'm going to compromise with you, but you're going to have to compromise with me." And they said "what do you want?" He says, "I'm tired. I've fought with you all I'm going to fight. If you want me to finish the book, give me the authority to do so. If you don't want to give me the authority, then you finish the book." They didn't want to give him that authority, but they didn't want to finish the book either, so they very reluctantly agreed to that.

What Bill knew that they didn't know, is that two pages later he's going to put **DIRECTIONS**, and **YOU**, and **MUST** right back in the book. He's had it in the book all the way up to 'How It Works', they jerked it out, then he puts it back. That ruins some of the continuity of the book, but now we see what happened it makes more sense. The other thing that is so apparent is when he says back here about the three pertinent ideas: "Our description of the alcoholic, the chapter to the agnostic, and our personal adventures before and after have been **designed to sell you** *(make clear)* three pertinent ideas…" He's talking about the Doctor's Opinion and the first four chapters and the stories in the back of the book. Now if we've been sold on those three pertinent ideas

(a) **"That we were alcoholic and could not manage our own lives."**
   Then we're through the First Step…

(b) **"If we've come to believe that no human power could relieve our alcoholism and that God can and will."**
   Then we're through Second Step…

WEEK #7 – How It Works *(Step 3)*
Joe and Charlie Transcript

Now the very next statement says if you are convinced then you are now at Step 3. You see the fallacy of trying to start somebody in Chapter 5 is that it starts at Step 3. And it's hard to start with Step 3 unless you've got 1 and 2 behind you. People come to us today and they say, well how do you work Steps 1 & 2? You don't, they are not working steps. There is no action involved here. These are conclusions of the mind that we draw based upon information presented to us in the Doctors Opinion and the first four chapters. I've always been powerless over alcohol and because of that, my life has been unmanageable. I just did not know that, nor did I know why, until I read the Doctor's Opinion and the first four chapters. There's always been a power greater than I am that could restore me to sanity, I just did not believe that He would nor did I understand the insanity until I read the Doctor's Opinion and the first four chapters.

If I can say to myself today, I'm powerless over alcohol and my life is unmanageable I'm through with Step 1. If I can say to myself today, I have come to believe there's a power greater than I am can restore me to sanity I'm through with Step 2. Now then I'm ready to look at Step 3. Now I might make a decision.

Big Book p. 60, par 3   *"Being convinced, we were at Step 3"*

We haven't took Step 3 yet we were just there

Big Book p. 60, par , cont. "which is that we decided to turn our will and our life over to God as we understood Him. Just what do we mean by that, and just what do we do?"

Well that's a very good question now isn't it? What does Step 3 mean? Well, we're going to make a decision, that's part of it. To do what? To turn our will, and what is our will? Our will is our thinking, and our life is our actions. We're going to make a decision to turn our will and our life over to the care and direction, is what the Step used to say, to God, as we understand him.

Our will is our thinking
Our life is our actions

We're going to make a decision to let God direct our thinking and direct our life in Step 3. We haven't done that yet, but we're getting willing to do that.

I've always heard a lot of people say one of the most misunderstood steps in the Big Book is Step 4, and I'll agree with that. But I don't think Step 4 is any more misunderstood that Step 3 is. I hear people today say, I've been in AA about 5 years, my life's still all screwed up and I don't understand why cause I turned it over to God three years ago when I took Step 3. Now

We don't turn anything over to God in Step 3. We make a decision to do something in Step 3, and the decision itself implies we're going to take some further action to carry it out.

Now one of the greatest examples I can think of is probably 4,5,6 years ago now Barbara and I made a decision to come to Los Angeles, California to visit some of our relatives. But we didn't do anything to carry that decision out, and sure enough we didn't get to Los Angeles that year either. Second year in a row we made a decision to come to Los Angeles and visit our relatives. Again we didn't do anything to carry that out and we didn't get to California either. Third year in a row we made that decision. Only this time it was a little different. This time I took the car down and had it serviced. Barbara packed the clothes and a little food, and we got in our car and we drove from our home to Tulsa, Oklahoma. Then we drove to Oklahoma City. Then we drove to Amarillo, Texas. Then we drove to Albuquerque, New Mexico. Then we drove to Flagstaff, Arizona. Then we drove to Barstow, California. Then we drove to San Bernardino, and then we drove to Los Angeles. And by golly one day we ended up visiting our relatives in Los Angeles. Not because we made a decision, but because we took the action necessary to carry out that decision.

Now what is it we're deciding to do? Well, we are making a decision to turn our will over to the care and direction of God as we understood him.

What is our will? Well, our will is nothing more than our thinking apparatus. Our will is nothing more than our mind. Our will is nothing more than this thing up here that tells us what to do, and what not to do.

A good example of the word will, tying it together with mind. Let's say that some of us are beginning to approach the end of our lives, which a few of us in here are. And we've gathered up a few material things and we've become concerned about what's going to happen to them when we pass on. We'll go down and sit down with an attorney and we'll tell that attorney what we want done with those things. I want this to be my spouse's, this to go to my daughter, I want this to be my sons, and etc. Now that attorney will take my thinking coming from my mind that day, write it down in legal terms on a piece of paper. I'll sign it, the attorney will sign it and we'll put it in a safe. Now a year or two or three later, sure enough I kick the bucket. If my family's like most of them they're going to call the undertaker and say come and get him, get him ready and let's get him out to that cemetery about as soon as we can.

A couple of days later they all gather out at the cemetery, they have me suspended over a hole in the ground, they're all standing around that hole. Somebody says a few words and gives a little prayer. And I hope it's somebody from AA that does it. And when the ceremony's over they start dropping me down in that hole. If my families like the rest of them they're not going to wait until I get to the bottom of the hole. As soon as I start down they jump in the car and they head for that attorney's office. And that attorney gets out that piece of paper and reads to them what my thinking was two or threes years prior to that time when I was sitting there in that office. We know they call that piece of paper a will. It's not by accident.

Will, Thinking and Mind; are all synonymous.

I'm making a decision to turn my thinking apparatus over to the care and direction of God as I understand him. What else am I deciding to turn over? Well I'm deciding to turn my life over to the care and direction of God as I understand him. And what is my life? My life is nothing more than my actions. What I am right now as of this moment is a sum accumulated total of all the actions that I've taken throughout my entire lifetime has made me what I am today.

All action is born in thought

You can say that again please. All action is born in thought. Sometimes we react to a situation so fast we think that we do it automatically but we don't. I can't even reach out and pick up this cup of water unless my mind tells my body to do so. So if all action is born in thought then it stands to reason my life is going to be determined by how I think.

WEEK #7 – How It Works *(Step 3)*
Joe and Charlie Transcript

If my thinking is okay, chances are my actions will be okay, chances are my life's going to be okay too.

If my thinking is lousy, chances are my actions I take will be lousy and chances are I'm going to have a fouled up life too.

When I got to this stage of the program I went to my sponsor and I said I don't think I'm going to be able to take Step 3. And he said Why? And I said because if I turn my will and my life over to the care of God as I understand him, I have no idea what he would have me be. And he may want me to be a missionary, and he may send me to China, and I sure as hell don't want to go there. And he just laughed and he said let's look at it this way, at least it wouldn't be in the hands of an idiot would it?

He said let's look back through your lifetime. He said you've always been a selfish, self-centered, self-willed human being. You've always done what you wanted to do whenever you wanted to do it and to hell with the rest of them. Is that right? We'll you know it is. He said the end result of that is that you almost destroyed your life and just as importantly, you've almost destroyed the lives of those around you that care for you. He said just think,

If God could direct your thinking it might become better.
If you're thinking becomes better, then your actions and your life's going to become better.
And just as importantly, the lives of those around you that care for would probably become better too.

Left on your own resources, you're always going to do the same things you've always done.
You're going to remain restless, irritable and discontented.
You're going to stay filled with shame, fear, guilt and remorse.
Sooner or later under those conditions, you're going to go back to drinking again.

If you don't find someway to be sober and have a little piece of mind, serenity and happiness, you'll never have any long lasting sobriety and
you can't do that on self will.

And he made if clear to me in such a manner that I was able to make the decision to turn my will, which is my thinking apparatus, and my life, which is my actions, over to the care of God as I understood him. It is absolutely amazing what has taken place since that time.

Remember in the area of the Foreword to the First Edition they said that "precisely, specifically, with clear-cut directions". You know Bill wrote down those precise, specific, clear-cut directions in the original "How It Works", but they forced some changes on him. And when these changes came out, what we see in the book now, those are the changes that we're make so a little continuity of the book gets mixed up here. Bill's precise, specific, clear-cut directions were altered a little bit but later on he puts them back in the book.

By the way, as far as we know, we're the only species on earth that's ever faced with this decision. It seems as though all the other species on earth don't have self-will. Whatever they do, at any given time, is always done on God's time at God's direction. It seems as though we human beings are the only species that God gave this thing called self-will to. Therefore you see very few of the other species here on earth in trouble. I've never seen a tree hit a car yet.

The one thing wrong with self-will is everybody's got one, that's one of the things wrong with it.

So our book says and he gives us these little instructions now and there going to come short and sweet and we have to be prepared to see them. And he says,

Big Book, p. 62, par 3   "The first"

he's going to tell us what to do first.

Big Book, p. 62, par 3 "The first requirement is that we be convinced that any life run on self-well can hardly be a success. On that basis we are almost always in collision with something or somebody, even though our motives are good. Most people try to live by self-propulsion. Each person is like an actor who wants to run the whole show; is forever trying to arrange the lights, the ballet, the scenery and the rest of the players in his own way. If his arrangements would only stay put, if only people would do as he wished, the show would be great. Everybody, including himself, would be pleased. Life would be wonderful."

Wouldn't that be nice if everybody would mind? They won't mind me they just won't do it, because they have self-will. My will for my wife and my children is one thing. Their will and their life is another. They have self-will and their thoughts are different from mine. Sometimes and most of the times they are in conflict. They just won't mind me. I know they'd be a lot better off if they would, but they won't. Now some twelve or thirteen years after Bill wrote the Big Book, and after many, many years experience with some of the great teachers and minds in the world, and after many, many years of experience with us alcoholics, Bill was forced to write the Twelve and Twelve.

And he was really trying to push the Traditions on the fellowship. He was hard selling the Traditions to the fellowship and they weren't buying a lot of it, but they needed the Traditions and he knew that. So he decided to write the Traditions and he thought well I'll put some short stories or short essays about the Steps in with the Traditions and maybe if they will read the Steps they will eventually read the Traditions. So he wrote the Twelve and Twelve for us. The Twelve and Twelve again is just the short essays, short stories about the Steps. It doesn't tell you how to work the Steps it is the short stories about the Steps

The only piece of literature in A.A. that tells you how to work the Steps, is the Big Book of Alcoholics Anonymous

But in the area of the 4th Step, in the Twelve and Twelve there is some of the best information the world's ever seen on self-will and what makes people tick. It's called, "The Basic Instincts of Life". And I always suggest to people that I sponsor that they go to the Twelve and Twelve, read the first three or four pages about the Basic Instincts of Life, get a working knowledge about the words that you see in there, and then look them up in the dictionary because they're very important words, and then we're going to use them a little later on in the third column when we get ready to do the 4th Step inventory. So I needed a working knowledge of that information, and Bill in his usual manner wrote some of the best information about the basic instincts of life. Very, very important information

WEEK #7– How It Works *(Step 3)*
Joe and Charlie Transcript

I think we have to face the fact that in 1937/38/39, when Bill was writing the Big Book he was not a spiritual giant. He was not a great student of human nature. Bill was a night school lawyer and New York City stock speculator yet he was able to write one of the most spiritual books the world has ever seen dealing with human nature. Surely, surely God took a hand in the writing of the Big Book and used Bill's hand to write the book.

But by 1950/51/52 Bill knew a lot more about spirituality, a lot more about human nature, a lot more about we alcoholics than he did back in the 30's. He'd studied with some of the greatest minds in the world for a period of years. And I think he felt that he had some new information that he could give us that would make it easier for us to work the steps according the Big Book Alcoholics Anonymous.

Basically that's what he says in the 12 and 12, that the Big Book has always been the basic text and always will be. You simply can not work the program out of the 12 and 12. I see lots of people try it. But they can't do it because there are no directions on how to work the steps. And I think that's why a lot of people love it. They can get in it and dance around and philosophies and they never have to do anything except talk. But there is some information in there that is absolutely invaluable, that if we can see it and understand it and accept it, it makes the working of the steps out of the Big Book so much simpler and so much easier.

And these three basic instincts of life that Joe's talking about, he taught me in step 4 in the 12 and 12 more about what makes me tick and what makes me do the things I do and act the way I act. He taught me there more in 2 or 3 pages than I had learned in some 40 years of living at that time. Let's look at them for just a moment. I think it will make it a lot easier to be able to see why we need to make our decision in three plus it sets us up really with information for step 4. Now in your handout sheets you've got a little picture in here about the middle in there somewhere I think it's page 7 and 8 in your handout material, which says the basic instincts of life which create self.

And he said that:
1. All human beings are born with three basic instincts of life.
2. They are God given,
3. They are absolutely necessary for survival of the human race
4. Therefore they are a good thing.

The first thing he talked about is the social instinct. And he said all human beings are born with the desire to be liked, to be accepted, to be respected by other people. He said all human beings ware born with the desire to come together in groups with other people. He said if we didn't have those desires and cared nothing for each other that the world would go into complete anarchy, dog eat dog situation would reign, and eventually under those conditions the human race would fail to survive.

Now he used several terms under the social instinct. He uses the term **companionship**…that's nothing more than wanting to belong or to be accepted.

WEEK #7 – How It Works *(Step 3)*
Joe and Charlie Transcript

So many of us grew up on the outside of the crowd looking in, wanting to be and knew we could not be.

He uses the term **prestige**…that is, wanting to be recognized or to be accepted as the leader of the group.

And the world needs leaders. I guess somebody back in the old caveman days had to say "John, get behind that tree with your spear. Jack you get over there with your club. And Mary-Jo and I will run this sucker through here and we'll have something". Somebody's got to do that. Most people will take one of two directions. Either let me be a part of or let me be the leader of. And in either case it's based upon what other people think of us.
Self-esteem: what we think of ourselves.

And that's usually high or low based upon what other people think of us or what we think other people think of us. If they seem to like us and accept us we feel pretty good towards ourselves. If it feels like they reject us and they don't want us, then we feel pretty lousy towards ourselves.
Pride… And I'm glad I got into the habit of going to the dictionary. I always thought pride was something you ought to have. All I ever wanted to be as a young boy growing up, I wanted to grow up to be a man who walked tall with pride and just a little bit sideways like John Wayne does. Until I looked it up in the dictionary and it says **pride**… is an excessive and unjustified opinion of oneself.

We either think too well of ourselves or too little of ourselves. In either case it's not the truth.
Personal relationships: our relations with other human beings and the world around us.
Ambitions: the plans for the future.

To be liked, to be accepted, so on and so forth. All human beings have these things. Now if I want to be liked and accepted and respected by the world and the people in it the first thing I've got to do is decide, well what do they want from me?

Society teaches us those things as we grow up. It'll vary in different parts of the world. One part of the world perhaps it's a good education. Another part of the world it's to be large landowner. Another part of the world it's to have a large family. Any number of things based upon where we live in the world. And as we grow up and they teach us these things and we ourselves set goals for ourselves as to what we want to become in the future. And if we're going to reach the goals that we set for ourselves we're going to have to work at it. You can't just be a bum and sit on your duff and be successful and people like you and accept you. If it's a good education you're going to have to work at, whatever it might be.

By the same token we're going to have to make some sacrifices. There are some things that I would really like to do as a human being that are very pleasurable and very exciting that if you catch me at it you're not going to like me at all. And I don't think you and I would do the work necessary to reach the goal nor make the sacrifices necessary unless we get a reward for doing so. And the great reward, Bill said it in his story when he said I had arrived.

God how many of us have done it. We set that goal and we just literally worked our tails off for years and the day we reach the goal and they pat us on the back and they say "Ah Joe you're a

WEEK #7 – How It Works *(Step 3)*
Joe and Charlie Transcript

fine fellow, you're a good man, you're doing great". There's a feeling that comes over us which is one of those indescribably wonderful feelings… a great, great feeling. The only thing wrong with it, it seems to be just a temporary feeling. No sooner do we reach the goal, we get the praise, we get the recognition, we get the prestige from it and we look around we say "Is this all there is to it?" And we set another goal. And we work and we work and we strive and we strive and we sacrifice and we reach the new goal and we get the praise and recognition, feels great, doesn't last long and we set another goal.

It seems to create within we human beings an insatiable desire for more and more power, more and more recognition and we're not getting it fast enough or they're not giving it to us the way we think they ought to, so what do we do about it? Well we start taking shortcuts. We start doing a little lying, a little conning, a little manipulating, a little stepping on other peoples toes and climbing on their backs and the instant we do so we create pain and suffering for others. They in turn retaliate against us and create pain and suffering for us.

It's plain to see, that a life run on self-will could hardly ever be a success.
Under those conditions we will always be in collision with people, places and things.

Second basic instinct he talked about is the **security instinct**. Now, I know that in AA we try to live one day at a time. But I also know that just about everybody in this room has got an insurance policy. The purpose of the insurance policy is to protect ourselves in the future. Bill said all human beings are born with the desire to be secure in the future. He said if we didn't have that desire we wouldn't provide the food, the clothing, the shelter, and the things that we need to survive. And next winter we would just simply freeze to death or the next drought season we would starve to death. So this desire that we have to be secure in the future is a God given thing and it is necessary for our survival. Now once again if you're going to be secure in the future you have to decide well what is it that I need in order to be secure?

Society usually teaches us those things as we grow up and it varies in different parts of the world. In one part of the world you only need $4. In another part of the world you need $4,000. In another part of the world maybe you need $4,000,000. In another part of the world you need 198 coconuts. Whatever it is that they use to measure, trade and barter with. Based up what we're taught, we set goals for ourselves and we begin to work at it. Now if you're going to be secure in the future you can't just sit on your duff and be a bum. You're going to have to work. You're going to have to make some money. You're going to have to invest it.

At the same time you've got to sacrifice. Hell we can't blow it all today and be secure tomorrow. And I don't think you and I would do the work necessary to reach the goal or make the sacrifices necessary if we didn't get a reward for it.

Once again the great reward is that great feeling that comes at the moment of successful completion of the goal. How many of us have done it? We set the goal for the new dress, for the new shoes, for the new suit, for the new drapes, for the new couch, for the new home, for the new car, for the new piece of property, for the new business and we work and we work and we strive and we strive and the day that sucker is paid for and nobody can take it away from us. What a great, great feeling that is. Hell back when I was a kid hardly anybody owned their own homes. Once in a great while somebody would buy a home and they would sacrifice everything they had to pay that sucker off and the day they paid it off the feeling was so great they would call in the neighbors and we would have a great party and celebrate it by burning the mortgage. How great that was. The only thing wrong with it is that it's just a temporary feeling. No sooner got the sucker paid off that I looked around and his house is bigger than mine. He has a Cadillac and I'm driving a Chevrolet. And he's got a Brooks Brothers suit and I bought mine at Kmart. And that causes us to set another goal. And we work and we work and we strive and we strive and we reach the new goal, feels good, doesn't last long, we set another....seems to create an insatiable desire for more and more and more and more. And we're not getting it fast enough. They're not giving it to us like we think they should. So what do we do? We take shortcuts. We lie, we cheat, we con, we manipulate, and the instant we do we hurt other people. They retaliate against us, creating pain and suffering for us.

Plain to see, that a life run on self-will can hardly ever be a success.

Third basic instinct he talks about is the sex instinct. He said all human beings are born with the desire to have sex. Now, it may get turned off by bad teachings or bad happenings but he said all human beings are born with the desire to have sex because if we don't have sex we can't reproduce ourselves. And if we don't reproduce ourselves, sooner or later the human race is going to fail to survive.

So just like the other two, if you're going to reproduce yourself through the sexual act you're going to have to work at it. Hell you can do more work in three minutes of sex, if you can last that long, than you'll do all day digging a ditch. Don't you older fellows remember how it used to be when we got through with it? My God you'd just fall over sideways, the sweat is just pouring off of you, and you can hardly get your breath. You feel like you've died, gone to heaven and come back two or three times. Gets excited doesn't he? And I don't think you and I would do that kind of work if we didn't get a reward for doing so. And the great reward is that great feeling we get both physically and emotionally at the moment of the successful completion of the sex act.

One of the greatest rewards that a human being can experience. But also just like the other two it seems to be just a temporary feeling. Hell you no sooner get through doing it that you get to thinking about doing it again. And it's such a pleasurable and exciting thing that the next thing you know you get to thinking about doing it in different ways. Then you get to thinking about doing it in different positions. Then you get to thinking about doing it with different people. And the next thing you know we're doing it at the wrong time in the wrong way with the wrong people and the instant we do so we create pain and suffering for others. They in turn retaliate against us, which creates pain and suffering for us.

It's plain to see, that a life run on self-will, can hardly be a success

The fulfillment of these things are so pleasurable
that all human beings from time to time will overdo in one or more of these areas
and create pain and suffering for others.

You'll notice on that little chart there's a circle called Self. That's where self-will comes from. It comes from these three basic instincts of life. You'll also notice coming out of the self circle there is one called '**wrongs**', which is another word we need to look at.

WEEK #7 – How It Works *(Step 3)*
Joe and Charlie Transcript

Somewhere we got the idea that wrongs meant a list of dirty filthy nasty items. But if you go to the dictionary and look it up you'll find several definitions of it.

Wrong - incorrect judgment of other people = resentment
Wrong - incorrect believing = fear
Wrong - are the harms and hurts that we do to other people

Now it's easy to spot a selfish, self-centered human being. One who is running on self-will, not running on God's will. A selfish, self-centered human being is always madder than hell. Damn him. Damn her. By God I'll show them. They're not going to treat me that way… A selfish, self-centered human being is always scared to death. They can't depend on God. They can't depend on other people. And if we're an alcoholic reaching the end of the road we can't depend on ourselves any longer and we're running absolutely scared to death all the time. . A selfish, self-centered human being, in order to fulfill the basic instincts of life are always overdoing and creating harms and hurts for others. Then we've got to be scared to death of what they're going to do when they catch us. And even if they don't catch us, if God dwells within each of us, we know the difference between right and wrong and guilt and remorse associated with those things begin to eat us up.

A person whose mind is filled with resentment, a person whose mind is filled with fear, a person whose mind is filled with guilt and remorse, does not feel good.

Eventually searching for a way to feel better we begin to think about the sense of ease and comfort that comes at once by taking a couple of drinks. Next thing you know we believe we can drink and we end up drunk all over again. So at the very least we're going to have to do something about this selfish self-centered human being and it seems the only way you can do anything about that is through God's help because God made self-will. And only God has the power to overcome that. And at the very least we're going to have to do something about these resentments and these fears and this guilt and remorse in order to find the peace of mind, serenity and happiness for good long term sobriety.

You know if every human being in the world today could fulfill these three basic instincts at the level that God intends there would be no conflict on earth today. But all human beings have self-will.

All human beings from time to time will overdo in one or more areas creating conflict for others and for themselves. I never knew that. I just knew I was always in trouble. I just knew I was always madder than hell. I just knew I was always scared to death. I knew guilt and remorse was eating me up but I didn't know where it came from. See they gave me the rules but they never taught me how to play the game. AA has taught me how to play the game. And now that I know how to play the game I don't break the rules anymore and I don't hurt other people and I'm not scared to death and I'm not filled with guilt and remorse. This is the greatest information I have ever seen about what makes me tick and what causes me to do the things that I do. Joe.

Big Book p. 62, par. 1, line 3 "Whatever our protestations, are not most of us concerned with ourselves, our resentments, and our own self-pity?"

WEEK #7 – How It Works (Step 3)
Joe and Charlie Transcript

It's not that I thought too well of myself, or that I thought too little of myself. It's that I thought of myself only. That was my problem.

Big Book p. 62, par 2., line 1 "Selfishness, self-centeredness! That, we think, is the root of our troubles. Driven by a hundred forms of fear, self-delusion, self-seeking, and self-pity, we step on the toes of our fellows and they retaliate. Sometimes they hurt us, seemingly without provocation, but we invariably find that at some time in the past we have made decisions based on self which later placed us in a position to be hurt."

You know alcoholism: I, self and me. You see if you don't have a God in your life, and I didn't, there's only one thing left to live by and that's the satisfaction of these basic instincts of life. And I tried to live my life based upon the satisfaction of those basic instincts. And I overdid in many, many of those areas.

Big Book p. 62, par 3, line 1 "So our troubles, we think, are basically of our own making. They arise out of ourselves, and the alcoholic is an extreme example of self-will run riot, though he usually doesn't think so. Above everything, we alcoholics must be rid of this selfishness. We must, or it kills us! God makes that possible."

I can't heal my sick mind with a sick mind. Only God can make that possible.

Big Book p. 62, par. 3, line 19 "And there often seems no way of entirely getting rid of self without His aid. Many of us had moral and philosophical convictions galore, but we could not live up to them even though we would have liked to. Neither could we reduce our self-centeredness much by wishing or trying on our own power. We had to have God's help."

Big Book p. 62, par 4, line 1   ***"This is the how and the why of it."***

You see he told how it works. Then he told us why it won't work because of selfishness and self-centeredness. And now he's going to tell us how it really works.

> ***Big Book p. 62, par 4, line 1***   ***"This is the how and the why of it.***
> ***...First of all, we had to quit playing God. It didn't work!"***

Everything I read leads me to believe that this is a God directed world. Now if it is a God directed world then those of us who have been self directed and those of us that have tried to direct everything and everybody around us ...we've been trying to do God's job for him. We're not God, we've just been playing at being God. And the book says we're going to have to quit doing that if we want any peace of mind, serenity and happiness in the future. I think

One of the great mistakes I see today in AA is people trying to force themselves to be better. And self-will cannot overcome self-will. Only God can overcome self-will. So if we want any peace of mind, serenity and happiness it looks like we're going to have to turn to God and let him be the Director. Let him do his job, which is direction.> Next direction.

Big Book p 62, par 4, line 28 "Next, we decided that hereafter in this drama of life, God was going to be our Director."

*Not our **suggestor**, our **<u>Director</u>**. From here on out, it'll be directions and not suggestions.*

WEEK #7 – How It Works *(Step 3)*
Joe and Charlie Transcript

Big Book p. 62, par 4, line 30 "He is the Principal; we are His agents. He is the Father, and we are His children. Most Good ideas are simple, and this concept was the keystone of the new and triumphant arch through which we passed to freedom.

And what is that idea of this concept. That he is the principle and we are his agents, He is the Father, and we are His children, he is the boss, I work for him. Now when I first got into this area of the 3rd Step I used God like you would an errand boy. I said, God please help me to stay sober, and by the way, while you're at it, help me get my wife back. Which one? The second one, I don't want that first one back. That first one didn't drink, she was mean and ugly. I like the one that drank.

God get me a job by the way pick up a little extra money for me, I need some money. I used God like you would an errand boy, send him out like that. And after I got sober I got to reading in that other book, that big, big book and in the front of that book

There's a story about this fellow he worked for six days and rested. Now to my knowledge he didn't have to go back to work anymore. So it looks as though if there's any work being done around here it's going to be me doing the work. He's the principle, we're the agents, He's the Father, we're the children, He's the boss, I'm the employee. Most good ideas are simple, and this concept was the keystone of the new and triumphant arch through which we passed to freedom. Now he's referring once again to that wonderfully effective spiritual structure.

Step 1 Willingness   Foundation
Step 2 Believing   Cornerstone

Now he tells us what we're building, "A triumphant arch through which we're going to pass to freedom". He said the keystone to that arch is a simple little idea that we're going to let God be the Director

You know in the old, old days when they built arches, the stones were all stacked loosely without mortar, and they began to lean together and there was a center stone up here called the keystone. If it was cut right, it would support the entire arch, but if it wasn't, it would slip out and the arch would collapse.

Well the keystone of the new and triumphant arch through which we're going to pass to freedom, is this simple little idea - that we're going to let God be the Director. For most of us that's the first time we ever had that idea. If we once had it as children we lost it somewhere. Instead of letting God be the Director, we we're the director, cause we told God what we wanted. God do this, God do that, God give me this, God give me that, God if you do this for me, I'll do that for you. And now only did we direct God we directed everybody around us. Now we can quit doing that. We're going to let God be the Boss from this day on. Now that is a radical idea for people like us. This is the decision that we're making

Big Book p. 63, par. 1, line 1 "When we sincerely took such a position, all sorts of remarkable things followed. We had a new Employer. Being all powerful, He provided what we needed, if we kept close to Him and performed His work well. Established on such a footing we became less and less interested in ourselves, our own little plans and designs. More and more we became interested in seeing what we could contribute to life."

WEEK #7 – How It Works *(Step 3)*
Joe and Charlie Transcript

You see I was always a taker. And takers are losers in life. Contributors are those that win I've noticed.

Big Book p. 63, par. 1, cont. "As we felt new power flow in, as we enjoyed peace of mind, as we discovered we could face life successfully, as we became conscious of His presence, we began to lose our fear of today, tomorrow or the hereafter. We were reborn."

You know they used to come over to my house on Monday night from that little church about two blocks from my house, and these guys wanted to talk to me about being reborn. And you know what I did for them, I'm drinking and man it's Monday night football, and they'll be talking about reborn about 8 o'clock they'd be knocking, and I'd run them off, I'd say you guys get out of here, it's Monday night football, I don't want to talk to you, get. And that's the way I did with those guys, and I didn't understand this reborn then at all. And I got to reading in that other book when I got sober and there's this story in there and this guy's name was Nicademus. And Nicademus was about like me, just dumber than a stump. And he asked that guy, what do you mean by being reborn. Do you mean I've got to go back into my mother's womb. See how dumb he was? And he looked at him and shook his head and said Nicademus don't you know you can't do that? Didn't you go to the University? Aren't you educated? You can't do that.

When I'm talking about being reborn
I'm talking about the renewing of your mind.
Old ideas cast aside, new ones accepted.
Reborn in my mind

I understood that then. And now I'm ready to do business, I'm ready to do the third Step.

And I knew what they did on Sunday morning at that little church up there about 11o'clock, and I couldn't wait till I got there. And they basically asked people to come down and do the third Step prayer. So I waited till next Sunday, got there about 3 or 4 minutes till 11:00, I didn't want to get there too early I might hear something that would help me. I got there about 3 or 4 minutes till 11:00 and sure enough they asked people to do that and I came down there and I did, just as the book says,

Big Book p. 63, par 2, line 1 "We were now at Step Three. Many of us said to our Maker, as we understood Him: God, I offer myself to Thee -- to build with me and to do with me as Thou wilt. Relieve me of the bondage of self, that I may better do Thy will. Take away my difficulties, that victory over them may bear witness to those I would help of Thy Power, Thy Love, and Thy Way of life. May I do Thy will always! We thought well before taking this step making sure we were ready; that we could at last abandon ourselves utterly to Him."

And I don't know what exactly happened that particular morning, but I do know this. From that Sunday morning till this moment, my life hasn't been the same. It's as if I been walking on the dark side of the street all those years and all of a sudden I'm on the sunny side of the street. And I don't know what happened except I do know that my life has changed. Thank God.

Big Book p. 63, par. 2, line 20 "We thought well before taking this step making sure we were ready; that we could at last abandon ourselves utterly to Him."

WEEK #7 – How It Works (Step 3)
Joe and Charlie Transcript

I think the word utterly means completely, whole heartedly, all the way, the entire ball of wax. I hope you don't make the mistake I did. The first time I took Step 3 I got on my knees, which I very seldom did in those days. I said

God, I offer myself to Thee -- to build with me and to do with me as Thou wilt.

Relieve me of the bondage of self, that I may better do Thy will.

Take away my difficulties..... so on and so on and so forth.

And as I finish it up I said now this applies to my alcohol, don't fool with my sex life. Stay out of my money. I can handle that too. God probably said, What an order, I can't go through with it. I said you take the alcohol and I'll take care of the rest. Today I realize the fallacy in that is as far as I know God doesn't even drink, he don't want the alcohol, He's wants me, and He wants all of me.

Just think. If God could direct my thinking in all areas, it might even become better in my sex life, if might even become better in my money areas. If might even become better in all areas. When my thinking becomes better in all areas then surely my life will become better in all areas too.

I think there's a valid reason behind this. I am told that we alcoholics are born to live in three dimensions. We are born to live with God, with ourselves, and with our fellow human beings.

And if we are praying with other human beings for the first time, we are beginning to get ourselves back together in all three dimensions the way God intended in the first place.

We alcoholics are the funniest people in the world. We'll let our families see us on our knees in the bathroom hugging the porcelain bowl, puking our guts up, morning after morning, after morning. We come to AA and try to straighten out our lives, and we're ashamed and embarrassed to let people see us prayer. Isn't that something?

Praying in the company of other human beings is always better. Anybody I work with that I sponsor I require that they take Step 3 with me for two reasons. Number one, if they take it with me I know they have taken it. That's the only way I know for sure. But the real reason is that every time we do it together it means more to me, and it has more strength and more power for me. I think it's a great idea.

We've made our decision, we've uttered our prayers, and the book says:

Big Book p. 63, par. 4, line 1 "Next we launched out on a curse of vigorous action, the first step of which is a personal housecleaning, which many of us had never attempted. Though our decision (Step 3) was a vital and crucial step, it could have little permanent effect unless at once followed by a strenuous effort to face, and to be rid of the things in ourselves which had been blocking us (Step 4). Our liquor was but a symptom. So we had to get down to causes and conditions."

Week Eight – Chapter 5

READ: Page 63, Paragraph 4: Page 64, top of page, end of paragraph.

There has always been God's will, and there has always been 'my will'. I could have been operating on God's will all the time but there seems to have been something within my will, within my mind, that blocked me off from God's will. If I'm going to turn my will and my loife over to the care of God as I understand him, I am first going to have to find out wihat is within me that is blocking me off from God's will, and do something about its elimination, before God can begin to direct my thinking. Then we can open up space in our head for God's will to come into our minds.

A time element is involved in this paragraph; it says that we "take this step at once". We heard a 'professional' counselor, counseling people not long ago telling them to wait two or three years to take their inventory. Our question to him was, "How many people have you killed with that advice?"

Picture this: You've just been shot 7 times in critical areas of the body; you're being wheeled into the E.R. bleeding profusely, do you want you surgeon to say: "let's give him 90 days to see if he heals up on his own"… or do you to hear him say "get him into O.R. stat, we've got a life to save today people!" Remember: this IS a matter of life and death.

We are trying to find a way to have peace of mind, serenity and happiness. As long as we are running our lives on self-will, we can't have pace of mind. We didn't have it before we got here on self-will and the longer I put off taking step four, the greater the chance of me getting drunk.

We think one of the reasons we procrastinate or "put it off", is FEAR. Fear that we dare not look at this stuff and we sure don't want to show it to someone else. Fear that we can't do it perfectly and we would rather wait until we could do it right. If that is our reason for not taking step four, what we are really saying is "Let's get well first and then we'll do it". But, the reality is we need to do Step Four IN ORDER to get well.

Another reason we put it off is that we really don't know how to do it. There is confusion about taking step four. Somewhere down the line someone was looking at step FIVE and there was a statement that said something about your entire life story. So we said "ah-ha, that's it". We took a statement out of Step Five and began to write our life story as our inventory on step four.

I did that when I first tried to take this inventory. But I didn't learn a thing because everything I wrote down I already knew. I learned nothing new by writing my life story. As I look back on it now, I realize that 95% doesn't have to do with my drinking anyway. That 95% of my story obscured the 5% that did have everything to do with my drinking.

READ: Page 64, Paragraph 1 to Page 64, Paragraph 2

Bill is going to tell us how to take a business inventory assuming that we know something about business. Then after he tells us how to take a business inventory, he's going to turn right around and say we do the same thing with our lives. In other words, we're going to take a personal inventory just like he tells us to take this business inventory. He says a business that takes no regular inventory usually goes broke. This is one of his first valid comparisons between business inventory and the personal inventory.

In our personal lives, you and I have a business, which to us is the most important business in the world, and that's the business of finding a way to live where we can be sober and peaceful and happy and free and not have to go back to drinking. If we don't inventory ourselves regularly, then we may as well end up going broke, which is going back to getting drunk all over again. So, the first comparison between the two would be that, without inventory, we would probably go broke or get drunk just like a business goes broke. Now Bill says, taking a commercial inventory is a fact-finding and a fact-facing process.

Step Four- Personal vs. Business Inventory Comparisons

On the right side, we put PERSONAL and on the left side we put BUSINESS. A commercial inventory is a 1) fact-finding and a 2) fact-facing process. It is an 3) effort to discover the truth about 4) the stock in trade. One object is to 5) disclose damaged or un-saleable goods, and to 6) get rid of them promptly without regret. It's the only way a business can be successful. We cannot fool ourselves about values. Were we have taken some key words and put them on the left side under BUSINESS: Fact Finding, Fact Facing, Truth about the stock in trade, Your effort to disclose damaged or un-saleable goods, To get rid of them promptly without regret.

Now Bill says "...we did **exactly** the same thing with our lives." We did with our lives what he told us t do with the business inventory. Now Bill loves words and he loves words that mean the same thing.

Let's look at our Step Four:

We made a 1) Searching: (we put this straight acroos from fact-finding; they basically mean the same thing) and a 2) Fearless: (we put this word straight across from fact-facing) 3) Moral: (we saw the word moral and we said uh-oh, there it is. There's that list of dirty, filthy, nasty items we don't want to look at, and we don't want anyone else to see them either. We dare not take this inventory.)

Bill went to the Dictionary again and looked up the word **Moral**. It doesn't mean a list of dirty, filthy nasty items. If he had wanted us to make a list of those things, he probably would have said "**immoral**". But he said moral and the dictionary says that means "the truth about the facts". That's all it is. The truth about something; the difference between right and wrong of a situation. *So we make a searching and fearless "truthful" inventory of ourselves, our 'stock-in-trade, we are going to inventory our 'thinking'.*

We set out to **4) Disclose damaged and un-saleable [thinking].** And **5) Get rid of it promptly without regret** (because that is the VERY thing that blocks us off from God's will. If my thinking is okay, then God can probably direct my will and I'll be successful in the business of staying sober. If my thinking is lousy, then God cannot direct my will and I will probably be unsuccessful and end up broke and getting drunk. So I'm going to do the same thing in step four that he told me to do with the business inventory.

READ Page 64, Paragraph 3 to Page 65, Top of Page.

We've learned we have a threefold disease: we are physically, mentally and spiritually sick.

>If I am physically sick I would go to the doctor. Whatever illness will have certain symptoms that would be readily identifiable to diagnose and treat.
>If I am mentally ill, I would go to a psychiatrist. My mental illness would have symptoms too that would make it possible to diagnose and treat.
>If I am spiritually ill, I will also display certain symptoms, The Big Book breaks these down so that we can readily identify them when they appear.

1.	**Resentment**
2.	**Fear**
3.	**Guilt & Remorse**

So if I want t get rid of what blocks me from God, I will have to get rid of resentment, fear, guilt & remorse. This is the process we are now beginning. So if those things can leave me head and stop being the underlying basis of all of my thinking and decision making; God's will can come in and start redirecting me to better things. This is the prescription the Big Book has to offer you to help you get well.

FOURTH STEP INVENTORY PROCESS

Resentments are the Number One Offender!

From these thoughts or mental attitudes "stem all forms of spiritual disease". We are instructed to list all of the people, institutions and principles with who we were angry or have resentments.

What is a Resentment?

"Webster's dictionary defines resentment as "indignation or ill-will felt as a result of a real or imaginary offense." Then Webster's refers the reader to the word anger and gives other examples of this thought or feelings which include rage, fury, ire, wrath, resentment, and indignation. These words denote varying degrees of displeasure from anger – string, intense, and explosive. The longer lasting resentment, ill-will and suppressed anger generated by a sense of being wronged or being wrong.".

B. In summary and broadly defined, we are dealing with a negative or unpleasant thought or feeling caused by the real or imagined act or failure to at of a person, institution or principle.
C. Persons institutions or principles may need some explanation. Remember you area person and your action or failure to act may very well cause you to think or feel badly (generally, this is called guilt) Institutions are any group of people, authorities, companies, government agencies or other organizations.

A Principle is a basic truth or natural law. Many of these principles have an do offend us because they get in the way of us getting what we think we want our need to fulfill some lack or inadequacy of our sense of self. For example:
*Alcoholism is an incurable, progressive and fatal illness.
*Honesty is the Best Policy.
*As you give, so shall you receive.
*There is no free lunch.
*When you are disturbed, there is something wrong with you.
*Live and let live or, forgive and forget.

PREPARING THE GRUDGE LIST

With the previous instruction in mind and before preceding any further with this inventory, a list should be prepared of the people, institutions and principles which have or now cause you to have resentment, as defined above.

Certain points to be remembered:

1) If you can remember the resentment, you should list it, even though you think you are "over-it". Go back through your life, "Nothing counts but thoroughness and honesty".

2) A review of family albums, school annuals, and previous jobs may be helpful. Some people write a short autobiography of their to jar the suppressed memories, but in no way would this take the place of the actual inventory. Usually, once you begin writing your grudge list, the heavens open up and names seem to fall from the sky if by magic. I personally like to do it the way Bill did it, by praying and being still, let God put the thoughts into your mind, it'll be what you're supposed to be working on at the present moment and not the 1001 distractions your mind is yelling at you – you'll see.

3) Throughout the taking of step Five, and at times thereafter, you will recall other people, institutions and principles that have caused you negative thoughts and feelings. You can add them to this list at anytime, but do not spend too much time searching your past, once the flood of names cease, its time to immediately move on. You will be doing this again in a year or two. Simply do your best. One week per section is more than enough time for someone who is really willing, others, if they're dragging their feet, maybe they really don't want to do this, in which case the Big book suggests sponsors moving on to someone more willing.

4) Do not concern yourself with whether you should or should not have the feeling. Just make the list. Nothing more is required of you at this point.

ASSIGNMENT: Read Page 65, Paragraph 1 to Page 66, end of Paragraph 3.

GLOSSARY WORDS USED IN STEPS FOUR & FIVE

- **Exact**: Very accurate, methodical, correct.
- **Nature**: The essential characteristic of an object or thing.
- **Wrong**: Acting, judging, or believing incorrectly.
- **Fault**: Something done wrongly, in error, or mistake. Being the cause.
- **Mistake**: To misunderstand or perceive incorrectly.
- **Defect**: Lack of necessity, incomplete, broken, handicapped.
- **Shortcoming**: Missing the mark, Falling short, Lacking ability.
- **Self-Centered**: Pre-occupied with ones own self and affairs. At the center of all occurrences to the degree everything negatively affects your world.
- **Selfish**: The complete and utter disregard for the welfare and mindfulness of others interests. Treating other people life, time or belongings as though they were yours to use, use, waste and disrespect.
- **Self-Seeker**: A person who seeks to personally gain from every encounter or situation.
- **Dishonest**: The act or practice of lying, cheating, stealing. The result of Insecurity.
- **Fear**: A feeling of anxiety, agitation, disease, apprehension over an idea either real or imagined to be real.
- **Frightened**: A temporary or continual state of fear and shock.
- **Inconsiderate**: Without thought for the welfare of others shown in your behaviors.

NOTES:

If there is EVER a word or a Concept that you do not understand, know this; you MUST look it up. You MUST find out its true meaning, because this will change everything for you. However, be aware that many ego's only pretend to know the true meaning of things. They will tell you a skewed definition, so be aware that there is no substitute for doing your own homework.

RESENTMENT INVENTORY PROMPT SHEET

Here is a list of people, institutions and principles that may hold the key to some of the latent grudges you've been hiding under the rug. They may also jar your memory of still others that aren't listed here. Add to this list as you see fit.

People	Institutions	Principles
Father	Authority	Adultery
Mother	Church	Bible
Sister	Correctional System	Death
Brother	Education System	Diety
Aunt	Government	Golden Rule
Uncle	Military	Heaven
Cousin	Police	Hell
In-Laws	Employer	Laws
Husband	Corporations	Life after death
Wife	Religions	No Free Lunch
God	Marriage	Original Sin
Jesus	Mental Health System	Philosophy
Satan	Divisions of Government	Retribution
Clergy	Congress	Seven Deadly Sins
Police	DMV	Ten Commandments
Parole Officer	Social Security	
Lawyer	I R S	
Judge	Welfare	
Doctor		
Employer		
Co-worker		
Creditor		
Childhood Friends		
Best Friends		
Lifelong Friends		
School Friends		
Teachers		
Acquaintances		
Girlfriends		
Boyfriends		
AA Friends		
Military		
Political Figures		
Neighbors		

Remember that these are merely suggestions to unlock a mind that has been sealed shut for almost an entire lifetime. This won't be easy if you are not completely convinced that you must do this in order to live and that without which you will surely die. Once begun, new ones will certainly come to mind along the way. Ask God to guide you and you will succeed.

STEP FOUR

Bill's Business Inventory Compared To a Personal Inventory

BUSINESS   **PERSONAL**

Fact-Finding -------------------------------------- Searching
Fact-Facing ------------------------------------- Fearless
Discover Truth   ---------------------------------- Moral
Stock in Trade ------------------------------------ Ourselves

1. **Business Inventory:** How to be successful in business.
2. **Personal Inventory:** How to be Successful at Making a Life.

OBJECTIVE

1. **Disclose Damaged Unsaleable Goods**
2. **Find Flawed Thinking Processes**

PURPOSE

1. **To get rid of them promptly without regret.**

DAMAGED GOODS

1. **Stock in Trade which is Damaged**
   A.   **Resentments**
   B.   **Fears**
   C.   **Guilt & Shame**

These block me off from God's will. Access to God's will is where the Power comes from that will help me to overcome my alcoholism. Of myself, trying to live a life based on self-reliance, I lack the power to succeed. I have proven this to myself over and over, which is why, without a thorough inventory I may never get over my drinking. Self-reliance has failed me. I cannot be free while these items are still stored inside of me. I cannot make sound rationale decisions while they are the basis of my reasoning. I cannot be recovered from a seemingly hopeless condition of body and mind while they are negatively, inherently affecting the course of my life.

A Businessman cannot fool himself about the value of his products.
Just as much as:
An Alcoholic cannot fool himself about the effectiveness of his thinking.

WEEK #9: Chapter 5 — HOW IT WORKS (Step 4)

READ: Page 64, paragraph 3   page 66, paragraph 2

After we have listed people, institutions, and principles in the first column, we come to the second column and look at **the cause**. What did they do? We put our answers beside each resentment. Again we go from top to bottom. What was the cause of that resentment? And we all remember that. If we didn't know this, we wouldn't remember the name. We all have that information. There may be one cause by one name and several causes by another name.

For instance in Bill's example, he is resentful at Mr. Brown and the cause is his attention to my wife; told my wife of my mistress and Brown may get my job at the office. I'd get a little upset with Brown, too. He's mad at Mrs. Jones. She's a nut and she snubbed me. She committed her husband for drinking and he's my friend. She is a gossip. He's mad at his employer. He's unreasonable, unjust, overbearing (he probably said, "Bill, where the hell were you Monday anyhow?"). He also threatens to fire me for drinking and for padding my expense account (now that's unreasonable). He's mad at his wife. She misunderstands and nags. She likes Mr. Brown and she wants the house put in her name. Now you tie together liking Brown and wanting the house in her name and it's about time to get a little upset here.

Very carefully beside each name, from top to bottom, we list the cause. I've never seen an alcoholic yet who does not only know whom he is mad at, but he knows exactly at why and what he's mad. *All we have got to do is take it out of our head and put it down on a piece of paper.* When we finish column 2, we are going to realize something. It's not really those people whom we're upset with; it's what they did to us that got us upset. So the first thing we realize is that it's not so much the people we're upset with, it's what they've done to us that got us upset. This is very valuable information. We're going to need this after a while.

DESCRIBE AND DISCUSS SECOND INSTRUCTION OF INVENTORY PROCESS

FOURTH STEP INVENTORY PROCESS
SECOND INSTRUCTION OF THE INVENTORY PROCESS

When you have completed your list (and not before) you must analyze each resentment. Step Four will mean very little unless you come to understand each resentment and learn from it. The following procedure has proven helpful in this understanding and analysis:

1. The columns on each page are labeled as follows: Column 1: Name

Column 2: Cause Column 3: Affects my

Column 4: What is the exact nature of my wrongs, faults, mistakes, defects, shortcomings?

2. Take the first name from your "grudge list" and write it in column 1 on the first page.

3. In column 2, write a few words which describe each and every event or circumstance you can recall which causes you to resent the person named in column 1. This is a very important part of the analysis. We learn from specific events, not general complaints.

FOR EXAMPLE: We learn little from the complaint that, "he was always lying", but we learn much from a specific, "he told me he wasn't married".

***NOTE:**

It is suggested that the homework be done soon after the workshop meeting and then reviewed with your sponsor before the next workshop meeting.

ASSIGNMENT: Read page 66, paragraph 3, to page 67, paragraph 1, and be prepared to discuss any problems you may be having with the second column.

Try not to think too much about these things, it is natural for the alcoholic mind to wander and fantasize, to go off on tangents and veer off target. **Especially when we are charged with emotionally driven sensations and 'feelings'.** They are like a drink to us; they often control us. By avoiding this, you're avoiding igniting your alcoholism.

We also frequently fall victim to boredom especially easily. Any thought you can catch your mind thinking about other than doing this work is your alcoholism blocking you from getting better. Just remember that **"All resistance is ego-resistance."** This process is an ego reducing process, that is through humility, will crush the ego into smaller, more manageable pieces, which is the point of the steps. The ego-will resist this process when you get to close to actually achieving the goal of the steps, otherwise, it will seemingly happily go along with the charades.

So the further you get closer to achieving the goal of the step process; the more difficult it will seem to get because the ego will become more aggressive at tricking you into believing its lies. Here is precisely why your relationship with God **MUST** be as authentic as possible.

WEEK #10: Chapter 5 — HOW IT WORKS *(Step 4)*

Read 64, paragraph 3 to page 66, paragraph 2 - Repeat this week.

Now we come to the second column. In column 3 ("Affects My" on our "Review of Resentments") we check off: Was it our Self-esteem, our Security, our Ambitions, our Personal or Sex relations which had been interfered with?

REFER TO BASIC INSTINCTS OF LIFE HANDOUT: Page 67 of this workbook

We go to the SELF-COLUMN (column 3). We take the Self-Esteem column and remembering always to work from top to bottom, beside each name and each cause we look to see if it was a threat to our self-esteem. Did it put us down in the eyes of other people? Did it embarrass us? If so, we put a little check mark there. We work from top to bottom with our mind on one thing only - is it a threat to self-esteem? Then we come back to the PERSONAL RELATIONSHIP COLUMN.

Starting at the top and working to the bottom, is it a threat to our personal relationships? Then we come back to the SECURITY COLUMN, do MATERIAL first and then EMOTIONAL SECURITY. Then to the SEX COLUMN: Is it a threat to my ACCEPTABLE SEX LIFE with my spouse? Is it a threat to my HIDDEN SEX LIFE with my girl/boy-friend? We work each column separately, from top to bottom. And then we look at the AMBITIONS COLUMN. Everybody has plans regarding their future. That's a part of our make-up. And I'll get just as upset with you if you threaten what I'm trying to get as I am if you threaten what I've already got. The only way I can be upset is if you threaten one of the two; my basic instincts or my ambitions in those areas.

As I fill these out I begin to realize that I'm making an awful lot of check marks under one particular column. I finish this column and I realize something that's very important for me to know. First, in the first column I realize it's not how many people I'm actually mad at but how much they control my thinking. In the third column I realize it's not really what they did, it's how I reacted to it based on my basic instincts of life. Today, for the first time in my life, I realize where my anger comes from. It's my reaction based on my basic instincts of life to what other people do to me or what I think they do to me.

Either one is just as bad! Now that I know where anger comes from I might be able to do something about it. But until I know that, I'll never get a handle on it, period, and that anger will keep giving me trouble for the rest of my life. I've learned three valuable things and all I've done is fill out the sheet. I have not analyzed it yet; I have only listed it.

DESCRIBE AND DISCUSS THIRD INSTRUCTION OF INVENTORY PROCESS

FOURTH STEP INVENTORY PROCESS
THIRD INSTRUCTION OF THE INVENTORY PROCESS

When you have completed your "CAUSES" Column, opposite each of the events you have listed in column two, you will check, "Which Part of Self is Affected" in column three. Start with SOCIAL INSTINCTS from top to bottom. To clarify these columns, refer back to your BASIC INSTINCTS OF LIFE HANDOUT. This will help with the definitions of the words such as self-esteem, etc. Then do SECURITY INSTINCT from top to bottom, also SEX INSTINCT top to bottom and finally AMBITIONS top to bottom. Once again to clarify these columns refer back to your BASIC INSTINCTS OF LIFE HANDOUT.

ASSIGNMENT: Continue to read page 66, paragraph 3 to page 67, paragraph 1.

BASIC INSTINCTS OF LIFE THAT CREATE SELF

SOCIAL INSTINCT	SECURITY INSTINCT	SEX INSTINCT
COMPANIONSHIP - Wanting to belong or to be accepted.	**MATERIAL** - Wanting money, things, property, clothing, etc. in order to be secure in the future.	**ACCEPTABLE** - Our sex lives as accepted by society, God's Principles or our own principles.
PRESTIGE - Wanting to be recognized or to be accepted as a leader.	**EMOTIONAL** - Based upon our needs for another person or persons. Some tend to dominate others, some are overly dependant on others.	**HIDDEN** - Our sex lives that are contrary to either Society, God's Principles or our own principles.
SELF-ESTEEM - How we think of ourselves, high or low.		
PRIDE - An excessive and unjustified opinion of one's self, either positive (self-love) or negative (self-hate).	**AMBITIONS** - Our plans to gain material wealth, or to dominate others, or to depend upon others.	**AMBITION** - Our plans regarding our sex lives whether acceptable or hidden.
PERSONAL RELATIONSHIPS - Our relations with other human beings and the world around us.		
AMBITIONS - Our plans to gain acceptance, power, recognition, prestige, etc.		

SELF → WRONGS

(INCORRECT JUDGEMENT)	(INCORRECT BELIEF)	(INCORRECT ACTIONS)
RESENTMENTS	**FEAR**	**HARMS OR HURT**
Feelings of bitter hurt or indignation which comes from rightly or wrongly held feelings of being injured or offended.	Feelings of anxiety, agitation, uneasiness, apprehension, etc.	Wrong acts which result in pain, hurt feelings, worry, financial loss, etc., for others and also self.

In the *Twelve & Twelve* there is some of the best information the world's ever seen on self-will and what makes people tick. It's referred to as, "The Basic Instincts of Life".

I've always suggested to the people whom I sponsor that they read the *Twelve & Twelve* regarding the Basic Instincts of Life. This is to get a working knowledge about the words there and look them up in the dictionary because they are very important words that we are going to use later in the third column when we get ready to do our Fourth Step inventory.

There have always been a lot of questions as to why Bill wrote the *Twelve & Twelve*. One reason I think he wrote the *Twelve & Twelve* is that he had so much trouble selling "The Traditions" to the groups and he felt if he could put the Twelve Traditions with the Steps in a book then it would be more acceptable to the groups. But I think one of the main reasons he wrote the *Twelve & Twelve* was that thirteen years later Bill knew more about what he was talking about. Let's face it, when Bill wrote *The Big Book* and finished it up in 1939, Bill was not a spiritual giant. He was not trained in those areas at all. Bill was not trained in human nature; he studied economics and business and he was a night school lawyer.

Yet, Bill was able to write one of the most spiritual books dealing with human nature the world's ever seen, even though he didn't know much about it. Surely God had a hand in the writing of *The Big Book*! Thirteen years later though, Bill had worked with many alcoholics. He had worked with and studied with some of the best minds in the world regarding spirituality and human nature and I think he felt he had more information that he could pass on to us that would make it easier to work the Steps according to *The Big Book*, of Alcoholics Anonymous.

Bill says in the *Twelve & Twelve* that the book is a series of essays that are designed to give us more information so we can better work the Steps. He also says the *Twelve & Twelve* is **not** designed to replace *The Big Book*. *The Big Book* has always been the basic text and always will be. You simply cannot work the program out of the *Twelve & Twelve*. Lots of people try, but they can't do it because there are no directions on how to work the Steps. Frankly, I think that's why they love the *Twelve & Twelve*. They can get in it and dance around and philosophize and they never have to do anything except talk. There is, however, some information in there that is absolutely invaluable. If we can see it, understand it and accept it, it makes working the steps out of *The Big Book* much simpler and much easier. Bill taught me more in *The Big Book* in two or three pages than I had learned in some 40 years of living.

Let's take a closer look at the Basic Instincts of Life, of what they are and how they affect us and those around us. For years while reading about "the actor" who wants to run the whole show on page 61 in *The Big Book*, I never really understood what Bill was talking about until I got into the *Twelve & Twelve* and read the information concerning the Basic Instincts of Life. Let's look at them for just a moment. **(See Chart "Basic Instincts of Life" page 67)**

All human beings are born with three basic instincts of life.
1. **They are God given**
2. **They are absolutely necessary for survival of the human race**
3. **Therefore they are good things**

The first thing he talked about is the **social instinct**. Bill said, "All human beings are born with the desire to be liked, to be accepted, and to be respected by other people and that we are born with the desire to come together in groups with other people." If we didn't have those desires and cared nothing for each other, the world would go into complete anarchy; a "dog-eat-dog" situation would reign and eventually under those conditions the human race would fail to survive.

Bill used several terms describing the **social instinct**:

Companionship: wanting to belong or to be accepted. So many of us grew up on the outside of the crowd looking in, wanting to be and knew we could not be.

Prestige: wanting to be recognized or to be accepted as the leader of the group. The world needs leaders. Somebody's got to do that. Most people will take one of two directions; either to be a part of or to be a leader of a group. In either case it's based upon what other people think of us.

Self-esteem: what we think of ourselves. That's usually high or low based upon what others think of us or what we think other people think of us. If they seem to like us and accept us we feel pretty good towards ourselves. If it feels like they reject us and they don't want us, then we feel pretty lousy towards ourselves.

Pride: is an excessive and unjustified opinion of one's self. We either think too well of ourselves or too little of ourselves. In either case it's not the truth. (I'm glad I got into the habit of going to the dictionary. I always thought pride was something you ought to have. All I ever wanted to be as a young boy growing up was to be a man who walked tall with pride and just a little bit sideways like John Wayne did!)

Personal Relationships: our relations with other human beings and the world around us. Friends, family, partners, employers, lovers, even acquaintances.

Ambitions: our plans for the future. What we would like to see manifest in our lives.

All human beings have these things. Now if I want to be liked and accepted and respected by the world and the people in it, the first thing I've got to do is determine, "What do they want from me?"

It varies throughout the world. In one part it's a good education, in another it's to be large landowner, and yet in another part of the world it's to have a large family. Society teaches us those things as we grow up and we set goals for ourselves as to what we want to become in the future. To reach these goals we have set we are going to have to work at it. You can't just be a bum and sit on your duff and be successful and people like you and accept you. You are going to have to work at whatever it might be.

By the same token we're going to have to make some sacrifices. There are some things that I would really like to do as a human being that are very pleasurable and very exciting but if you catch me at it you're not going to like me at all. I don't think you and I would do the work needed to reach the goal or make the sacrifices necessary unless we get a reward for doing so. And the great reward? Well Bill said it in his story when he said, ***"I had arrived."***

How many of us have done it? We set our goal and we just worked our tails off for years. The day we reach the goal, they pat us on the back and say "You're a fine fellow", "You're a good man", and "You are doing great". There's a feeling that comes over us which is one of those indescribably wonderful feelings. The only thing wrong is it seems to be just a temporary feeling. No sooner do we reach the goal, get the praise, the recognition and the prestige from it, we look around we say "Is this all there is to it?" So we set another goal, and we work and work, and we strive and strive, and we sacrifice and we reach the new goal, and we get the praise and recognition, feels great, doesn't last long, and we set another goal.

It seems to create within we human beings an insatiable desire for more and more power, more and more recognition and we're not getting it fast enough or they're not giving it to us the way we think they ought to, so what do we do about it? Well we start taking shortcuts. We start doing a little lying, a little conning, a little manipulating, a little stepping on other peoples toes and climbing on their backs and the instant we do so we create pain and suffering for others. They in turn retaliate against us and create pain and suffering for us.

It's plain to see, that a life run on self-will could hardly ever be a success. Under those conditions we will always be in collision with people, places, and things.

The second basic instinct he talked about is the **security instinct**. Now, I know that in AA we try to live one day at a time. But I also know that just about everybody in this room has got an insurance policy. The purpose of the insurance policy is to protect ourselves in the future. Bill said, "All human beings are born with the desire to be secure in the future. If we didn't have that desire we wouldn't provide the food, the clothing, the shelter, and the things that we need to survive. Then next winter we would just simply freeze to death or the next drought season we would starve to death. So this desire that we have to be secure in the future is God-given and it is necessary for our survival." Now once again if you're going to be secure in the future you have to decide "Well, what is it that I need in order to be secure?

Society usually teaches us those things as we grow up and it varies throughout the world. In one part of the world you only need $4, in another you need $4,000, in another you need $4,000,000 and in another part of the world maybe you need 198 coconuts, or whatever it is that they use to measure, trade, and barter. Based on what we're taught, we set goals for ourselves and we begin to work at it. Now to be secure in the future you can't just sit on your duff and be a bum. You're going to have to work. You're going to have to make some money. You're going to have to invest.

At the same time you've got to sacrifice. Hell, we can't blow it all today and be secure tomorrow. Again, I don't think you and I would do the work necessary to reach the goal or make the sacrifices necessary if we didn't get a reward for it.

Once again the reward is that great feeling that comes at the moment of successful completion of the goal. How many of us have done it? We set the goal for the new dress, for the new shoes, for the new suit, for the new drapes, for the new couch, for the new home, for the new car, for the new piece of property, for the new business, and we work and we work and we strive and we strive for the day that sucker is paid off and nobody can take it away from us. What a great and wonderful feeling that is.

How great that was. The only thing wrong with it is that it's just a temporary feeling. No sooner had I gotten that sucker paid off I looked around and his house is bigger than mine; he has a Cadillac and I'm driving a Chevrolet; he's got a Brooks Brothers suit and I bought mine at Kmart. That causes us to set another goal. And we work and we work and we strive and we strive and we reach the new goal, feels good, doesn't last long, we set another. It seems to create an insatiable desire for more and more and more and more yet we're not getting it fast enough. They're not giving it to us like we think they should. So what do we do? We take shortcuts. We lie, we cheat, we con, we manipulate, and the instant we do we hurt other people. They retaliate against us, creating pain and suffering for us.

It's plain to see that a life run on self-will can hardly ever be a success.

The third basic instinct he talks about is the **sex instinct**. Bill said "All human beings are born with the desire to have sex." Now, it may get turned off by bad teachings or bad happenings but he said "All human beings are born with the desire to have sex because if we don't have sex we can't reproduce ourselves, and if we don't reproduce ourselves, sooner or later the human race is going to fail to survive."

So just like the other two basic instincts, if you're going to reproduce yourself through the sexual act you're going to have to work at it. Hell, you can do more work in three minutes of sex, (if you can last that long), than you'll do all day digging a ditch! Don't you older fellows remember how it used to be when we got through with it? My God you'd just fall over sideways, the sweat is just pouring off of you, and you can hardly get your breath.

You feel like you've died, gone to heaven and come back two or three times. But I don't think you and I would do that kind of work if we didn't get a reward for doing so. The great reward is that great feeling we get both physically and emotionally at the moment of the successful completion of the sex act. It's one of the greatest rewards that a human being can experience. But, just like the other two it seems to be just a temporary feeling. Hell, you no sooner get through doing it that you get to thinking about doing it again; it's such a pleasurable and exciting thing that the next thing you know you get to thinking about and doing it in different ways. Then you get to thinking about doing it in different positions. Then you get to thinking about doing it with different people. The next thing you know we're doing it at the wrong time in the wrong way with the wrong people and the instant we do so we create pain and suffering for others. They in turn retaliate against us, which creates pain and suffering for us.

It's plain to see, that a life run on self-will can hardly ever be a success.

The fulfillment of these basic instincts is so pleasurable, that all human beings from time to time will overdo it in one or more of these areas and create pain and suffering for others.

You'll notice on that little chart there's an object called **'SELF'**. That's where **self-will** comes from. It comes from these three basic instincts of life. You'll also notice coming out of the **'self'** object there is another called **'wrongs'**, which is another word we need to look at. Somewhere we got the idea that wrongs meant a list of dirty filthy nasty items. But if you go to the dictionary and look it up you'll find several definitions:

- o   Wrong - incorrect judgment of other people = **resentment**
- o   Wrong - incorrect believing = **fear**
- o   Wrong - are the **harms and hurts** that we do to other people

Now it's easy to spot a selfish, self-centered human being,
…the one who is running on self-will, not running on God's Will.
A selfish, self-centered human being is
always madder than hell.

Damn him; Damn her. By God I'll show them. They're not going to treat me that way. A selfish, self-centered human being is always scared to death. They can't depend on God. They can't depend on other people. If we're an alcoholic reaching the end of the road we can't depend on ourselves any longer and we're running absolutely scared to death all the time.

A selfish, self-centered human being, in order to fulfill the basic instincts of life, is always overdoing it and creating harms and hurts for others. Then we've got to be scared to death of what they're going to do when they catch us; even if they don't catch us. If God dwells within each of us, we know the difference between right and wrong. The guilt and remorse associated with those things begin to eat us up.

A person whose mind is filled with resentment, a person whose mind is filled with fear, a person whose mind is filled with guilt and remorse, does not feel good. Eventually searching for a way to feel better we begin to think about the sense of ease and comfort that comes at once by taking a couple of drinks. Next thing you know we believe we can drink and we end up drunk all over again.

So at the very least we're going to have to do something about this selfish, self-centered human being and it seems the only way you can do anything about that is with God's help because God made self-will and only God has the power to overcome that. At the very least, we have to do something about these resentments, these fears and this guilt and remorse in order to find the peace of mind, serenity and happiness for good long term sobriety.

If every human being in the world today could fulfill these three basic instincts at the level that God intends there would be no conflict on earth today. But all human beings have self-will and from time to time will overdo it in one or more areas, creating conflict for others and for themselves.

I never knew that. I just knew I was always in trouble. I just knew I was always madder than hell. I just knew I was always scared to death. I knew guilt and remorse was eating me up but I didn't know where it came from. You see, they gave me the rules but they never taught me how to *play the game*. A.A. has taught me how to play the game and now that I know how I don't break the rules anymore and I don't hurt other people and I'm not scared to death and I'm not filled with guilt and remorse. This is the best information I have ever seen on what makes me tick and what causes me to do the things I do.

The delusional nature of alcoholism is the process of painting us into a corner that we cannot get out of, then poking us with a stick until the fear and frustration, anger and self-doubt, culminate into a pinnacle of pressure so great our only viable option seems to be to take a drink to release the pressure. This of course sets off the terrible phenomenon of craving resulting in more debacles.

WEEK #11: Chapter 5 — HOW IT WORKS *(Step 4)*

READ: Page 66, paragraph 3   page 66, paragraph 3

Now we see why we had to have a written inventory. If you only had a mental inventory, you would have already lost it. So we can turn back to this list and look at it again, for it holds the key to the future. We've been looking at the past according to resentments, but the past resentments are going to hold the key for the future, <u>if we can</u> <u>see what to do with them</u>.

Before I looked at my resentments to see what people had done to me. Today I'm looking at my resentments to see what those resentments had done to me. If the resentment blocks me off from God's Will and causes me to get drunk, then I can't afford to have that. It doesn't make any difference whether it's a justified or an unjustified resentment; either one of them effectively blocks me off from God's Will.

"We began to see that the world and its people really dominated us.
In that state, the wrongdoing of others, fancied or real, had power to actually kill."

When I read that I thought, "My God, how dumb can I be?" All my life I've been proud of the fact that I stand on my own two feet. "Yes sir, I run my show. Nobody tells me what to do. I make my own decisions." But when I read that statement, I suddenly realized that other people have been telling me what to do all my life through my resentment toward them.

When I'm resenting them, they have control of my thinking. If they control my thinking, they effectively control my decisions and my actions and my entire life. I always thought I controlled my thinking, my decisions, my actions and my entire life. I realize today that I never have. They've always controlled me through my resentments. Then I thought, "Man, I really am sick!

Some of these people have been dead and buried for years and they've been reaching out from the grave and they've had me by the ying-yang as far back as I could remember." When I saw that I said, "The hell with that! I'm not going to let those people live in my head rent-free anymore!" I made a decision in Step Three to let God direct my thinking. Now if I let other people, dead or alive, direct my thinking, then obviously God isn't. I did not know that until I took this inventory.

Resentments come from self-will. God makes self-will and only God has the POWER to overcome self-will. Self cannot overcome self. But the instant I see what those resentments are doing to me, I'm just about willing to do anything to get rid of them rather than let them get me drunk.

READ: Page 66, paragraph 4   page 67, paragraph 1

We write our resentments down on paper and analyze them. We have these three columns there and we read them across. We can learn a lot about them. We can analyze them. We can't analyze them when they're only in our minds. Only when we get them down on paper can we analyze them. This is sort of like a little computer. You have the first column down.

If the name is down, you can extract the cause. Once we get the cause, we can trace the cause and find out which part of self it affects. Then for the first time we can get a pretty good picture of the truth of the resentment. Now when we do this, we're getting rid of about 95% of these resentments simply by listing and analyzing them. When you list and analyze the resentments, about 95% of them are going to look dumb.

They appear stupid on paper. So we get rid of them. There will be some, however, that we will hold onto - especially those deep-seated resentments. Bill suggests that we use prayer on those. There is no way that you can enter into a relationship with God and the communion with God in prayer about the well-being of another individual and at the same time continue to resent him. One will remove the other.

In the program we tend to focus on the Third Step and Seventh Step Prayers and hardly anyone ever mentions the Fourth Step Prayer that appears on the top of page 67. If you have resentment and you're re-playing it over and over again, then you are cutting yourself off from God's Will working in your life. The Fourth Step Prayer is the prayer you should be praying. Also there's an example Bill uses in "Freedom from Bondage" on page 551 in *The Big Book*. It's a classic example of using prayer on resentments.

READ: Page 67, paragraph 2   page 67, paragraph 2

It's so simple you may think it won't work. But if you follow these simple instructions and do what *The Big Book* says, I guarantee you that your resentments will be removed so God can direct your thinking in that area of your life.

But it will do no good to get rid of them if I don't know how to keep them from coming back because the world is full of sick people and tomorrow they're going to do something to me; I'm sure of it. And if I'm not careful, I'll resent once again. And I can't have one. If I have one resentment, then almost immediately I'll have two, three, twenty, thirty, and I'm a basket case all over again.

I've got one more thing to do before I'm through with resentments. We've got to get down to the cause of this thing. We've got to get rid of the real things within ourselves that started it all.

DESCRIBE & DISCUSS FOURTH INSTRUCTION OF INVENTORY PROCESS

FOURTH STEP INVENTORY PROCESS
FOURTH INSTRUCTION OF THE INVENTORY PROCESS

THE BEGINNING OF GROWTH: As noted earlier, it is a spiritual axiom that when I am disturbed, no matter what the cause, there is something wrong with me. Now that you have listed and understand the resentment and how it affected you, having stopped blaming or "putting out of your mind the wrongs others have done", you can now look for your own mistakes and learn from them. Take the following action:

D. For each person, institution or principle and for each event, ask yourself, **where have I been**.......

SELFISH: Caring unduly or supremely for one's self, regarding one's own comfort in disregard to that of others

SELF-SEEKING: Act or habit of seeking primarily one's own interest or happiness

INCONSIDERATE: Not adequately considerate; ill-advised, not regarding the rights or feelings of others; thoughtless

DISHONEST: Lacking honesty, willful perversion of the truth, stealing, cheating, or defrauding, lying by omission; (even people pleasing is living a lie)

FRIGHTENED: Fear excited by sudden danger; alarm. State of habit of fearing; anxious concern about losing something I already have or not getting something that I want

E. Answer the following questions for each item in column two in the space provided or on the back of your worksheet or on a separate piece of paper. This will help in sharing with your sponsor in Step Five.

4th **Column: What was MY WRONG in all this?**

5th **Column: What did I do initially to get the ball rolling?**

6th **Column: How could I have done things differently?**

ASSIGNMENT: Continue to read page 67, paragraph 3. If you are having problems with your Fourth Step, please be sure to call someone in the group or the leader and share so you won't get stuck or discouraged.

WEEK #12: Chapter 5 — HOW IT WORKS *(Step 4 - Fears)*

The first symptoms of spiritual illness are resentments. We have taken our inventory of resentments. Many of us are holding on to resentments from the past. We are sitting around tables trying to analyze why they did *that* to us. It doesn't make any difference *why* they did it, they did it. Then we try to analyze why those resentments made us the way we are today, and it doesn't make any difference that we are the way we are. Why don't we get rid of the resentment, freeing our mind of it, releasing our mind, and letting God begin to direct our thinking?

Our Steps are to be used not to discuss all these problems, but to solve these problems. You and I can get rid of all our resentments, if we want to. If we can see in the fourth column what we need to change in ourselves, (our personality), then with God's help we can change those things. If I become less selfish, I'm not going to hurt as many people. If I'm more honest, I'm not going to be in hot water all the time.

If I get a little more courage instead of fear, maybe I can quit doing some of those things I used to do. If I can consider other people, then surely my relationship with them is going to be better. If I have less conflict I'm going to have more peace of mind, serenity, and happiness, and I'm less likely to take a drink.

In the fourth column I have the exact nature of the wrong that I will be discussing with someone in Step Five. I have the defects of character that I'm going to become willing to get rid of in Step Six. I have those shortcomings that I'm going to ask God to take away in Step Seven. It doesn't matter if I call them a wrong, mistake, defect, or shortcoming; they are the things that cause my problems.

The second common manifestation of "self" is fear. Self-willed, self-centered people know of no God to depend upon and cannot depend on other people. If we are practicing alcoholics we can't depend on ourselves either, and we are riddled with fear.

READ: Page 67, paragraph 3   page 68, paragraph 1

We're going to start looking at the second common manifestation of self, the second symptom of spiritual illness, the second thing that blocks us off from God's Will. I think we're going to find as we look at fears, some of the same things we found with resentments. First we're going to see how much fear really does dominate our thinking, and by dominating our thinking it controls our actions and controls our lives just like resentments did. I think we're going to find that a lot of our fears originate from something we ourselves have done in the past based upon our old selfish, self-centered, self-seeking character.

If fear dominates our thinking, then obviously God can't.

Fear will be just like resentments. We will not get rid of all fears because fear also serves a useful purpose in life. If we didn't have any fears, we probably couldn't exist at all. We wouldn't be able to walk across a crowded street without getting run over. If we didn't fear what others think then we probably couldn't hold this meeting. We'd probably start telling each other the truth and what we really think and the meeting might break up in a hurry under those conditions. Fear brings caution and it is useful.

But when fear dominates us and causes us to do things that end up bothering other people or when fear causes us to rationalize our thinking and make excuses for not doing things we should do, then fear is really dominating our life.

If fear dominates our thinking, then obviously God doesn't.

DESCRIBE & DISCUSS INVENTORY PROCESS OF OUR FEARS

INSTRUCTION FIVE OF THE FOURTH STEP INVENTORY PROCESS

ANALYSIS OF FEAR
FEAR -- TOUCHES EVERY ASPECT OF OUR LIVES

Webster's dictionary defines "fear" as the feeling of alarm or disquiet caused by the expectation of danger, pain, disaster, or the like. (Being found out, being known for what you know or think you are). It is said that the driving force in the life of most alcoholics is the self-centered fear that we will lose something we have or that we will not get something we need or want.

We use the same instructions to review our fear as we had to review our resentments except it's worded just a little bit differently, which was Bill's way of doing things. We made up a worksheet even though *The Big Book* does not show a worksheet for fear. We followed the same pattern that we had for resentments and used the same procedure to review our fears:

Column 1: What am I Fearful of? List all of your fears. We fill this out the same way we did the resentments, from top to bottom. I think as we list our fears, we might be amazed at how many fears we really do have. We men like to be tough and macho and say, "Well, we don't have much fear." But we're not talking as much about physical fear as we are about the fears of the mind. I said, "I don't have much fear but I'll put them down like I'm supposed to". I began to list my fears and I was surprised to see I was filling out worksheet, after worksheet.

Column 2: Why Do I Have the Fear? In column two, write a short description of each fear you have experienced. Now this is not an attempt to psychoanalyze ourselves. Some fears I'm supposed to have. I'm supposed to be afraid of the dark, because I don't have built in headlights and I can't see at night. That kind of fear brings caution. But if it prevents me from going outside at night, then it's an unreasonable fear and I probably need to do something about it. I'm supposed to be afraid of heights, I don't have wings and I can't fly. That fear brings caution. But if it keeps me from riding in an elevator, then it's going to rule and dominate my life entirely. In most fears I find that I have set something in motion to produce that fear. I have fears connected with many different things and most of them have a good root cause, and most of them stem from something I have set in motion.

Column 3: Which Part of Self Is Threatened? ANALYSIS OF FEAR: We cannot have a fear unless one of our Basic Instincts of Life is threatened or involved. Refer to your BASIC INSTINCTS of LIFE HANDOUT **(workbook p.67).** Check off which part of "self" was affected. It is said that each of these fears set in motion chains of circumstances which brought about or caused us misfortunes. If you threaten my ambitions, you create fear. I think in filling out this sheet we're going to find out just how much fear drives us, how much it dominates and how it keeps us from doing the things we really should do. Many of us would like to go back to school to finish up an education and get a degree. But most of us won't do that. The reason we won't is that we're afraid to fail or afraid we can't compete or afraid of what people will think of us if we fail, or we will be embarrassed.

Column 4: What is the exact nature of my wrongs, faults, mistakes, defects, shortcomings? Check off the box that pertains to your part in the fear, just like in the fourth column of the resentment inventory:

1) Selfish & Self-Seeking ☐

2) Dishonest ☐

3) Inconsiderate ☐

4) Frightened ☐

Fear *is* the wrong. That's what separates me from God. But what's the nature of the fear? I'll find the nature of it in practically every case; that is if I wasn't so selfish, so self-seeking, so dishonest, so frightened, or inconsiderate of other people, I wouldn't be putting myself in positions where I have to experience that fear.

If I wouldn't be so greedy, I wouldn't be so afraid I'm not going to have enough money. If I wasn't dishonest, if I wouldn't steal and write bad checks and tell lies, then I wouldn't have to worry about what they are going to do with me when they catch me. If I wasn't so frightened in the first place, I wouldn't have to do those things I've been doing. If I was more considerate of other people I wouldn't be hurting them and experiencing fear.

If I don't find a way to change that old character out there in column 4, I'm going to have to live with this stuff for the rest of my life blocked off from God's Will and eventually go back to drinking. Fear does the same thing to me that resentments do, they effectively block me off from the *Sunlight of the Spirit*. You can use fear just as you can resentments to justify not doings things you should really go ahead and do.

Most of my fears will disappear when we look at them and see what we have been doing. Those that don't disappear I can handle with prayer. With God's help I can change out of that fourth column and I will have less fear in the future.

STUDY AND PRAYER: When our fears have been listed and the above questions answered, the book *Alcoholics Anonymous* gives us the solution to fear in the second and third paragraphs appearing on page 68. We are also given a short prayer in which we ask ***"Him to remove our fears and direct our attention to what He would have us to be."*** This solution and prayer should be directed toward each fear.

There is no way to enter into communion with God about fear and at the same time continue to have that fear. Now this will remove fear - if we pray about that fear, ask God to remove the fear then at once we commence to outgrow that fear. We ask Him to remove all our fears and to direct our attention to what He would have us be instead. God will remove that fear - *IF WE ASK*! I think this is one of the greatest promises in this book, it says He will do so; and at once we commence to outgrow our fears.

ASSIGNMENT: Continue to read page 68, paragraph 4, to the end of Chapter 5, and be prepared to discuss any problems you may be having with your inventory so far.

Instructions for completing our "FEAR Inventory"

1. **Column1**: When dealing with our fears, we put them down on paper. Complete column 1, from top to bottom. Do nothing on columns 2, 3, & 4 until column 1 is complete.

2. **Column 2**: I asked myself; "Why do I have this fear?" Complete column 2, from top to bottom. Do nothing on columns 3 or 4 until column 2 is complete.

3. **Column 3**: I ask myself: "Which part of self caused my fear?" "Was it my self-esteem, my security, my ambitions, my personal or sex relations that had been interfered with?" Complete each sub-column within column 3, going from left to right, starting with "companionship" and finishing with the "sexual ambitions". Do nothing on column 4 until column 3 is complete.

4. **Column 4**: Referring to our list again and putting out of our minds the wrongs others had done, we resolutely looked for our own mistakes asking: "Where had we been selfish, self-seeking, dishonest, inconsiderate, and/or frightened?" We ask ourselves this question and complete each area of column 4.

   On the far right side of your worksheet, the back of your worksheet, or on a separate sheet of paper, write down your faults as revealed by column 4; i.e. "What was MY PART in all this?", "Where did I set the ball rolling?" and/or "What should I have done differently?"

   Reading from left to right; we now see:

   Column 1: The Fear

   Column 2: Why I have this fear

   Column 3: The part of self that has caused this fear

   Column 4: The exact nature of the defect within me, which allows this fear to surface and blocks me from God's Will.

LETTING GO

To let Go doesn't mean to stop caring, It means I can't do "it" for someone else.

To Let Go is not to cut myself off, it's the realization that I can't control a situation or other people.

To Let Go is not to enable, but to allow a learning process to occur from natural consequences.

To Let Go is to admit your own powerlessness placing the outcome in God's hands.

To Let Go is to not try and blame or change someone else, but to change only myself.

To Let Go is not to care for a specified outcome, but to care about a bigger picture.

To Let Go is not to try and fix a person or their situation, but to support them in correcting it themselves.

To Let Go is not to judge, but allow God to work in His time, Miracles in both of your lives.

To Let Go is not to be the director, but to be the agent of the master.

To Let Go is not to be unProtective, but to allow another to grow through facing their own reality.

To Let Go is not to deny help, but to Accept giving help. Yet being wise enough to see how help needs to be given.

To Let Go is YOUR healing process and is why the other person is having to go through what you are having to be a witness to.

To Let Go is breaking away from self-reliance that has always failed you – and learning to trust in the Power of God and real Love.

REVIEW OF FEARS

"SELF"

COLUMN 1	COLUMN 2	COLUMN 3: Which Part of Self Was Affected?		COLUMN 4	Questions
THE FEAR:	WHY I HAVE THIS FEAR:			What is the exact nature of my wrongs, faults, mistakes, defects, shortcomings?	What was MY PART in all this? What did I do initially to get the ball rolling? How could I have done things differently?

Column 3 sub-categories:

Social Instinct	Companionship
	Prestige
	Self-Esteem
	Pride
	Personal Relationships
Security Instinct	Material
	Emotional
Sex Instinct	Acceptable Sex Relations
	Hidden Sex Relations
Ambitions	Social
	Security
	Sexual

Column 4 categories:

- Self-Seeking & Selfish
- Dishonest
- Inconsiderate
- Frightened

136

WEEK #13: Chapter 5 — HOW IT WORKS
(Step Four – Sex Conduct / Harms Done)

"Now about sex: Many of us needed an overhauling (change) *there. But above all, we tried to be sensible on this question."* (*The Big Book* page 68, paragraph 3) We're going to be dealing with how we *think* about sex more so than how we *perform* sex. This "sex thing" is quite a bit different with human beings than it is with the other animals of the earth. You have to remember that all the other species are **God directed**. Whatever they do, whether it is sex, eating, sleeping or where they shelter, **is all dependent upon God's direction…period**.

When it comes time for them to reproduce, whenever it might be, God usually signifies this by some change in the female species. There is physical change. The male of the species senses this change. The male prepares himself and the two join together. Then, they go their separate ways. They really don't have any choice in their sex life. They can't decide when they're going to do it. That's decided by God, usually at certain times of the year, depending on which species they are. They cannot decide who they're going to do it with. That is usually decided by God also. They can't decide how many times they're going to do it. They can't decide in what position they're going to do it. For them, it is primarily a reproductive thing; period. **It's all done with God's direction.**

God made us human beings a little bit different. Because he gave us this thing called **self-will**. He gave us the ability to *think* about not only sex, but every aspect of our lives as well. So he gave us the ability to make decisions about it. Of course he wanted us to use sex for reproduction of the human race, but he also made it very enjoyable for us so we would do it. He also gave us the ability to choose who we were going to do it with, where we are going to do it, when we were going to do it, and how many times we were going to do it and in what position we were going to do it.

We think that most of the troubles with the human race, which are sex related, originate not so much from the physical act itself, as from the way we *think* about sex. Because it's through sex that we become **emotionally** involved with each other. If we couldn't think and reason and have this intelligence, our emotions would not be involved. Therefore, most of the troubles that we have are not so much from the physical act of sex, as it is from the **emotional or mental side of sex**.

What we are going to do by using our book is to take a look at our past sex life. We will see that some of the things that we have done in the past (and are maybe still doing) end up hurting other people. If we hurt others, it's likely they are going to retaliate against us and that in turn is going to cause more pain and suffering for us.

We are also going to find out how to look at our sex lives. If we are not doing it the way we think we should, or as often as we think we should, it tends to make us irritable, restless and discontented. It is very difficult for us to get a handle on a future sex life where we can be relatively free of worry or fear concerning it. The analysis is like what we had to do with fear and resentments. We had to see what fear and resentments did to us. Now we are going to see how sex really affects us.

READ: Page 68, paragraph 4   page 69, paragraph 2

We heard those "voices" all of our lives. There are those who say sex is dirty, and you ought to do it one time in one position with one person only, and the only purpose for doing it is to reproduce, and if you enjoy it, there must be something wrong with you. And I've heard those voices over and over and over. This is the extreme on one end of the scale.

I read that last statement above with complete relief, because I just knew that this book was getting ready to condemn me for what I had done in the past and I knew it was getting ready to tell me what I was going to have to do in the future. I had already made up my mind I wasn't going to pay any attention to it at all. I was relieved to see that *The Big Book* was not going to do that, and thank God it doesn't because if *The Big Book* tried to tell me what was right and what was wrong in the sex area and what I had to do in my sex life, then *The Big Book* could not match all human beings anywhere in our world. Our book is designed to be helpful for any alcoholic, anywhere in the world. So thank God it stays out of that kind of controversy.

READ: Page 69, paragraph 3   page 71, to end of page

We see the same set of instructions in *The Big Book* on page 69, paragraph 2, for the sex inventory that we saw for the fears and resentments inventory except they are worded slightly different. By looking at the past and writing it down on paper and analyzing it, we can develop an ideal for the future. We reproduce and multiply, it's a part of life. Just like our resentments and fears, our sex drive is the same way. It's a great battle, the battle of life:

Either we can let God control these things or these things can dominate us.

DESCRIBE & DISCUSS INVENTORY PROCESS OF SEX CONDUCT

INSTRUCTION SIX OF THE INVENTORY PROCESS

Analysis of Sex Conduct

Let's look at the worksheet; **"REVIEW OF OUR OWN SEX CONDUCT & HARMS DONE" (see Workshop Workbook, page 89).** *(We will use this sheet for both the analysis of our own sex conduct and again for harms done to others that are not related to sex. We will start with the analysis of our own sex conduct.)*

Preparing a List of Sex / Relationships:

COLUMN 1: Who Did I Harm?
We make a list of those people we have harmed by our conduct of the past. Most of us know exactly what we have done and who we have hurt. There's a thing inside ourselves that usually tells us the difference between right and wrong, between what to do and what not to do. Usually when we've harmed someone by our sexual misconduct, we know we have.

COLUMN 2: What Did I do?
    Ask yourself these questions:
        a. Did I arouse jealousy?
        b. Did I arouse suspicion?
        c. Did I arouse bitterness?

There are many ways that we hurt people in a sexual manner. Sometimes when we are in a relationship and emotionally involved as in a marriage, and we go outside the marriage and do things we shouldn't be doing and our partner finds out about it, we have hurt that individual. If there are children in the home and our escapades have created problems in the home, then surely we have harmed our children. If the partner outside the home becomes common knowledge, then they too are hurt. If she is married we've hurt her husband and her children. With one sexual act we can hurt 4, 5, 6, 8, 10 people very easily.

Sometimes we hurt people simply by demanding more than our fair share. We are using sex to the extent that we have to have more and more of it. Maybe our partner doesn't want to do it that much, and we selfishly demand that they do it any time that we want to and we end up hurting them emotionally, not just physically. We also hurt people by withholding sex from them using it as blackmail to get something else we want.

COLUMN 3: Affects My…

In column 3 we look at what part of "self" is affected. We think this will be the most revealing thing in this sexual inventory. Refer again to your **BASIC INSTINCT OF LIFE HANDOUT (Workshop Workbook p. 67).** We might think that most of the troubles that we cause for others would come from the sex instinct. Once in a while that's probably true, to get the physical release, the emotional gratification that comes at the moment of successful completion of sex. Maybe we are doing it at the wrong time and the wrong place with the wrong person and we hurt each other because of the sexual instinct. But, we think that we are going to find in most cases, our **sexual harms** don't come from the **sexual instinct**, but from the *social* **or the** *security instinct*.

We found out a long time ago as boys growing up, that you could use sex to build self-esteem. The more members of the opposite sex you could get, the more of a man you were, and some of the girls had the same problem. **If that is what we are using sex for, not to reproduce the human race, nor to enjoy, it is to build self-esteem and that falls under the *social instinct*.**

Sometimes we use sex to obtain **security**, or maybe we are just **lonesome**; maybe we just want someone to pay attention to us. We found out a long time ago that we can **give sex to get, or get back, a personal relationship and to build our emotional security. If that is what we are using sex for, that is not to reproduce the human race, not to enjoy then it is to fulfill the *social and security instincts* of life.**

Sometimes we use sex for **material security**. Maybe we are in a sexual situation that we really would rather not be in. We find we have become **overly dependent** upon that person for **material security**. We are afraid to not have sex even though we may not want to do it. **If that is what we are using sex for, not to reproduce the human race, or to enjoy then we are using it to build *material security*.**

Sometimes we use sex to **get even with another human being**. They go out and do something and that infuriates us, and we say we will show them. Then we go out and do the same thing to get even with them. The fallacy with that is that we can't afford to tell them that we did it. But there we are using sex to get even with another human being, not to reproduce or enjoy.

Sometimes we use sex to **force our will on another human being**. They aren't doing what we want them to do, so we say we'll show them. We'll just cut them off from sex. We won't let them have any until they come around to our way of thinking. There we are again using sex not to reproduce or enjoy but to force our will on another human being.

COLUMN 4: My Defects
What is the exact nature of my wrongs, faults, mistakes, defects, shortcomings?
1   Self-Seeking – what I can get out of a relationship or situation.
2   Selfish – taking without giving, hording or hiding, not sharing or reciprocating.
3   Dishonest – lying, cheating, stealing, omitting truth, allowing injustice.
4   Frightened – fearing the result of an action or inaction into anxiety
5   Inconsiderate – not thinking about the affect your behavior will have on another

What is the nature of the wrong? What is the inherent characteristic of it? What is at the core of it? If I wasn't so "**selfish**", I wouldn't be demanding more than my fair share. If I wasn't so "**selfis**h", I wouldn't be demanding that they do it in ways that they don't want to. I wouldn't be doing things that I shouldn't be doing in the first place.

If I wasn't so "**dishonest**", I wouldn't be doing those things and sneaking around and lying about them. If I wasn't so "**self-seeking**" or "**frightened**" that I wasn't going to get all I wanted before I died, I wouldn't be out there doing all those things.

If I don't change those things in the fourth column, I'm going to keep doing the same things I've always done. I'll keep hurting other people, and they will continue retaliating against me and I'm never going to have any peace of mind.

Analysis of Harms Done Other than Sexual

Referring to our inventory sheet again, we follow it just like we did on all the other inventory sheets focusing on **"Other Harms Done" (non-sexual)**.

Column 1: Who Did I Hurt?

These are the people I might have hurt financially, or I may have undercut them and taken their jobs away. I may have stolen from them or hurt them physically in various different ways. If we have hurt other people (we know who we have hurt), we make a list of them.

Column 2: What Did I Do?

Column 3: Which Part of "Self" is Affected?

I really can't do anything to hurt another human being unless one of my Basic Instincts of Life is out of control. If my desire for personal relationships is too great, it may cause me to hurt another human being in some way. If my desire for security or sex is too great, it may cause me to hurt another human being. *Always*, there will be a part of self affected.

Column 4: My Defects

If I stay **selfish, self-seeking, dishonest, frightened, and inconsiderate**, I'm going to keep right on hurting other people. Fear, guilt, and remorse will eat me up and eventually cause me to drink.

Once again we are doing Step Four: this last sheet is part of the inventory process. In taking all the worksheets together; resentments, fear, sexual conduct, and harms done, in the fourth column we have listed the exact nature of the wrongs for Step Five, the defects we are willing to turn loose of in Step Six, and the shortcomings we'll ask God to take away in Step Seven. Column one has all the names that will come from these worksheets to be used for Steps Eight and Nine at a later date.

When I'm through with this last worksheet, then I will have completed the entire Step Four Inventory. In *The Big Book* page 70, paragraph 3 says, ***"If we have been thorough about our personal inventory, we have written down a lot. We have listed and analyzed our resentments."***

I hear in A.A. some people say "utilize and don't analyze". Well I think in some places that is a good idea. What it means is let's quit doing so much talking and start working. **To analyze something really means to get down to the truth of it**. You know when a detective comes to the crime scene he analyzes the crime scene; he's trying to see the truth of it. ***Analyze* is just another word that Bill uses which means *truth*.**

We've made a searching and fearless, moral, truthful, honest, analytical inventory. Bill doesn't say so but we've listed and analyzed our fears. We've listed and analyzed our sexual conduct. We've listed and analyzed all harms we've done other than sexual.

The Big Book page 70, paragraph 3: ***"We've begun to comprehend their futility and their fatality. We have commenced to see their terrible destructiveness. We have begun to learn tolerance, patience and good will toward all men, even our enemies, for we look upon them as sick people."***

You see, there is a positive result in every Step. For an alcoholic to begin to learn tolerance, patience, and goodwill towards all men, even his enemies, is one hell of a personality change already! *And all we have done so far is Step Four!*

The Big Book page 70, paragraph 3: ***"...We have listed the people we've hurt by our conduct and are willing to straighten out the past if we can.***

In this book you read again and again that faith did for us what we could not do for ourselves. We hope that you are convinced now that God can remove whatever self-will has blocked you off from Him. If you've already made a decision (Step Three), ***and an inventory of your grosser handicaps*** (Step Four), ***you have made***

a good beginning. That being so, you have swallowed and digested some big chunks of truths about yourself."

I think one of the greatest mistakes in AA today is that everybody is sitting around waiting to get well so they can do Step Four perfectly and *The Big Book* recognizes we're not going to do it perfectly.

We've looked at our grosser handicaps for:
Resentments, Fear, Sexual Harms Done, Harms Done to Others - Other than Sexual

What are the grosser handicaps?
Selfishness, Self-Seeking, Dishonest, Frightened, and Inconsiderate Attitudes (Emotions)

We've looked at all those things!

Instructions for completion of the "Sex Conduct & Harms Done" Inventory:

1. We listed all the people we had harmed. Complete column 1, from top to bottom. Do nothing on Columns 2, 3, and 4 until Column 1 is complete.

2. We asked ourselves: "What Did I Do?" Complete column 2, from top to bottom. Do nothing on columns 3 or 4 until column 2 is complete.

3. We ask ourselves: "Was it my self-esteem, my security, my ambitions and/or my sex relations which caused this harm?" Complete each sub-column within column 3, going from left to right, starting with "companionship" and finishing with the "sexual ambitions" section. Do nothing on column 4 until column 3 is complete.

4. Referring to our list again and putting out of our minds the wrongs of others, we resolutely looked for our own mistakes, asking: "Where had I been selfish, dishonest, self-seeking, frightened, and inconsiderate?" We ask ourselves this question and complete each area of column 4.

5. In the far right column, on the back of the worksheet, or on a separate sheet of paper, write down your faults as revealed by column 4.

    A. *"Where did I set the ball rolling?"*
    B. *"Where was I at fault?"*
    C. *"What should I have done differently?"*

6. Reading from left to right, we now see the harm (column 1), what we did to cause this harm (column 2), the part of self that caused this harm (column 3), and the exact nature of the defect within us that allowed the harm to surface and block us off from God's Will (column 4).

Congratulations, you have completed Step Four!

ASSIGNMENT: Read pages 72 through the second paragraph page 75. Be prepared to discuss the material you read. Start looking for someone to take the Fifth Step with and set a specific date.

REVIEW OF OUR OWN SEX CONDUCT & HARMS DONE

COLUMN 1	COLUMN 2	COLUMN 3: Which Part of Self Was Affected?				"SELF" COLUMN 4		Questions
WHO DID I HURT?	SEX: Where Did I Unjustly Arouse Jealousy, Suspicion or Bitterness? WHAT DID I DO? (SEX / HARMS)	Social Instinct		Companionship		What is the exact nature of my wrongs, faults, mistakes, defects, shortcomings?		What was MY PART in all this? What did I do initially to get the ball rolling? How could I have done things differently?
				Prestige				
				Self-Esteem				
				Pride				
				Personal Relationships				
		Security Instinct		Material				
				Emotional				
		Sex Instinct		Acceptable Sex Relations				
				Hidden Sex Relations				
		Ambitions		Social				
				Security				
				Sexual				
						Self-Seeking & Selfish		
						Dishonest		
						Inconsiderate		
						Frightened		

143

WEEK #14: Chapter 6 — INTO ACTION *(Step 5)*

READ: Page 72, paragraph 1

Note that in this Step, it says: **"<u>the exact nature of our wrongs</u>."** But here in the narrative, Bill uses the word <u>**defects**</u> for Step Five. A little later on, in Step Six he uses: **"<u>All the things we have admitted are objectionable</u>."** Then in Step Seven, instead of using <u>**shortcomings**</u>, he uses <u>**defects of character**</u>. He used those words in the Steps, but here in the narrative he was not concerned where these words fall. People always asked Bill, "What's the difference between a *wrong*, a *defect*, and a *shortcoming*?" Bill said, "It doesn't make any difference what you call them, **they are all the same**."

READ: Page 72, paragraph 2   page 73, end of top paragraph

There is a statement which messed us up in Step Four, because we read, **"all your life story"** then we went back and began to write our whole life story. But as we have seen, 95% of our life story doesn't really have anything to do with our drinking. What does have something to do with our drinking are **resentments**, **fears**, and **harms done**. If I am listing all my resentments, I am listing my entire life story as it pertains to resentment. If I list all my fears, I am listing my life story as far as fear. If I list all my harms done, then I am listing my life story as far as harms done. It is *those* things that really count.

READ: Page 73, paragraph 1   paragraph 3

Now I'm going to take my inventory to another human being, someone that is not involved in my personal life, who can look at this thing from an **outside view** and help provide an **objective and truthful picture** of it. That human being will help me see those **character defects** that I need to get rid of. I'm amazed at how often my sponsor would change those things in my inventory. He could point out character defects which I was unable to see. **He helped me, truthfully look at *me*.** I know in Step Five confession is good for the soul. It helps me to share these resentments, fears, and harms done with someone. However, **the real purpose of Step Five is to learn all I can learn about myself and to truthfully see those things that I need to work on and change in the future**. Left to my own resources I simply cannot do that.

READ: Page 73, paragraph 4   page 74, paragraph 2

These three paragraphs are as they were originally written. When *The Big Book* was written there were no sponsors to go to. Bill was giving suggestions as to whom to do the Step with. We think **it is important that one find a person who has done the work as outlined in this book**. Being knowledgeable as to our inability to be honest with ourselves, they can be objective and help point out our shortcomings.

READ: Page 75, paragraph 1   page 75, paragraph 3

My sponsor says, **"This is the most magical page in the book of Alcoholics Anonymous. Page 75 is the beginning of the whole deal."** It is sandwiched in between Step Five and Step Six, as a Gift from God. There are only two things you can do with a gift: You can take it and make it yours, and be eternally grateful or you can throw away what I believe to be the greatest gift that God gave to humanity. It is right there on page 75.

There are ten Promises on page 75. It says we are preparing an arch through which we will walk a free person. I'm free today by the definition of *The Big Book*, which says. *"Freedom is doing what I have to do because I want to do it."* There isn't anything in this world I have to do if I don't want to do it, as long as I am willing to pay the price.

The Big Book goes on to say, *"The feeling that the drink problem has disappeared will often come strongly."* It goes on to say, *"All fears will fall from us."* You may not realize this until some time later in your sobriety, but when you get up the courage to do something which used to terrify you, it is then you will find out that fear has been removed from you.

It continues to say on that page: *"You will begin to feel the nearness of our creator." "We will begin to feel we are on a Broad Highway, walking hand in hand with the Spirit of the Universe."* My sponsor says: "You will have brushed the face of God and established a conscious contact with a Power Greater than yourself." It's all right there on page 75, along with five more promises.

For God's sake, hurry on, lest the test comes before you are ready!

While giving your Fifth Step to your sponsor, you will be making a **list** of your **character defects**, as you and your sponsor have analyzed and discussed them.

ASSIGNMENT: Read Chapters Six and Seven in the Twelve Steps and Twelve Traditions. Also read the first two paragraphs of page 76 in *The Big Book*. Be prepared to discuss the material **WILLINGNESS** and **HUMILITY**. It might help to look up the definition of these words and discuss what they mean in the context with these Steps with the group next week.

Yesterday is lost and gone forever,
While tomorrow is but a guess...
What is real is: 'what is here and now'.
And "Here and Now" is all that we possess.

Stay awake and aware in the present moment.

WEEK #15: Chapter 6 — INTO ACTION *(Steps Six and Seven)*

READ: Page 76, paragraph 1

That's all of Step Six. You will notice that he didn't mention **"defects of character"** in there at all. What he did mention were those things which **"we have admitted are objectionable."** Now surely in taking Steps Four and Five, when we saw resentments, fears harms done to other people, when we saw that those things stemmed from our basic character defects of selfishness, self-seeking, dishonesty, frightened and inconsiderate character and when we could see what those things did to us, that caused us to do the things that hurt other people and caused them to retaliate against us and **blocks us off from God**, then surely by now those things have become objectionable to us. If they aren't, then the book, recognizing that **self cannot overcome self**, says **we ask God to help us be willing to be willing to have those things removed.**

Let's face it, sometimes during Step Six, even though we see what those old **defects of character** are doing to us, sometimes we don't want to turn them loose for a couple of reasons:
Number One - some of them seem fun or stimulating…
Number Two - we don't know what life's going to be without them. I went to my sponsor and I said, **"If God removes all my character defects, I won't have any personality left!"** And he said, **"You are just about 100% correct."** "But", he said, **"What you don't understand is that when God takes those away, God replaces them with something better."** That something better will be better than you've ever had before, and you are going to have a lot better life by doing so." But I'm still afraid. Sometimes we human beings would rather sit here in today's pain than take a chance of changing for the future because we don't know for sure what that's going to be - and we understand today's pain.

My mind is nothing more than a set of mental habits. Throughout my lifetime those habits have been ingrained in my head. It's automatic for me to **react with fear**. It's automatic for me to **react selfishly** and it's automatic for me to **react dishonestly**. It's automatic for me to be **inconsiderate** of other people. I don't know how life will be if I'm reacting differently. How can I now react different? I have been that way before but I've forgotten how.

Sometimes fear stops us from reacting differently if we are not ready and if my reactions are not objectionable by now, then the only thing to do is to ask **God to help us be willing to get rid of those things. Slowly, as God takes one away and I practice the other, my character changes**. Contrary action is required. **Actions against my will, actions contrary to the way I have always lived my life**.

Step Six is a very difficult Step to do. If you want to **change**, then Step Six says **don't do what you want to do**, because **if you feed action to your old thought patterns and your old character, they're going to grow and grow**. But if you feed action to your new thought patterns and your new character, the old patterns and character will die in your mind. It is very, very hard. Just don't do what you want to do. We can only do that with God's help.

READ: Page 76, paragraph 2

We have then completed **Step Seven**, and Bill didn't even mention "shortcomings". Bill uses "shortcomings" and "character defects" interchangeably. I have found my character defects and shortcomings in **Step Four**, I talked about them to another human being in **Step Five** and became ready (willing) to turn loose of them in **Step Six**. I asked God to remove them in **Step Seven**. Now I have completed Steps Six and Seven. But if I'm not careful, I'll fall into a trap. We tend to feel after Steps Six and Seven that God is going to reach in and pluck out these defects of character and just make us as pure as the driven snow. We turn to God and hand them over and say, "Here you are; give me the $29.95 special" and everything will be all right. NO! These were not the Steps God took.

God doesn't need these Steps, He's okay already. God does not reach into my head and remove these character defects leaving another hole in my head. God replaces them with the opposite. If I want God to take away my **selfishness**, then I'm going to have to start to practice being **unselfish** with God's help and all the willingness I can muster through prayer. **Slowly, over a period of time, an old habit will die and it be replaced with a new habit**. If I'm willing to let God take away **dishonesty**, then I'm going to have to try in every given situation to be **honest** with God's help and all the willingness I can muster through prayer. Now that's hard for me to do. It's alien to my nature. But, when God helps me by removing these character defects and I practice the opposite, slowly the old habit dies and it's replaced with a new one.

Sometimes we wind down on Steps Six and Seven, maybe because *The Big Book* has only two paragraphs on these Steps. However, we begin to see that Steps Six and Seven are the **real tools of change in the program**. Steps One, Two, Three, Four and Five are seeing the problem and solution and making that decision and then the inventory, and once we take the inventory we see these things and then talk them over with another person. The first five Steps prepare us for these two great tools to apply to our lives daily. **Our future life is really based on how we apply these Steps**. God doesn't take these steps, He doesn't need to, but *we* do need these Steps to change. They are very difficult steps to work at first. Easy to understand but they are very hard. *The Big Book* says, "**Simple, but not easy**."

Our mind is a set of mental habits that we have used all our lives. We have developed old patterns. The way we got these mental habits is that we worked on them. We worked for years to get sick. We didn't get sick overnight. So we are going to have to work the same way to make these changes. It's with the use and application of these two tools (Steps Six and Seven) that we can change. Step Seven can be a hard tool you use. When you don't do what you naturally want to do and make yourself do what you naturally don't want to do, pretty soon, your old ideas will begin to fade away and a new set of motives will begin to dominate your mind. When we begin to do the things we naturally don't want to do, we begin to see the good results we get from doing those things.

Those things will become a part of our personality, and the old things will become less important and the new part will become your way of life. It's just a matter of working against yourself.

There was a student years ago in the BIG, BIG, BIG BOOK, who said that saving your life meant **daily dying to self**. You have to die somewhere in your life, so that you can live somewhere new. Only we can do that job on a daily basis and that's what Step Six and Step Seven are:

Daily dying somewhere, so we can live somewhere new.

We have to do that job!

LEADER: Discuss **Willingness** and **Humility** with the group and what they mean in context with these Steps.

This is a program of perpetual nature, or perpetuity.

We get help and we can't keep it unless we are giving it away.

In fact, the freedom from the bondage of the false self , the selfishness and self-centeredness we suffer from, that which is the cause of all our problems today, is only relieved through and by helping others.

The program, the steps themselves, are practice for this very job. They train us to help others, to get trained to help others, to train others to help others. All of this gets us out of ourselves where we can see truth.

The illness, the spiritual malady, is the separation from a God consciousness, from which we suffer. This place is also known as ego, but it is simply a separation from God's love. This is the Power that we lack, although it is there and has been there all along, we've merely lacked a connectivity to it, a relationship with it.

In this place we are the most fearful because we have to be the most self-reliant; and it's a reliance that we know in our heart of hearts is the task that we cannot live up to. Our history shows us plainly for all to see, that our self reliance had failed us dreadfully.

We know our own shortcomings and failures, and we know that we cannot survive on our own resources alone; yet ego insists on not getting the needed help from God to survive. It would rather see you die a miserable death than to admit failure and accept assistance because then it would feel that it could lose its position of significance; a status that it wrongly thinks would lessen its inherent sense of insecurity.

All of our thoughts, feelings and actions are based on this one premise; that our ego's might feel insignificant and therefore insecure. This is the thinking that precedes our actions, the premise behind our character defects, that we should never fall short, that we should always win, that we can never been seen as human, typical or average.

The ego always wants to be above average and 'special' in the eyes of others. This is pride; the protector of the ego. The pride is like ego's armor and whenever ego's is attacked with a weapon of insecurity, it is the pride that reacts, as armor usually does, with a chilling clang that's sets in motion (through e-motion) a pre-learned reaction.

This program will teach us that humility is the pathway to peace and that all you think that 'what will save you' isn't so at all. It hasn't worked so far, and a good honest look at your entire life through a fearless and thorough inventory will prove that to you.

You will come to find your life isn't working because your reaction to external and internal stimuli has been the exact opposite of what would and will work for you. So in steps 6 and 7 we will start to learn how to change everything in our lives by changing ourselves.

Yet, we do have a way out that has worked for many thousands of people who were once in the same position of despair as you are in right now, and now they're free people, they're at peace and living in the sunlight of the spirit.

BIG BOOK WORKSHOP HOMEWORK ASSIGNMENT

D. Read Chapter 6 **"Into Action"** (p.76-p84 par.1) in *The Big Book* (1st time) – USE HIGHLIGHTER! (Just read and highlight the 1st time you read through the chapter.)

E. Read Chapter 5 **"Into Action"** (p.76-p.84 par.1) in *The Big Book* (2nd time). Answer the "Work Assignment Questions" below as you read the assignment the 2nd time.

F. Be prepared to discuss the material.

WORK ASSIGNMENT QUESTIONS
"INTO ACTION – Step Eight and Step Nine"

PAGE: 76

G. Do you have any misgivings about these Steps?

H. Do you feel diffident (distrustful or unduly timid) about going to some of these people?

PAGE: 77

7. What is your real purpose?

8. Can you approach the people on your Eighth Step list in a helpful and forgiving spirit?

PAGE: 78

21. Do you see that nothing worthwhile can be accomplished until you clean your side of the street?

22. Is it important that you be praised for your Ninth Step efforts?

23. Do you understand the importance of losing your fear of creditors?

24. Have you discussed any criminal offense you may have committed and which may still be open with your sponsor? If not, should you do so?

PAGE: 79

18. Do you understand how your Ninth Step may harm other people?

19. Have you studied your domestic troubles and the harm that may have been caused in these areas?

PAGE: 81

17. Do you understand the importance of not creating further harm by creating further jealousy and resentment in a "tell-all" session?

PAGE: 83

13) What does Bill mean when he says that the spiritual life is not a theory – we have to live it?

14) Do you see that in taking the Ninth Step you should be sensible, tactful, considerate and humble, without being servile or scraping?

15) Are you experiencing the promises set forth on pages 83 and 84?

WEEK #15 – INTO ACTION (Step 6 & Step 7)
Joe and Charlie Transcript

Now if you've done (Step) 4 and 5 according to the Big Book you've done a lot of work and you're probably tired and need a little rest. The book's going to give us a little rest stop…

Big Book, p. 75, par. 3: *Returning home we find a place where we can be quiet for an hour,*

J & C Now he didn't say seventy-two days. You see they mean for us to get on with this thing, between (Steps) 3 and 4 - at once**, now we get an hours rest here but that's all.

> ** Big Book pg. 64 line 1: *Though our Decision (Step 3) was a vital and crucial step, it could have little permanent effect unless at once followed by a strenuous effort to face, and to be rid of, the things in ourselves which had been blocking us (Step 4).*

Big Book, p. 75, par. 3: *We thank God from the bottom of our heart that we know Him better.*

J & C We don't know him yet, but we know him better.

Big Book, p. 75, par. 3: *Taking this book down from our shelf we turn to the page (59) which contains the twelve steps. Carefully reading the first five proposals we ask if we have omitted anything, for we are building an arch through which we shall walk a free man at last. Is our work solid so far? Are the stones properly in place? Have we skimped on the cement put into the foundation? Have we tried to make mortar without sand?*

J & C And once again we are referring to the wonderfully effective spiritual structure, the personality change we're building.
> Step 1 - Willingness was the foundation (pg. 23, par. 5)
> Step 2 - Believing was the cornerstone (pg. 47, par. 2)
> Step 3 - Arch that we pass through to freedom - 3 is the keystone (pg. 62, last line)

Now we've put two more stones in place (Step 4 & Step 5)

Big Book, p. 76, par. 1: *If we can answer to our satisfaction, we then look at Step Six. We have emphasized willingness as being indispensable. Are we now ready to let God remove from us all the things which we have admitted are objectionable? Can He now take them all, everyone? If we still cling to something we will not let go, we ask God to help us be willing.*

J & C And that's all for Step 6. And if you notice he didn't say a thing about defects of character did he? He did say those things that we admitted were objectionable. Now surely, surely in Step 4 and 5 when we looked out into that fourth and fifth columns and we saw that old selfish, dishonest, self-seeking, frightened, inconsiderate character that we have become, when we saw that those were what cause us to do the things that hurt people.

They in turn retaliate, we in turn resent, we're afraid, we're filled with guilt and remorse which causes us to drink then surely those things in the fourth and fifth column have now become objectionable to us. Are we ready to turn them lose, if we are we're thru with Step 6. The book recognizes though that self cannot always overcome self, because it says if we're not ready we ask God to help us be willing to turn these things loose. Now you would think when we see what they do to us we'd be more than willing, but sometimes we're not. You know we human beings are funny people; sometimes we would rather sit in today's pain and suffering cause we've come to learn how to take care of that. Sometimes **we'd rather sit in today's pain and suffering than take a chance on changing in the future because we don't know what change will bring.**

WEEK #15 – INTO ACTION (Step 6 & Step 7)
Joe and Charlie Transcript

If I have to get rid of my selfishness and become unselfish, then how am I going to get what I want in the future?

If I'm going to have to get rid of my dishonesty and start operating honestly, then how the heck am I going to make a living? I don't know nothing about honesty when I get here.

If I'm going to have to start getting rid of my self-seeking and frightened character and start operating on courage that scares the hell out of me. I don't know nothing about that.

If I'm going to have to start considering other people and their needs and their wants, then who is going to take care of me?

Sometimes we would rather sit in today's pain than take a chance on changing in the future.

The Big Book recognized that and said if you're not ready,

Big Book, pg. 76, par. 1: *...we ask God to help me be willing*.

J & C And with God's help we become willing with (Steps) 3 through 6. When ready we say something like this, (Step 7 Prayer)

Big Book, pg. 76, par. 2: *My Creator, I am now willing you that you should have all of me, good and bad. I pray that you now remove from me every single defect of character...*

J & C Whoop, whoop. We're at Step 7 now and it said "shortcomings", but here he calls (it defect of character).... see what he's done to us. He confused the heck out of us didn't he?

Big Book, pg. 76, par. 2: *I pray that you now remove from me every single defect of character which stands in the way of my usefulness to you and my fellows. Grant me strength, as I go out from here, to do your bidding. Amen.*

J & C We've then completed Step 7.

Are you ready to have God remove them (defects of character)? If you are, you're through with (Step) 6. Have you humbly asked him to take them away? If you have, you've done Step 7.

But I hope you don't make the mistake I did. I assumed that now that I'm ready, and God being all powerful, that all I've got to do is turn to God and say okay God here I am, warts and all, does that mean give me the $29.95 special and I'll never have to worry about this stuff again. I found out it don't work that way. God will do for me, what I can't do for myself. I simply do not have the power to remove a character defect - only God has the power.

God will not do for me, what I can do for myself. And what I can do for myself is find out the opposite of that character defect, and then with God's help and all the willpower I can muster, in every situation it comes up, try to practice the opposite.

WEEK #15 – INTO ACTION (Step 6 & Step 7)
Joe and Charlie Transcript

Because you see, God can't take away my selfishness and leave another whole in my head. It's going to have to be replaced with the opposite, which is unselfishness. And when I first got here my mind was a set of mental habits ingrained in 38, 39, 40 years of living. The habitual thing for me was to react selfishly.

The only way to break a habit is to work against your self.

If I ask God to take away selfishness and I start trying to practice unselfishness, then **slowly the old habit dies and a new habit takes its place.** Over a period of years I have become an unselfish human being. I am not what I was when I first got here.

If I want God to take away dishonesty, then I must do my part, which is to practice honesty in every situation that comes up and that's hard for me to do. That is so alien to my nature that I can't practice honesty without Gods help. But with God's power and all the willpower I can muster I can force myself to be honest and **slowly the old idea dies and a new one takes its place**. The habitual thing for me today is to react to any situation with honesty.

If I want God to take away fear then I've got to kick myself in the butt and practice courage.

If I want Him to take away inconsideration, then I must start considering other people and their needs and their wants and **slowly the old idea dies and a new idea takes its place**.

Big Book, pg. 63 par. 1: … ***We were reborn.***

J & C I am not what I used to be. Now I'm not completely unselfish. I never will be. I'm not always completely honest. Sometimes I'm afraid and other times I'm inconsiderate but the majority of the time I'm an unselfish, honest human being with courage, considering other people first. You know I think you and I are the luckiest people in the world. We have the opportunity through these two little steps right here (6 & 7) to live two lifetimes in one lifetime. Most people out there are sick; most of them are going to their grave sick; not even knowing they're sick. We not only know we are sick, we know what's wrong with us we found it in Steps 4 & 5 and in Steps 6 & 7 we can do something about it. We can change it and we become entirely different human beings.

Most people don't get that opportunity. Now be careful, for God's sake be careful! **Because if you really accept this as the correct thing and the right thing then that means from this day on you are responsible for what you are**. I can't blame it on Barbara any longer, I can't blame it on Mother and Dad, I can't blame it on God and I can't blame it on society.

If I stay selfish, dishonest, self-seeking, frightened and inconsiderate it's got to be because that's the way I want to be. I no longer have the luxury of blaming it on others 'cause I don't have to be that way.

WEEK #15 – INTO ACTION (Step 6 & Step 7)
Joe and Charlie Transcript

You know what I found out?

> I found out that when you become unselfish people start kind-a liking you a little better than they did before.

> I found out when you start becoming honest, well, you feel better about yourself. **That's the way you build self-esteem is to do the right thing for a change!**

> I found out when I practice with courage and I operate on courage instead of fear I do things that makes me feel better and I quit doing things that made me feel so bad.

> I found out there's real pleasure in considering other people first and giving to others before you take for yourself.

I didn't know that. How in the hell could I know that? I've never been that way before. This thing really amazes me in what happens to us and the simplicity of this thing if we will just do what the book says.

Joe?

You know there's always a paradox in AA. To give you an idea what a paradox is: How many of you have ever called your sponsor so you could listen? We always call him so we can talk, right? That's the paradox.

The paradox here in these two steps is that they use:

> The Doctors Opinion (p. xxiii) and the first four chapters to do Steps 1 & 2
> 3 ½ pages for Step 3
> 8 pages for Step 4
> 4 pages for Step 5

and a whole chapter devoted with "Working with Others".

The paradox is that two of the biggest steps in all of Alcoholics Anonymous are in two little paragraphs, (Steps) 6 & 7.

These are the tools of change.
These are the tools of acceptance.

A lot of people talk about just running around accepting things - I accept this, I accept that. Well I can't do that.

Acceptance comes after some actions…
Acceptance comes after the actions of Steps 6 & 7.

You know there's a story in that other Book (Bible) about this guy named Judas.

Judas could not accept what he had done. (Betrayal) So what did he do? He killed himself. That's the importance of acceptance. You can't accept anything unless you take some action. He didn't do Steps 6 & 7 - didn't have them

WEEK #15 – INTO ACTION (Step 6 & Step 7)
Joe and Charlie Transcript

There is another story in this other Book (Bible) about this guy, his name was Saul. Saul was riding his ass on the way to Damascus. A big bolt of lightening came down and knocked him off his ass, on his ass. That's the way I read it. He gets up and he dusted himself off and this big voice came out of the sky and said, "Saul, can we talk?"

"Yeah, we can talk. What you want to talk about?"

Had to get his attention didn't he? Maybe alcoholism has to get our attention.

"Saul you've been a very selfish individual and you've harmed a lot of people and you're very resentful and angry. You've harmed a lot of people by those attitudes and I want you to quit doing that!"

Saul asked, "How do you quit doing that?"

"Do THESE things instead and if you will do that, then you'll make a change, and when you change then we'll call you Paul."

Well he did those things and became Paul. Now we know that Paul was one of the greatest writers the world's ever known. The Corinthians, (those from the town of Corinth, Greece), they asked Paul one day, "Paul, what is this secret to living?"

Paul answered, **"The secret to living is daily dying."**

The old Saul had to die so the new Paul could come alive.

By the time I got to Steps 6 & 7, I could see what I had become as a result of the previous steps and I didn't like what I had become and a little doubt crept in my mind.

Can God really change me from what I had become to what he intends for me be? And then I had to reaffirm and rethink about this idea on page 53. It said,

Big Book, pg. 53, par 3: *God either is, or He isn't?*

J & C He either can or he can't

Big Book, pg. 53, par 3: *What was our choice to be?*

J & C And I chose to believe that he could.
The tools of change…

To change from what I had become to what God had intended me to be.

Steps 6 & 7 - Two of the biggest Steps in all of Alcoholics Anonymous!

WEEK #15 – INTO ACTION (Step 6 & Step 7)
Joe and Charlie Transcript

Just before the break I want Joe to tell you one little story about buying some salad to show you practicing this thing. A few years ago I went into a grocery store to buy some salad and some stuff to fix for a salad - that night I was having steak. I went in there and bought this stuff and came back up to the register and I was going to pay up and I gave this lady ten dollars and she took the ten dollars and stood right there and counted me out change for a twenty, and I watched her do it. And I picked up that money and I put it in my pocket and I got out to my car and I sat there and I said well you big dummy you sold out for ten bucks. I thought I was worth more than that! I'm glad it wasn't less than that!! So I took the money back in there and I told the lady I said "You know I'm a member of a fellowship that requires me to be honest. You gave me too much money and I want to give you this ten dollars back." And she said, "You know I never heard of a fellowship like that." I said, "Well I hadn't either till a few years ago, so here's your ten bucks back." The whole point of this story, when I walked out with that ten dollars, and believe me I don't need ten dollars; I mean I do not need ten dollars. And I'm walking out I felt about that big (tiny), sneaking out the door. You see then I went back in there and gave her that ten bucks back and I walked out and I feel good again. I did the right thing. If you practice that enough times the next time she gives change for a twenty you do it right there you don't even go out the door with it. That's what we're talking about when we change and only we can do it.

Only we can slay ourselves, with God's help, and become different human beings.

If you stay dishonest, self-seeking, frightened and inconsiderate it must be because you want to!

We've completed our first seven steps knowing full well we're going to be working on (Steps) 6 & 7 for the rest of our lives really, trying to change as the opportunity comes up.

Now we've read in the book where we are:
1. Spirituality sick
2. Mentally sick
3. Physically sick

…when the spiritual malady is overcome we straighten our mentally and physically (p. 64, par. 4)

We begin to look at those things and begin to realize that all human beings really are born to live in three dimensions of life.

If God dwells within each of us we're going to have to live with God, whether we like it or not is beside the point. (<u>Spiritual Dimension</u>) The only question is: **Do we live with Him in harmony or disharmony?** I don't know of anybody that ever got in more disharmony with God than we alcoholics have.

We also have what we call the <u>Mental Dimension</u>. We've all got a mind, sometimes we act like we don't but we do. We have to live with our mind, whether we like it or not is beside the point, we don't have a choice. And again: **Do we live there (with our mind) in harmony or disharmony?** I don't know of any group of people that ever got more fouled up in their heads than we alcoholics have.

WEEK #15 – INTO ACTION (Step 6 & Step 7)
Joe and Charlie Transcript

For years I thought the <u>Physical Dimension</u> was my body only. Today I realize the Physical Dimension is the world and everything in it. We alcoholics don't have any place else to live except here on earth, we don't have any choice in the matter, whether we like it or not is beside the point. The only question is: **Do we live on earth with our fellow man in harmony or disharmony?**
And I don't know of any group of people that ever got more fouled up in a relationship with the world and everybody in it than we alcoholics have.

So we were sick spiritually, mentally and physically.

The book talks about a design for living, and it looks (seems) to us that:
> **These steps are designed in such a manner to put us back together and make us well in all three dimensions of life as God intended for us to be in the first place.**

Steps 1 & 2
> We got right with the Spirit.
> Because we were powerless, we saw the need for the power.

Step 3
> We decided to go after that power
>> We made a decision that God was going to be the Director.
>>> He's the Father, we're the children.
>>> He's the Employer, we are the employee (we work for him)

For most of us that's the first time we've had that relationship with God for a long, long, long time. We got the right relationship in (Steps) 1, 2 & 3. That removes self-will, to let us begin to look into our own minds.

Step 4 & 5
> We found out those things
>> that: Block us off
>> from God,
> Block us off from our fellow man,
> Creates the resentments and the fears and the guilt's etc.

Steps 6 & 7
> We begin to work on those things that block us off

We begin to get right in our minds through Steps 4, 5, 6 & 7. That removes just enough self-will, to begin to look at our relationship with the world and everybody in it. Through Steps 4, 5, 6 & 7 we got rid of these resentments, we got rid of these fears to the level that God intended for them to be. But, we haven't really done anything about the storeroom back here that's filled with guilt and remorse associated with the harms we've done in the past.

If we want to get right in the Physical Dimension, (our relationship with the world and everybody in it), it has long been known that the way you do that, is to make restitution for the things done in the past.

WEEK #16: Chapter 6 — INTO ACTION *(Steps Eight and Nine)*

READ: Page 76, paragraph 3

I think we have really **laid the groundwork in recovery**. We have gone through Steps One, Two, and Three. **In Step One, we saw the Problem. Step Two, we found the Solution to our Problem**. Then in **Step Three, we made a Decision**. That decision was vital. That decision was to turn our will and our lives over to the care of God, as we understood Him based on Steps One and Two. Step Three (once we made this decision) was the first time that we were in a correct relationship with God in our lives. Thus we actually laid the spiritual foundation on which we were going to build our lives.

We know that **human life emanates from the inside out** and that there is a design for living. There is a design to everything on the face of this earth and there is a design to our lives. *The Big Book* **talks about this throughout, and gives us a design for living that really works.** We saw as a result of Steps One and Two that in Step Three we make a decision. When we made the decision, for the first time, we were in a correct relationship with God in our lives. That's the spiritual foundation. Once we laid that foundation, we went to work in Steps Four, Five, Six, and Seven where we deal with ourselves. **We learned that we're a product of our minds, not our bodies**. So, in Steps Four, Five, Six, and Seven we worked on the mind.

Now we are going out into the third dimension of life; our relationship with others. That is a major part of human life. Now we have to go out into that area and deal with it. It is the final work we are going to do. It does not only deal with us physically but also deals with the sociological. We are talking about our relationship with everything else in the world that's physical; other people, our jobs, and anything else. Everything in life will fit into one of these areas.

This is a design for life.

We say that alcoholism is an inside job. So we started on the inside and we're working our way out. We are headed into the **third dimension**, which is our relationship with other people (Steps Eight and Nine). We have guilt and fear which will cut us off from the sunlight of the Spirit (Steps One, Two, and Three) and if that happens we're going to lose all our work we started. You know, **half measures availed us nothing**. We agreed to go all the way so we don't lose what we have done!

Steps Eight and Nine are talking about the third dimension of life and we all know about that.

THE THREE DIMENSIONS OF LIFE
STEPS 1 THRU 9

PHYSICAL - SOCIAL
MENTAL
SPIRITUAL
GOD
1-2-3
4-5-6-7
8-9

In order for us to complete the job, and completely get rid of those things in our mind that block us from God's will, it's going to become necessary now to do something about that fear, guilt and remorse associated with the past.

READ: Page 76, paragraph 4   page 78, paragraph 1

There's no way I can become willing to make amends at all unless I have really worked a good Step Four, the way our book tells us to. Even then, some people have harmed us as badly as we have harmed them and we say to ourselves, "By golly, they had it coming and I really don't think I owe them an amends." We're going to find a few like that and it's going to be very difficult even then for us to become willing to make amends to them all, so then I can't make amends to any of them, period. Step Eight will block us off entirely from Step Nine if we aren't really careful.

My sponsor didn't let this happen to me. He said, "Some of these people on these lists, you know them and they know you, and you love them and they love you, and you would like to get things straightened out with them right now, wouldn't you?" And I said, "Sure I would." My children were on there and my brother was on there, and my mother and my father and some of my friends. I wasn't sure about my wife, she was on there, but I didn't know about her. So he said, "I'll tell you what you ought to do." Why don't you get a separate sheet of paper and start a list and put **RIGHT NOW** on it.

Those people on your amends list that you're willing to do something with them, right now, take their names off of there and put them on that **RIGHT NOW** column. Then there are some people on there that you know that you're going to make amends to sooner or later. You don't particularly care about it, but you know you're going to do it. Take their names off of there, put another column labeled **LATER** on the paper and put their names under it. There are only a few on there that you aren't sure about. You may or may not make amends to them. Take their names off of there and put them in a third column and just put there at the top, **MAYBE**. Now the only ones that are going to be left on there are those that you don't ever intend to make amends to. Take them off and put them in a fourth column and title that **NEVER**.

Now what I'd like you to do is start making amends to the **RIGHT NOW's**. By the time you're through with that, you're ready to do some of the **LATER's**. Then you do your **LATER's** and then you might be ready to do some of the **MAYBE's**. Probably by the time you're through with the **MAYBE's**, you'll be ready to do some **NEVER's**. He led me right into this thing and did not allow me to use the fact that there were some I did not intend to make amends to anybody at all. If you have trouble in that area, you might try this. It really does work.

RIGHT NOW	LATER	MAYBE	NEVER

READ; Page 78, paragraph 2

After we have become willing Step Nine very clearly tells us what to do. It tells us the kinds of amends to make. It says we make **DIRECT AMENDS** to such people. It tells us when to make the direct amends: "...*except when to do so would injure them or others"*. The only thing I really need to truly understand is, what does it mean by **"Direct Amends"**, what does it means by, **"wherever possible"**, and what does it mean by, **"except when to do so would injure them or others"**?

We start on Step Nine by looking at what it is talking about when he says **"Made Direct Amends"**. Making direct amends, we're going to look at them two different ways. First, we're going to look at them as direct**; face-to-face**. That is the best way to make an amends. When we make our amends face-to-face, there's no doubt about the result. This thing really does work if we're willing to do what the book tells us to do. Sometimes it's not easy to do those things, but the book continuously reminds us that **self cannot overcome self**, and we may have to **ask for God's help to be willing to be willing to do these things**. I think we will find the benefits far, far outweigh whatever pain we are going to have in doing it.

There are many, many things that can come up in making amends. That's why we have so much in the book on Step Nine. It has paragraphs that deal with just about everything that could come up. Now we're going to talk about **past criminal offenses**, and how we handle those.

READ: Page 78, paragraph 3   page 80, paragraph 4

Here again, **we considered other people who will be involved**, talked to them, got their okay before he made his amends. Undoubtedly, I need to make some amends to my wife or husband. In fact the only thing I can really do is say, "Look, I know what I was and you know what I was and I really hurt you while I was drinking and I'm truly sorry about that, but I'm trying to live a decent life now and with God's help, I don't intend to do those things anymore." And that's about all I can do with my children too. I tell them that I know what I was and they know what I was and I really hurt them and I'm truly sorry about it, but I'm trying to live a different life and with God's help, I'm going to try to be a decent husband/wife and a decent father/mother from now on. To some of those, these are just about all the amends we can possibly make. We don't have to keep trying to make them for the rest of our lives. **Sometimes we feel so guilty about these things so we keep on trying to make amends forever and go far beyond what we probably should do in the first place.** <u>This requires very careful consideration</u>.

READ: Page 80, paragraph 5   page 83, paragraph 1

There will be some amends that we can never make. Maybe we don't know where these people are. Maybe they are dead or maybe the case would be that it would injure other people. So we have to live with those, but we will not hurt. There is no pain. We know we would do it if we could. If we are willing, this will free us. If we're willing, even if we cannot do it, then there is no guilt or remorse or anything bothering us. That's why we are doing all this, so it doesn't bother us.

A mistake we see a lot of people make in our zeal to have everybody like us, is to expect for everyone to forgive us. Sometimes, they don't accept our amends. We leave there feeling crushed, and then we tend to want to go back again and again and literally force those people to forgive us. We don't need to do that. **As God's people, we stand on our own two feet. We make our amends to the best of our ability, and if they don't want to accept our amends we are at peace anyway.** There is nothing we can do about that. All we can do is make our amends.

I think **there's one person we owe an amends to as much as anybody, and that's ourselves**. I'm not about to say that I never hurt anybody with my drinking, because I hurt everybody who came in contact with me when I was drinking. And I'm positive I hurt myself as bad as I ever hurt anybody else. I think **the finest amends that I can possibly make to me is to free myself from the past. The only way I found to do that is by making my amends to other people wherever I possibly could. Through the making of my amends to others, my guilt and my remorse and my fears associated with the past have disappeared**.

READ: Page 83, paragraph 2   page 84, paragraph 1

Joe McQ, in The Big Book Comes Alive Seminar, reads the promises in the following manner and is **the way Alcohol made him feel before it turned against him**:

When I drank alcohol, I would know a new freedom and a new happiness. When I drank alcohol, I would not regret the past, nor wish to shut the door on it.
When I drank alcohol, I would comprehend the word serenity and I would know peace. When I drank alcohol, no matter how far down the scale I had gone, I would see how my experience could benefit others.
When I drank alcohol, that feeling of uselessness and self-pity would disappear.
When I drank alcohol, I would lose interest in selfish things and gain interest in my fellows. When I drank alcohol, fear of people and of economic insecurity would leave me.
When I drank alcohol, I intuitively knew how to handle situations which used to baffle me. When I drank alcohol, I suddenly realized that alcohol is doing for me what I could not do for myself.

My God, no wonder I loved to drink! Alcohol did that for me for many, many, many years. **Alcohol was my friend**. I doubt that I could have lived in normal society growing up without alcohol or some other drug as it did for me exactly what I wanted it to do.

One day it turned against me. It began to get me drunk, in trouble and it caused me to do things that I didn't want to do. From that day on, I spent the rest of my drinking career searching for a way to drink and recapture the good feelings.
- **Not knowing that I was alcoholic**.
- **Not knowing that I have a progressive disease**.
- **Not knowing that there was no way to recapture those good feelings**.

I almost destroyed me and everyone in my life.

"We feel that our program can benefit yet others…"

"We too feel that the benefits of our program can benefit others. How? When we actually work these principles into all of our affairs, into our behaviors and everyday thinking; we will become less selfish, more helpful, less self-seeking, more kindly, less intolerant, more understanding, less spiteful and more loving… by us changing… others will benefit; it is in this way, first and foremost, that these steps will benefit others…" Joe McQ.

161

I came to A.A. and you showed me a Big Book and nine Steps. I applied them in my life and to my absolute amazement I found that I got all the good things from these first nine Steps that I ever got from alcohol. Now if I can feel as good from the first nine Steps as I did from drinking alcohol in the beginning, then I most certainly do not need to take a drink in order to change the way that I feel. I think the amazing thing about it is this:

So far, the first nine Steps have never turned against me! I've never been placed in jail because of the first nine Steps. I've never been drug into a divorce court because of the first nine Steps. I have never vomited from the first nine Steps. You see they have given me all the good that alcohol gave me, but none of the bad. That's why I don't need to drink. Now if I don't want to receive these promises, sooner or later my mind is going to start searching for a sense of ease and comfort. It's going to take me right back to the idea that I've got to drink to change the way that I feel. You see, that's what this is all about.

Now why did we get The Promises? We got The Promises because we have fit ourselves back into the design for living that God made us to live in the first place. And when we do that, then we're not in conflict with God. We're not in conflict with our fellow man, and we're not in conflict with ourselves. Then we can have these promises. If you'll notice, every promise in there deals with the mind. None of them deal with the body. Surely if I've had these promises then I have become a different human being. Surely my personality has changed entirely from what it used to be to what it is if I've received these promises.

We have effectively recovered from a hopeless condition of the mind and of the body at the end of Step Nine, if we have received these promises.

Isn't that great?

I did that, and I received these promises and today I realize that they make me feel exactly the way alcohol used to make me feel in the beginning. They give me all the good things that alcohol ever gave me. So, if I get all the good things in the first nine Steps that alcohol gave me, then I don't have to drink alcohol in order to feel better.

– Once Again –

The beautiful thing about the first "nine Steps" is:
- **They have never turned against me like alcohol did.**
- **I've never been drug into a divorce court because of the first nine Steps.**
- **I have never vomited ... damned near did a time or two.**

This is the miracle of Alcoholics Anonymous.

Through the first Nine Steps we get all the good things alcohol ever gave us. Therefore we don't need to drink to change the way we feel and yet we receive none of the bad things from the first nine Steps that alcohol did to us. .

We have RECOVERED from a seemingly hopeless state of body and mind by the end of step 9.

Every promise in here deals specifically with the mind, not the body. If you receive these promises in your mind, you have become a different human being, thus, they will resonate into the body.

WEEK #17: Chapter 6 — INTO ACTION *(Step 10)*

READ: Page 84, paragraph 2

I think as we left the first nine Steps, it was clear that we were **halfway through this stage of our development**. Then we were about to enter another plane of continuous growth through the last three Steps. **A lot of times the last three Steps are called maintenance Steps**, I think because the word maintenance is mentioned here that we have tied that term on to them. It gives us the idea that we stay where we are. **But, we like to look at these last three Steps as continuous growth Steps; Steps that we can grow with for the rest of our lives.**

As we read the Step Nine Promises you'll see they all deal with the mind. None of them deal with the body. **We came here restless, irritable, discontented, filled with shame, fear, guilt, remorse, worry, anger, depression, etc. We work the steps, we receive the promises. Certainly we have undergone a change in our personality. We have undergone a spiritual awakening already**.

Now if that's true then what is the purpose of the last three steps? Many people will tell us that the last three steps are to maintain our sobriety. I will agree that they will help us stay sober. **But the word maintenance itself is a misnomer… to maintain something is means to keep it "as is".** Another natural law applies:

Nothing in our universe ever stays "as is"
- Everything in our universe is in a constant state of change It's either growing or it's dying
- It's progressing or it's regressing It's going forward or it's going back

Like a tree, it's continuously growing and when it stops growing it starts dying. So our lives are the same way; we have to continue to grow and this is what these last three Steps are all about. They are about continuing to grow. Now the tremendous amount of spiritual growth we have made through the first nine steps is that we've got the Promises.

But if we just tried to maintain this, eventually we start slipping back and we start having trouble with people, then with our self, then with God then we end up drunk all over again.

Now how do I know that? I see it happen in A.A. over and over and over and over again. That's what happens when people like us who had a good program go back and get drunk again, it's because we stopped growing.

We can't stop growing! If you do you start dying. Let's look at the last three steps. Not as just maintenance steps… Not just to keep us sober… but to see, that we must actually continue to grow in our relationship with God, with ourselves and with other human beings.

Last week we talked about the **normal three dimensions of existence**:

*The Dimension of the Spirit   (God, Higher Power, Creator)
*The Dimension of the Mind   (mental, thinking, perception)
*The Dimension of the Physical
(our physical and sociological relationship with the world and everything in it)

We saw where the first nine Steps had put us back together in these normal three dimensions of living. However, **twice in *The Big Book* Bill mentions a "Fourth Dimension of Existence"**: Once in his story and once in Chapter Two. The Fourth Dimension is a dimension of living far beyond the normal three. You can't explain it. You can't describe it. You can only feel it. And that's what the last three Steps do… they move us into another dimension of living.

For just a moment, let's look back on page eight in *The Big Book* and see a reference here of another dimension of living. Bill says, ***"I was soon to be catapulted into what I like to call the Fourth Dimension of Existence."*** In other words, a dimension of living far beyond the normal three dimensions.

On page 25, where he talks about the spiritual experience, again he refers to a Fourth Dimension of Living: ***"The great fact is just this, and nothing less; that we have had deep and effective spiritual experiences which have revolutionized our whole attitude toward life, toward our fellows and toward God's universe. The central fact of our lives today is the absolute certainty that our Creator has entered into our hearts and lives in a way, which is indeed miraculous."*** Now just before that paragraph he says, ***"We have found much of heaven and we have been rocketed into a fourth dimension of existence of which we had not even dreamed."***

From this we see there is another dimension far beyond the other three. **I think we might be the luckiest people in the world, because most people will never realize there is another dimension of living. Even if they do realize it, most of them do not have the tools necessary to get them into that dimension of living.** We need to look at the fact that the last three Steps are most certainly not maintenance steps, because, as we said before, to maintain would mean to keep "as is". We can see that the last three Steps are growth Steps which will put us into another dimension far beyond the promises found on pages 83 - 84.

Now if we could stop at the end of Step nine and if we could stop with those promises of Pages 83-84, we would be absolutely great for the rest of our lives. But that isn't the case since we can't stay there. The reality is one of two things will happen:

We are going to have to continue to grow, or we are going to begin to regress back.

Studying our text book, *The Big Book* of Alcoholics Anonymous, we see that **Step Ten is the ongoing continuous practice of Steps Four, Five, Six, Seven, Eight, and Nine.** Remember these are the Steps that give us our personality change (growth). We didn't get any change from Steps One, Two, or even Three. All the change came through the "action" Steps Four through Nine

So, **continuous practice of these "Action Steps" will bring about continuous growth**. The more we take Step Five and see things and then discuss them with other people, the more we'll learn about ourselves. And if we ask God to remove these things that we find in Step Four which "block us off", they will become less and less.

Then as we make amends to other people, our relationships with other people will grow and get better. So, in the practicing of these "Action Steps", we will not remain the same, we will have to grow into the Fourth Dimension. Step Four has prepared us for Step Ten. That's why we said, if we didn't do a good Step Four, if we don't learn the Step Four process, we really can't do a good Step Ten.

What we're really doing is using those "Action Steps" that gave us all the growth in the first place and we are practicing them over and over on a daily basis for the rest of our lives. Our growth will continue into another Dimension of Existence that we never even dreamed of, there is no way you can describe it. The only way you can know what it is, is to experience it.

Working Step Ten will definitely put you into another Dimension of Living.

READ: Page 84, par. 3 - page 85, end of paragraph

Everyone talks about the promises of pages 83-84, but very few talk about the promises here on pages 84-85. There are twelve promises after the Ninth Step and twelve more after the Tenth Step. These are the promises we really were looking for when we came to the program.

WE HAVE CEASED FIGHTING ANYTHING AND ANYONE – EVEN ALCOHOL
FOR BY THIS TIME SANITY WILL HAVE RETURNED

Remember we said in **Step Two - Came to believe that a Power Greater than ourselves could restore us to sanity**. Remember that insanity didn't mean we were crazy. We were insane in one area - when it came to alcohol we were insane to take that first drink. Let's look at how we see alcohol now. Remember, that little piece that was missing? It's going to come home to us now. We've got it!

This is the real double miracle of Alcoholics Anonymous. Back on page 45, it said the main objective (purpose) of this book is to enable us to find a Power greater than ourselves which **WILL** solve our problem. We emphasized then, that it doesn't say, which will help us solve, or will enable us to solve... It says, **"WHICH _WILL_ SOLVE YOUR PROBLEM."**

Somewhere between page 45 and page 85, I woke up one morning and I said, "There's something strange in my life today." And I asked myself, "How long has it been since you've wanted to take a drink?" And you know I couldn't remember.

Somewhere between page 45 and 85, God reached in my head and He plucked out the OBSESSION TO DRINK ALCOHOL, and it's never returned since then. **God replaced the OBSESSION TO DRINK with the OBSESSION TO STAY SOBER.** This obsession is a good one. It will make me see the truth and that idea will be so strong that it will overcome the idea to drink.

God did for me what I couldn't do for myself...
I believe this is the real miracle of Alcoholics Anonymous.

READ: Page 85, paragraph 1

In this paragraph we see the word maintenance and it is done only on a **ONE DAY AT A TIME** basis. You can spend millions of dollars on this building we are in but can maintain it only **ONE DAY AT A TIME**, but sooner or later it's going to shut down on you anyhow.

The rest of this paragraph shows us the proper use of the will. It doesn't say anything about saying to God: God, where shall I work? Or God, tell me who I ought to be married to, or God, show me a sign. It says, ***"How can I best serve Thee? Thy will, not mine, be done."***

When the obsession to drink is removed entirely and if we have received these promises, for the first time in our life,

We are in a position where we can really serve
God and our fellow man,
AND, unless we are willing to do so,
chances are we're going to end up losing what we have.

I love the idea of exercising our willpower along this line all we wish. In Step Three we "made a decision to turn our will and our life over to the care of God as we understood Him." In Steps Four through Ten, we removed enough self-will that our mind became pretty well normal and straightened up.

Now that we can use our will properly, they have given us our will back here at the end of Step Ten. But, I'd like you to notice the perfect sequence of *The Big Book*. They give us our will back on page 85, but they restored our sanity on page 84. We would have been in a hell of a shape if we had gotten our will back before we got sanity back.

READ: Page 85, paragraph 2

We are talking here in this paragraph about a sixth sense of direction.

Most of what you and I know, we learn through our normal five senses of direction. For instance, everything I know today on a conscious level, I learned through hearing, through seeing, through tasting, feeling or touching.

That's the only way we human beings have of learning anything. We gather information from those five senses and that information then lodges in our mind at a conscious level, and then we use that information to run our lives.

For those of us who learned from just those five senses and ran our lives on that information, we almost destroyed ourselves.

If God dwells within all human beings, and I'm convinced He does, and if God has all knowledge and all power, and I'm convinced He does, then that means that you and I have within ourselves all the knowledge and all the power that we could ever possibly need to solve any problem that we could ever have -- If we could learn to tap into that Power.

There's another sense of direction somewhere inside ourselves that if we could tap into that, then we'll have another sense of direction referred to as a sixth sense of direction, which is all knowledge and all power. Human beings have known forever that the way to do that is through prayer and meditation. Most of us alcoholics have problems with prayer and meditation.

Even though I was raised in church, I found when I came to A.A. I knew very little about prayer and nothing at all about meditation. I had two prayers, one was, "Now I lay me down to sleep" and the other was, "God, get me out of this damn mess and I swear I'll never do it again." The only other prayer I knew was "God, if you'll do this, I'll do that." I always tried to bargain with God. Today I realize that God has the controls and doesn't need to bargain with me at all.

Let's see if we can find a way to <u>tap into that unsuspected inner resource of strength</u>, and see if we can continue our spiritual growth through Step Eleven next week.

BIG BOOK WORKSHOP HOMEWORK ASSIGNMENT

1) Continue to read page 85, last paragraph to the end of Chapter Six, and try doing your new work around Step Ten in your daily life and see if you can catch your character defects and try to correct them as you live your new life One Day at a Time.

2) Be prepared to discuss the material.

WORK ASSIGNMENT QUESTIONS
"INTO ACTION – Step 11"

PAGE: 86

9. What do you watch for?

10. Do you practice this Step on a daily basis?

11. Do you follow the procedures pages 86 & 87 which outline your daily morning meditation and the way you progress throughout the day?

PAGE: 87

4. Has your attitude about a Power greater than yourself changed?

PAGE: 88

5. Do you believe **"It Works – It really does!"**?

Step Eleven

Step Eleven is the culmination of all the previous Steps. We have taken all the other Steps so that they can lead us to Step Eleven.

Step One had to be taken so we could take Step Two, because we couldn't see the solution until we understood the problem.

Steps One and Two gave us what we needed to make a decision. The decision was Step Three; to turn our will and our lives over to the care of God as we understood Him. This decision was an important turning point.

Next we had to carry out the decision. There were certain things that blocked us from God, and we could not get on with turning our will and our lives over to the care of God until we removed those things that were blocking us off from God. Therefore we took the action Steps: Steps Four, Five, Six, Seven, Eight, Nine, and then Ten, which is the continuation of Steps Four through Nine.

As a result of the actions of Steps Four through Ten we removed, with God's help, the things that were blocking us from God. Now we can carry out the decision we made in Step Three. Steps Three and Eleven are the pillars of the Steps. We could say that the Steps have two crucial points; the turning over of our will in Step Three and the receiving of God's will in Step Eleven. This amounts to changing the direction of a human life. This is not to say the direction can be changed by these two Steps alone, because the others are necessary before we can complete these two.

When we change the direction of a life, we change the life. We said in Step Three we were willing to turn our direction over to God, who had always been there even when we were blocked from Him. Our lives become different as a result of this process. Anyone who can begin to use Step Eleven effectively has had a spiritual awakening. He or she has "tapped that unsuspected inner resource" of strength. (*The Big Book*, p. 569-570) This shows that the Steps have worked for this person.

After Step Eleven, comes the Twelfth and final Step, which tells us to carry this message to other people.

Step Eleven takes a lot of work. First, it takes the work of the first ten Steps, and then it takes continuous practice over a long period of time.

HOW OUR WILL INTERACTS WITH GOD'S WILL

In Step Three:	In Step Eleven:
We **give up our** directions We turn our will and our lives over **to** God as we understand Him.	We **receive God's** directions We receive God's will in our lives, and the power to carry it out **from** God as we understand Him.

WEEK #18: Chapter 6 — INTO ACTION *(Step Eleven)*

READ: Page 85, paragraph 1   READ AFTER: Page 86, paragraph 1

If we have taken Steps Four through Nine and **continued to take the same action in Step Ten over and over again**, we should have now removed the things that block us off from God and our fellow man. Now we should be able to receive God's will and to tap that unsuspected inner resource of the Spirit.

That's what the previous Steps are about… to get us to Step Eleven. Once we work Step Eleven, then we have it and we carry this to another person. So Step Eleven is the pinnacle. (According to the Webster's Dictionary, pinnacle is "summit"; "the highest point") **Now that we have worked these other Steps, we can tap this unsuspected inner resource of the Spirit with the simple program of prayer and meditation**.

When I got to this section of the Book, I was amazed at what Bill wrote, because he was not a spiritual giant at this point. Bill was only three years sober. He had been around people of the Oxford Group and Dr. Bob's wife, Ann, would read to him from the Bible. Now here he was faced with the task of writing something on prayer and meditation.

He didn't have that experience and he was writing to a group of people who were spiritually bankrupt. I am really glad and thank God he did not have a great spiritual life, because most people, who are founded in theology and in spiritual education, talk over the heads of people who are spiritually bankrupt.

Bill lays out a simple daily plan that anybody can adopt and apply to their lives. Anybody that will take this plan in Step Eleven from *The Big Book* and apply it **will teach themselves a personal life of prayer and meditation on an individual basis**. Anyone who can use this outline and apply it on a daily basis, regardless of whether or not you are spiritually bankrupt, you can tap into the unsuspected inner resources of the Spirit. You will be able to see God's direction and develop this sixth sense of direction in a personal way on a daily basis.

We see now that this thing we do at night is in Step Eleven, not in Step Ten.

REFER TO THE DAILY INVENTORY HANDOUT – See pages 115 - 116
These sheets in the handout are suggested formats for a daily inventory, so that when we go to bed at night, we can review what we've been through that day.

The first sample: (p.115)
On the left-hand side of the sheet: **Personality Characteristics of a Self-Willed person**.
On the right-hand side of the sheet: **Personality Characteristics of a God-Willed person**.

The second sample: (p. 116) is taken from the A.A. Grapevine Volume 3 of June, 1946
On the left-hand side of the sheet: **Liabilities – "Watch For…"**
On the right-hand side of the sheet: **Assets – "Strive For…"**

These character defects are nothing new. We have talked about them throughout *The Big Book*, such as **Selfishness, Self-Seeking, Frightened, Dishonesty and Inconsiderate**. Then we went into the *Twelve and Twelve*, and made a more detailed list which really are offshoots based on those five from *The Big Book*. It only takes a couple of minutes at night to run down this list and see which side of the sheet we are on, or have been on that day.

Invariably, we will find ourselves partially on one side and partially on the other side. I've never yet found myself completely on either side altogether. I vary back and forth from day to day, but, it gives me another opportunity to **stop and look and see what I need to continue to take to God**.

Then after I've done the review, I can ask God again to remove those things and give me the strength and the Power to do the opposite. It's almost impossible to do this and stay the way you are. Almost all of the real successful people I've ever met usually tell me that one of the reasons for their success is this ability to stop and inventory themselves from time to time.

Through doing this, we can very definitely continue our growth on a daily basis. I find it takes less time and energy to do this every evening than it does to wait until I get really, really sick and *then* try to dig myself out from under that mess I'm in. This daily inventory keeps me on a daily basis realizing the things I need to do in order to continue to grow.

READ: Page 86, paragraph 2

When we get up in the morning, we clear the day. I remember as a new person I had to go to a meeting at 6:00 o'clock in the morning and meet my sponsor. One morning I went down and he said: "Why don't you get your life together in the morning?" I said: "What are you talking about?" He said: "You're just like a damn goose. You just get up in the morning and squawk and crap and say, "Here I come, mean old world." And this is true. We humans, what do we do in the morning? We get up in the morning, begin a day, and we have to go take a shower probably, then you comb your hair, women have to put their faces on and men have to shave and take care of all that stuff. Then we get down to that important stuff, what we're going to wear, shoes, belt, underwear and this takes a lot of time. Maybe we eat and then we run out the door to the car and off we go for the day...right? Beat the Day!

I wonder what we have done about our lives... our mind... our mind *IS* our lives. I often wonder if we humans could spend as much time on our minds as we do on our clothes, what our lives would be like. Our minds run the whole show. It takes time... it takes that quiet time in the morning to get our lives... our minds together. ***THIS IS* the beginning of a great day**. *The Book* says, *"Our Thought-Life will be placed on a much higher plane."*

We have great minds! I've never seen a dumb alcoholic, but then I ask myself, is my life as good as my mind? NO! I have a better mind than my life, because it seems like there's something always blocking me from the real quality I could be. So to stop in the morning and have that quiet time, then I find that my thinking gets better. *When my thought-life gets better, then my thinking is cleared of wrong motives.*

Now we can see if we did that each morning... every morning... in just a short period of time, it would completely change our lives. This is a very good and definitely valuable suggestion. The thing that makes this really effective is to use both of these suggestions together each day not just a morning meditation or just a night meditation, we need to do both.

READ: Page 86, paragraph 3   page 87, end of paragraph

Throughout each day we have to face indecision. We have to begin to realize that we are humans, and being humans we have character flaws. We are on the face of this earth for only a short period of time, when we think about it in the expanse of God's universe we are not that significant. During the time that we are on the face of this earth, we experience some things and we learn some things. We don't know it all and we're going to face things each day that we don't know how to handle. I think one of the greatest gifts this program has given me is the ability to say, "Hell, I don't know, I just don't know." That is a very hard thing for a self-centered person to do! Each day when a problem comes up I turn it through the computer in my head looking for the answer, and it doesn't take it long to kick it back out and say: "I don't have an answer to or for that!" Then frustration starts. People in A.A. say, relax, take it easy and realize it isn't in your computer. Turn it over to God's computer because God knows all.

God has a covenant with me; He will allow me to struggle on the basis of self-knowledge or I can let go and plug into this Ultimate Source of Information; His master computer, which is found within each and every one of us. When I relax and take it easy and say "I don't know", then my computer is free to operate on other things that day. When I have that problem I can't seem to do anything else. But, *now* I can listen to other people and I know that _God uses other people to speak to me and they may have the answers_. We have this ability, know that we have come this far, and we can receive these answers from other people, and from deep down within ourselves where our God lives with His master computer.

Our book says, "What used to be a hunch..." We all have hunches, but they come when they want to, seemingly, but by practicing this definite and valuable suggestion, the occasional inspiration gradually becomes a working part of the mind. If we practice this, it will be something we can use at all times to receive answers in our lives. Now, today, I can rely on this source of information. I can receive answers for problems in my life through the application of this very good, definite, and valuable suggestion. **This one suggestion will change your life, but, you have to practice and practice.**

READ: Page 87, paragraph 1   page 88, end of Chapter Six

Page 87, paragraph 1 deals with prayer. Bill had a way of doing things differently and Step Eleven says prayer and meditation, but of course Bill wrote in the Book about meditation first and then prayer.

Here we are going to begin to work on an effective prayer life. He gives us a very good, definite and valuable suggestion. Step Eleven says, "We pray..." and there's a word in there that we say real fast – "*We pray __only__*"..."**_ONLY_** *for God's will and the power to carry that out*". It takes time for us to effectively develop praying just like that. That's what we need in our lives as alcoholics who have lost their way in life, through our undisciplined lives. **What we really need is God's direction in our lives and the Power to carry that out.** That's all that we really need. So we pray only for that. It's very difficult to do that. It's very difficult to fashion that type of healthy prayer life. It takes time and work.

Now we are going to talk about our personal life and a personal communication with God... God, as we understand Him, to deal with our specific lives and our specific problems. So we have to fashion a prayer to fit God as we understand Him and say our needs as we see them with God. And surely as alcoholics, who have lost direction, the only thing we need to pray for is: **"God's Direction in our lives and the Power to carry that out".**

Anyone, who will use the valuable suggestions that Bill has laid out for us here, should be able to develop a specific prayer life to focus on our specific needs and our specific problems on an individual basis and we will see that God's Direction in our life will grow and God's Will, will become very clear.

ASSIGNMENT: Read the Chapter "Working with Others". This entire chapter is devoted to twelve-Step work, because "Faith without works is dead". Be ready to discuss what you will be doing to be of service to God and your fellow man in a twelve-Step manner.

An invitation to a GREAT Eleventh Step experiment
"We alcoholics are undisciplined."
The Big Book, page 88

Read pages 86 through 88 every day for 30 consecutive days

Morning

In the first hour of your day, read from page 86:

"On awakening let us think about the twenty-four hours ahead..." to the END of p 88. Put a / line through "today" below.

Evening

Before going to bed, read the paragraph on page 86:

"When we retire at night ... what corrective measures should be taken" Put a \ line through "today" below to make an X.

In passing on what has been so freely given to us, we PROMISE that if you will simply read this material for 30 consecutive days, your life will change.
It will HAVE TO BE on a more spiritual basis.

The "catch": If you miss a day, you got to start over! (An axiom to "EASY WON'T do it"!)

1	2	3	4	5	6	7	8	9	10	11	12	13	14	15	16	17	18	19	20	21	22	23	24	25	26	27	28	29	30	31

Feel better? Want to try doing it again?

1	2	3	4	5	6	7	8	9	10	11	12	13	14	15	16	17	18	19	20	21	22	23	24	25	26	27	28	29	30	31

Within EACH and every action or inaction I reveal to myself and to others in my life the true extent of my willingness to work the steps, the true extent to how committed I am to change and live a happy, useful and sober life today. When someone says they want to get sober, but then don't take the recommended actions; what they're really saying is that they want someone to take away their problems so that they can continue to live the way they are. Another FREEBEE, handout or sacrifice.

We've been lying, cheating and stealing from others our entire lives. We've been always looking to get something for nothing, cut corners or get full pay for half-a-days labor. "Why not", we think, "Others are doing it?" The time to stop comparing ourselves to others has arrived. To time to start realizing our truth and getting honest within ourselves about ourselves is now. This escape plan will only work for us if we are willing to go the extra mile and stop making excuses for our thinking, our behaviors and our defects.

Morning Meditation

"God please direct my thinking today and keep my thinking clear of dishonest or self-seeking motives. Lord, please keep me divorced from self-pity and help me employ my mental faculties, that my thought-life might be placed on a higher plane; the plane of inspiration."

Now, I am ready to do the first two items:

1. I think about the 24 hours ahead – Here I meditate about what I would like to be and I think about what God wants me to be.

2. Consider my plans for the day – Here I think about what God wants me to do and how I am to live His will. I come up with my vision for what God's will is for me today. I already have a list of amends from last night's 10th Step. I plan to start out my day with this list of amends and I ask myself, what else would God want me to do today?

In thinking about our day we may face indecision. We may not be able to determine which course to take; here we ask God for inspiration.

This is the prayer I say...

"God please give me inspiration. Help me have an intuitive thought or a decision about this problem I face. Help me Lord, not to struggle, instead, help me to relax and take it easy."
(From the thoughts on page 86)

Finally, Bill gives us a prayer to end our period of meditation with. He writes:

We usually conclude the period of meditation with a prayer...

This is the prayer I say:

"God, please show me all through this day, what my next step is to be. Give me the strength, faith and courage I need to take care of the problems in my life today. I ask especially Lord, that you free me from self-will and fear."

Bill then gives us some things to watch out for while considering the previous prayer:

We are careful to **make no request for ourselves** only. We may ask for ourselves, however, if others will be helped. We are careful **never to pray for our own selfish ends**. Many of us have wasted a lot of time doing that and **it doesn't work**.

Now, we are supposed to go out and live our day, doing God's will for us. What are we to do, when things start to go wrong for us? Bill writes:

As we go through the day we pause when agitated or doubtful, and ask for the right thought or action. We constantly remind ourselves we are no longer running the show, humbly saying to ourselves many times each day, *"Thy will be done."*

In the form of a prayer, it could look like this:

"God, please give me an intuitive thought or decision to help me with this problem. Help me know what I should do and keep me mindful, that you are running the show. Free me from my bondage of self. Thy will be done always. Amen"

11th Step Evening Review

"When We Retire at Night, We Constructively Review Our Day...
Were we Resentful, Selfish, Dishonest, or Afraid? Do we owe an apology? Have we
kept something to ourselves which should be discussed with another person at once?
Were we kind and loving toward all? What could we have done better?   Were we
thinking of ourselves most of the time? Or were we thinking of what we could do for
others, of what we could pack into the stream of life?"

"After making our review, we ask God's forgiveness and inquire what corrective
measures should be taken." (Big Book P.86)

Were We Operating on Self-Will or God's Will?

PERSONALITY CHARACTERISTICS OF:			
SELF-WILL		GOD'S WILL	
Selfish and Self-Seeking		Interest in Others	
Dishonesty		Honesty	
Frightened		Courage	
Inconsiderate		Consideration	
Pride		Humility, Seek God's Will	
Greed		Giving or Sharing	
Lust		What We Can Do for Others	
Anger		Calmness	
Envy		Gratitude	
Sloth		Take Action	
Gluttony		Moderation	
Impatience		Patience	
intolerance		Tolerance	
Resentment		Forgiveness	
Hate		Love, Concern for Others	
Harmful Acts		Good Deeds	
Self-Pity		Self-Forgetfulness	
Self Justification		Humility, Seek God's Will	
Self Importance		Modesty	
Self Condemnation		Self-Forgiveness	
Suspicion		Trust	
Doubt		Faith	
ACTION PLAN:			

175

EVENING REVIEW -- DAILY INVENTORY

"When we retire at night, we constructively review our day. Were we selfish, dishonest or afraid?" (Last column Step 4 process)

"Do we owe an apology?" (Step 8 list and Step 9.) We add, "Do we need to make any DIRECT AMENDS?"

"Have we kept something to ourselves which should be discussed with another person at once?" (Step 5 and SPONSORSHIP)

"Were we kind and loving towards all?" ("God will show us how to take a kindly and tolerant view of each and every one." p67)

"What could we have done better?" (We suggest UNDERSTANDING! Our job is to "grow in understanding and effectiveness." p84)

"Were we thinking of ourselves most of the time?" ("...we became less and less interested in our little plans and designs." p63)

"Were we thinking of what we could do fo others, of what we could pack into the stream of life?" (move from "taker" to "giver".)

"But we must be careful not to drift into worry, remorse or morbid reflection, for that would diminish our usefulness to others."

"After making our review, we ask God's forgiveness and inquire what corrective measures should be taken."

LIABILITY	1	2	3	4	5	6	7	8	9	10	11	12	13	14	15	16	17	18	19	20	21	22	23	24	25	26	27	28	29	30	31	ASSET
Self Pity																																Self Forgetfulness
Self Justification																																Humility
Self Importance																																Modesty
Self Condemnation																																Self Valuation
Dishonesty																																Honesty
Impatience																																Patience
Hate																																LOVE
Resentment																																Forgiveness
False Pride																																Simplicity
Jealousy																																Trust
Envy																																Generosity
Laziness																																Activity
Procrastination																																Promptness
Insincerity																																Honesty, Sincerity
Negative Thinking																																Positive Thinking
Criticizing																																Look for the GOOD
Vulgar, Immoral, Trashy Thinking																																Spiritual CLEAR Thinking

Another useful tool: put a "+" or "-" on each line for each day. This is for you! Nobody is keeping score, so just go for it!

WEEK #19: Chapter 7 — WORKING WITH OTHERS *(Step Twelve)*

READ: Page 89, through 103

"Having had a spiritual awakening as the result of these steps, we tried to carry this message to alcoholics and to practice these principles in all our affairs."

Let's look at Step Twelve for just a moment. There are three parts to Step Twelve.
The *first* part of Step Twelve is probably the greatest promise to be found anywhere in *The Big Book*: ***"Having had a <u>spiritual awakening</u> as the result of these steps..."***

I think that is a promise to me if I will put the first eleven Steps to work in my life to the best of my ability, then I can have a spiritual awakening.

What is a spiritual awakening? *A personality change sufficient to recover from alcoholism.*
Bill tells us in *The Twelve and Twelve* there are as many different kinds of "spiritual awakenings" as there are people in A.A. But, people who have had a spiritual awakening all have certain things in common, that is, they are able to *feel, believe, and do* things that they could never do before on their own strength unaided. Now if that is the criteria for a spiritual awakening, then I believe I must have had one of some kind because I certainly feel things that I never felt before.

Today I *feel* true love. I never knew what love was. I always had love mixed up with sex and things like that. Today I realize that doesn't have anything to do with love. Love is compassion, tolerance, patience, and goodwill towards my fellow man. Today I feel some of that. Before AA I never felt any of that and I could have cared less about you. You could have some after I got what I wanted, but I was going to get mine first every time. Those feelings have changed. So, if that's the criteria, then surely I've had some form of spiritual awakening.

Today I *believe* things I never believed before. I believe God is a kind and a loving God.
I believe He stands ready to help any human being anywhere in the world the instant they are ready to give self-will back to Him and begin to follow His will. Before, I always thought He was hellfire and brimstone. **I believe God disciplines us**. Sometimes we are so hard headed that it takes a big blow to us to get our attention. But I think we are the ones that punish ourselves, not God, but, we blame Him for how we feel. My belief about God has changed entirely. So, if that's the criteria, then surely I've had some form of spiritual awakening.

Today I can *do* things that I couldn't do before I came to A.A. I can stay sober. I could never do that before, and because of the fact that I'm sober, I'm allowed to do many, many things I could never do while I was drinking. So, if that's the criteria, then surely I've had some form of spiritual awakening.

Now, let's look at the *second* part of Step Twelve:
   "...we tried to carry this message..."
What am I supposed to do with it? Not a message, not the message, not some message, but **this** message to others. What is **this** message? Very simple...*"Having had a spiritual awakening as the result of these steps..."*

That's the **only** message that we carry to other people. Sometimes we get to thinking we're healers in A.A. Or we get to thinking we're marital advisors, economic advisors, sex advisors. I don't know of any group of people in the world that screwed that mess up worse than we did, yet we think we can advise other people in those areas. We only know one thing. But I'll guarantee you, that one thing we know, we know better than anybody in the world and that is: ***An alcoholic armed with the facts about himself can help another alcoholic learn about the disease of alcoholism.*** We know more about it than anybody alive, because we are the only people in the world who have experienced the disease of alcoholism. Same thing with the **recovery** process... we are the only people in the world who have experienced the *recovery* from the disease of alcoholism.

Now we can take that very unique knowledge and carry that to another human being and help them understand what their problem is: *the disease of alcoholism*. Help them understand what their solution will need to be: a vital spiritual experience. Help them walk through the program of action, so they also can have a spiritual awakening and recover from their disease. *We are the only people in the world who can do this.*

I've got to believe that in the 1930's God got tired of seeing people like us die. He had to take Bill, Bob, Ebbie, Dr. Jung and Dr. Silkworth... and even the Oxford Group and all the others concerned put this thing together. **God has always worked with people, through people.** Very seldom does He speak to one of us directly. (We've got one back home who says he does, but he won't give anyone else God's telephone number, he's keeping it for himself.) If God worked through people in the 1930's to set this up, it stands to reason that He will work with people today and through people to continue to carry this message to those who are still suffering. There's no alcoholic in this room that shouldn't be dead. How many times did we wake up the next morning and say, weren't we lucky the night before? I don't think luck had anything to do with it. I think we are a ***chosen people***. Not as a race, but, ***to do a job***.

They tell me today that 96-97% of the alcoholics that are alive today will die from their disease, never even knowing that they are alcoholics. Three or four percent of us manage to stagger into A.A. and less than 25% of that three or four percent of us are recovering, so we are talking about one out of one hundred have recovered from this disease. I used to say, "God, why am I an alcoholic? Today I say, "God, why am I not one of those dying from the disease?" I don't have any trouble with God's will. I don't think God is concerned with where I work.

I don't think He's concerned with where I live. I doubt whether He's concerned with whom I'm married to, in any great extent. But, I think there is one thing God is concerned with: *"What are you doing with what I've given so freely?"* If we can take this unique knowledge that we have, then you and I together, can avert death in countless thousands and thousands of people. Not many people in this world have that privilege. I think we are very unique. I think we are very, very lucky individuals.

The *third* and last part of Step Twelve says:
    "...to practice these principles in all our affairs"

Well, what are the *principles*? We've heard arguments go on for hours about this, just like the difference between a defect and a shortcoming and a wrong. In the chapter "How It Works", Bill said: *"No one among us has been able to maintain anything like perfect adherence to these principles. We are not saints (Bill says) the principles we have set down are guides to spiritual progress, not spiritual perfection."*

The Full Version of the Serenity Prayer

God, grant me the Serenity

To accept the things I cannot change...

Courage to change the things I can,

And Wisdom to know the difference.

Living one day at a time,

Enjoying one moment at a time,

Accepting hardship as the pathway to peace.

Taking, as He did, this sinful world as it is,

Not as I would have it.

Trusting that He will make all things right

if I surrender to His will.

That I may be reasonably happy in this life,

And supremely happy with Him forever in the next.

Amen.

What did he set down just before that statement? *The Twelve Steps of Alcoholics Anonymous*
In the Forward of *The Twelve and Twelve* he says: *"The Twelve Steps of Alcoholics Anonymous are a set of principles, spiritual in nature, which if practiced will expel the obsession to drink."*
I have never yet seen Bill write about the principles except when it was in connection with:

The Twelve Steps… THEY ARE A SET OF PRINCIPLES

Now it's easy for me to *practice* them here in AA. I love you and you love me and we're going to do our best not to hurt each other. And through practicing these principles here in AA, that hour a day we're in AA we can be happy, peaceful, and free. But what do we do with the other 23 hours a day? If I practice these principles in my own home, where I am 10-12 hours a day, and I *practice* these principles with my spouse, I realize how powerless I am over her. I realize the insanity of this. She is mature… she's not going to listen to me anymore at all.

I make a decision to turn her will and her life over to the care of God, as I understand Him. And I inventory *me* to see why I still have the need to control her, I find those defects of character that cause this, and I talk it over with another human being and I ask God to take them away. I make amends quickly to her when I have harmed her. There are times I'm really ashamed of me. There are times I treat absolute strangers with more courtesy than I treat my own spouse in my home. If I *practice these principles in my home with her*, I could be happy, peaceful and serene another 8-10 hours a day.

How about my children? Can I realize how powerless I am over them? Can I realize the insanity of me trying to control their lives for them? They're not going to listen to daddy anymore. Can I make a decision to turn their will and their lives over to the care of God, as I understand Him? Can I inventory me and see why I need to control them? Can I find those defects and do something about it? Can I make amends quickly when I smart off to them once in a while? If I could practice these principles with my children, I could be happy when I'm with them. If I don't, I don't stand a chance with them. All we will do is argue and fight from then on. If I can practice them with my kids, I can be happy there another hour or two a day.

How about on the Job? Can I see how powerless I am over my coworkers? Do I realize the insanity of me trying to control them? Can I make that decision? If I can do this on the job, then I could be happy there another 8 to 9 hours a day. We're down to about 23 hours now.

I have one hour left. How about the supermarket check-out line? I'm in the express line. I've got three items. There's a little old lady in front of me with her whole basket full. She has about 50 things in there. She shouldn't be in this damn line anyway. She needs to be over there. I'm in a hurry and I want to get through here. It takes them about 10 or 15 minutes to add up her bill, and I'm in a hurry and I want to get through here and she shouldn't be in this line in the first place. Then after they add up the bill, she pulls out her coupons. It takes another 10 minutes to add up her bill again and I'm in a hurry and she shouldn't be in this damn line in the first place. They get her new bill added up and she gets out her checkbook. It takes her about 10 minutes to write the check and she shouldn't be in this line in the first place and I'm in a hurry. Then she stands there and balances her checkbook. Now if I could practice these principles in the supermarket check-out line, I could be happy there, too.

What we're saying is: *it's really up to us. We have the tools*, haven't we? *We've got eleven Steps* that if we will use them in our lives on a daily basis, we can be happy, peaceful, and serene, 24 hours a day, 7 days a week, 4 weeks out of the month, and 12 months out of the year, *IF* we choose to do so, but, it's entirely up to us. Nobody can do it for us. Nobody will do it for us.

We will have to do this with God's help for the rest of our life if we want to be happy, peaceful and free.

It really does work, if we're willing to work for it.

After reading this chapter, discuss these questions with your group:
1. What are the step-by-step requirements for a twelfth Step?
2. Have you ever tried this? (Share your experiences with the group).
3. In cases where the alcoholic has not responded, have you worked with his family?
4. Did you offer them your way of life and what results did you have in this situation?
5. Do you believe that you should "Burn the idea into the consciousness of every man that he can get well regardless of anyone"?

Chapter Eight, "To Wives" Chapter Nine, "The Family Afterwards" Chapter Ten, "To Employers" Chapter Eleven, "A Vision for You" – are all chapters to teach you how to practice these principles in all your affairs.

These chapters contain many spiritual truths which apply to all of us and should be read.

FINAL ASSIGNMENT: Find some new members of Alcoholics Anonymous who need and want this program and do another Step Study team with them.

READ: "A Vision for You" on page 164. As it is a fitting way to end your Step Study.

A VISION FOR YOU – P.164

"Our book is meant to be suggestive only. We realize we know only a little. God will constantly disclose more to you and to us. Ask Him in your morning mediation what you can do each day for the man who is still sick. The answers will come, if your own house is in order. But obviously you cannot transmit something you haven't got. See to it that your relationship with Him is right and great events will come to pass for you and countless others. This is the Great Fact for us.

Abandon yourself to God as you understand God. (We did this in Steps 1, 2, and 3) *Admit your faults to Him and to your fellows.* (We did that in Steps 4, 5, 6, and 7.) *Clear away the wreckage of your past.* (We did that in Steps 8 and 9) *Give freely of what you find and join us.* (We do that in Steps 10, 11 and 12)…

We shall be with you in the Fellowship of the Spirit, and you will surely meet some of us as you trudge the Road to Happy destiny.

May God bless you and keep you – until then."

BIG BOOK WORKSHOP HOMEWORK ASSIGNMENT

Note: At this point the Book assumes that you made a list of people you had harmed when you did your Fourth Step Inventory. If this has not been done, you should certainly make such a list at this point and review it with your sponsor. God will provide the proper time and place if you pray for the willingness to make amends *"...Sometimes quickly sometimes slowly."*

I. Read Chapter 6 **"Into Action"** (P84 par2 – P85 par.2) in the "Big Book" (1st Time) – USE HIGHLIGHTER! (Just read and highlight the 1st time you read through the chapter.)

J. Read Chapter 5 **"Into Action"** (P84 par2 – P85 par.2) in the "Big Book" (2nd Time). Answer the "Work Assignment Questions" below as you read the assignment the 2nd time.

3) Be prepared to discuss the material.

WORK ASSIGNMENT QUESTIONS
"INTO ACTION – Step 10"

PAGE: 84

12. What are the specific instructions outlined for taking of Step Ten?

13. What do we watch for?

Note: *"By this time sanity will have been returned - we will seldom be interested in liquor."*

3. Is this the sanity referred to in Step Two?

PAGE: 85

25. What is the proper use of will power?

26. What is the suggestion for taking the Eleventh Step on a daily basis?

Special Fourth Step Inventory Bonus Package

Use the information in this special bonus material to help aid you in doing a more through 4th step. The prompt sheets and additional 4th step column worksheets will help give you're the room you need to be thorough.

One of the requirements for sobriety is the need for confession of personality defects, a moral inventory, and step four is designed to be just this. There is a lot of hype and fear surrounding this step (mostly created by those who are yet to do it), and these worksheets are designed to make this task as easy and simple as possible. Everything contained in these sheets is directly from the Big Book 'Alcoholics Anonymous', there is no opinion, just fact. To be able to start on this step, the previous three steps must of course have been completed, so before starting check with your sponsor, spiritual advisor, counselor, etc. to make sure you are ready.

Many people get loaded or act out in some way when they reach this step. Why? They will tell you that the pain of dredging up memories long buried was too much to endure, or any one of a thousand other excuses. The plain and simple fact is just this, the pain does not come in writing this inventory, the pain comes in resisting the writing. Alcoholics and addicts, time after time, would rather get loaded again than have to face some inner truths. The freedom from self is made impossible by holding on to fears and secrets we've harbored all our lives, the way of strength, paradoxically, is in becoming vulnerable.

Here are some tips to help you with this moral inventory:

Try and list resentments in groups, i.e.; Family, school, relationships, work, etc.

If you are not sure in any area, call somebody and ask them for their experience.

Get into the habit of writing every day, even if it's only for ten minutes.

In the resentment inventory, don't write across, do it in columns, i.e; ALL names first, ALL causes second, etc.

Be honest! The only person to truly benefit from this exercise is you, don't cheat yourself out of this incredible experience.

RESENTMENT INVENTORY PROMPT SHEET

Here is a list of people, institutions and principles that may be helpful in your resentment inventory. Feel free to add to the lists if you need to.

PEOPLE	INSTITUTIONS	PRINCIPLES
Father (Step)	Marriage	God-Deity
Mother (Step)	Bible	Retribution
Sisters (Step)	Church	Ten Commandments
Brothers (Step)	Religion	Jesus Christ
Aunts	Races	Satan
Uncles	Law	Death
Cousins	Authority	Life After Death
Clergy	Government	Heaven
Police	Education System	Hell
Lawyers	Correctional System	Sin
Judges	Mental Health System	Adultery
Doctors	Philosophy	Golden Rule
Employer's	Nationality	Original Sin
Employee's		Seven Deadly Sins
Co-Workers		
In-Laws		
Husbands		
Wives		
Creditors		
Childhood Friends		
School Friends		
Teachers		
Life Long Friends		
Best Friends		
Acquaintances		
Girl Friends		
Boy Friends		
Parole Officers		
Probation Officers		
A.A. Friends		
C.A. Friends		
N.A. Friends		
U.S. Service Friends		

FEAR INVENTORY PROMPT SHEET

Here is a list of fears that may be helpful in your fear inventory. Feel free to add to the lists if you need to.

Fear Of God	Fear Of Drowning
Fear Of Dying	Fear Of Men
Fear Of Insanity	Fear Of Women
Fear Of Insecurity	Fear Of Being Alone
Fear Of Rejection	Fear Of People
Fear Of Loneliness	Fear Of Crying
Fear Of Disease's	Fear Of Poverty
Fear Of Alcohol	Fear Of Races
Fear Of Drugs	Fear Of The Unknown
Fear Of Relapse	Fear Of Abandonment
Fear Of Sex	Fear Of Intimacy
Fear Of Sin	Fear Of Disapproval
Fear Of Self-Expression	Fear Of Rejection
Fear Of Authority	Fear Of Confrontation
Fear Of Heights	Fear Of Sobriety
Fear Of Unemployment	Fear Of Hospitals
Fear Of Employment	Fear Of Responsibility
Fear Of Parents	Fear Of Feelings
Fear Of Losing A Wife	Fear Of Getting Old
Fear Of Losing A Husband	Fear Of Hurting Others
Fear Of Losing A Child	Fear Of Violence
Fear Of Animals	Fear Of Writing Inventory
Fear Of Insects	Fear Of Being Alive
Fear Of Police	Fear Of Government
Fear Of Jail	Fear Of Gangs
Fear Of Doctor's	Fear Of Gossip
Fear Of Stealing	Fear Of Wealthy People
Fear Of Creditors	Fear Of Guns
Fear Of Being Found Out	Fear Of Change
Fear Of Homosexuals & Lesbians	
Fear Of Failure	
Fear Of Success	
Fear Of Responsibility	
Fear Of Physical Pain	
Fear Of Fear	

FOURTH STEP INVENTORY

RESENTMENTS, FEARS & SEXUAL CONDUCT/HARM DONE TO OTHERS

RESENTMENTS

Please read from the bottom of page 63 through page 65 before beginning.

Column 1: Resentments
List all people, places, things, institutions, ideas or principles with whom you are angry, resent, feel hurt or threatened by.
Column 2: The Cause
What happened? Be specific as to why you were angry.
Column 3: Affects My......
How did it make me feel? Specifically, how did it affect the seven parts of self?
Column 4: Where Was I To Blame
Read through the second paragraph on page 67 before answering this.
What's the truth here? Where was my responsibility in this relationship? What might I have done instead? Where was I at fault?

FEARS

Read the Big Book, page 67, last paragraph through first paragraph on page 68.

List your fears. Then write about why you have each fear. Has self-reliance failed you?

SEXUAL CONDUCT/HARM DONE TO OTHERS

Read carefully Big Book pages 68-70.

Again, make a list for yourself. What happened in each instance? How did it make you feel.

The Seven Parts Of Self Defined

Self Esteem - How I think of myself

Pride - How I think others view me

Pocketbook - Basic desire for money, property, possessions, etc.

Personal Relations - Our relations with other people

Ambition - Our goals, plans and designs for the future

Emotional Security - General sense of personal well being

Sex Relations - Basic drive for sexual intimacy

REVIEW OF FEARS

"SELF"

Questions

COLUMN 4 — What is the exact nature of my wrongs, faults, mistakes, defects, shortcomings?

What was MY PART in all this? What did I do initially to get the ball rolling? How could I have done things differently?

COLUMN 1	COLUMN 2	COLUMN 3: Which Part of Self Was Affected?		COLUMN 4	Questions
THE FEAR:	WHY I HAVE THIS FEAR:				
		Social Instinct	Personal Relationships		
			Pride		
			Self-Esteem		
			Prestige		
			Companionship		
		Security Instinct	Emotional		
			Material		
		Sex Instinct	Hidden Sex Relations		
			Acceptable Sex Relations		
		Ambitions	Sexual		
			Security		
			Social		
			Frightened		
			Inconsiderate		
			Dishonest		
			Self-Seeking & Selfish		

REVIEW OF FEARS

"SELF"

COLUMN 1	COLUMN 2	COLUMN 3: Which Part of Self Was Affected?			COLUMN 4	Questions
THE FEAR:	WHY I HAVE THIS FEAR:	Social Instinct	Personal Relationships		What is the exact nature of my wrongs, faults, mistakes, defects, shortcomings?	What was MY PART in all this? What did I do initially to get the ball rolling? How could I have done things differently?
			Pride			
			Self-Esteem			
			Prestige			
			Companionship			
		Security Instinct	Emotional			
			Material			
		Sex Instinct	Hidden Sex Relations			
			Acceptable Sex Relations			
		Ambitions	Sexual			
			Security			
			Social			
				Frightened		
				Inconsiderate		
				Dishonest		
				Self-Seeking & Selfish		

REVIEW OF FEARS

"SELF"

Questions

What was MY PART in all this? What did I do initially to get the ball rolling? How could I have done things differently?

COLUMN 4

What is the exact nature of my wrongs, faults, mistakes, defects, shortcomings?

- Frightened
- Inconsiderate
- Dishonest
- Self-Seeking & Selfish

COLUMN 3: Which Part of Self Was Affected?

Ambitions	Sexual
	Security
	Social
Sex Instinct	Hidden Sex Relations
	Acceptable Sex Relations
Security Instinct	Emotional
	Material
Social Instinct	Personal Relationships
	Pride
	Self-Esteem
	Prestige
	Companionship

COLUMN 2

WHY I HAVE THIS FEAR:

COLUMN 1

THE FEAR:

REVIEW OF FEARS

COLUMN 1	COLUMN 2	COLUMN 3: Which Part of Self Was Affected?		COLUMN 4	Questions
		"SELF"			
THE FEAR:	WHY I HAVE THIS FEAR:	Social Instinct	Personal Relationships	What is the exact nature of my wrongs, faults, mistakes, defects, shortcomings? — Frightened	What was MY PART in all this? What did I do initially to get the ball rolling? How could I have done things differently?
			Pride	Inconsiderate	
			Self-Esteem	Dishonest	
			Prestige	Self-Seeking & Selfish	
			Companionship		
		Security Instinct	Emotional	Ambitions — Sexual	
			Material	Security	
		Sex Instinct	Hidden Sex Relations	Social	
			Acceptable Sex Relations		

REVIEW OF FEARS

COLUMN 1	COLUMN 2	COLUMN 3: Which Part of Self Was Affected?		"SELF" COLUMN 4	Questions
THE FEAR:	WHY I HAVE THIS FEAR:			What is the exact nature of my wrongs, faults, mistakes, defects, shortcomings?	What was MY PART in all this? What did I do initially to get the ball rolling? How could I have done things differently?
				Frightened	
				Inconsiderate	
				Dishonest	
				Self-Seeking & Selfish	
		Ambitions	Sexual		
			Security		
			Social		
		Sex Instinct	Hidden Sex Relations		
			Acceptable Sex Relations		
		Security Instinct	Emotional		
			Material		
		Social Instinct	Personal Relationships		
			Pride		
			Self-Esteem		
			Prestige		
			Companionship		

REVIEW OF FEARS

"SELF"

COLUMN 1	COLUMN 2	COLUMN 3: Which Part of Self Was Affected?		COLUMN 4	Questions
THE FEAR:	WHY I HAVE THIS FEAR:			What is the exact nature of my wrongs, mistakes, faults, defects, shortcomings?	What was MY PART in all this? What did I do initially to get the ball rolling? How could I have done things differently?
			Frightened		
			Inconsiderate		
			Dishonest		
			Self-Seeking & Selfish		
		Ambitions	Sexual		
			Security		
			Social		
		Sex Instinct	Hidden Sex Relations		
			Acceptable Sex Relations		
		Security Instinct	Emotional		
			Material		
		Social Instinct	Personal Relationships		
			Pride		
			Self-Esteem		
			Prestige		
			Companionship		

REVIEW OF FEARS

COLUMN 1	COLUMN 2	COLUMN 3: Which Part of Self Was Affected?		COLUMN 4	Questions
THE FEAR:	WHY I HAVE THIS FEAR:	"SELF"		What is the exact nature of my wrongs, faults, mistakes, defects, shortcomings?	What was MY PART in all this? What did I do initially to get the ball rolling? How could I have done things differently?
		Social Instinct	Personal Relationships	Frightened	
			Pride	Inconsiderate	
			Self-Esteem	Dishonest	
			Prestige	Self-Seeking & Selfish	
			Companionship	Sexual	
		Security Instinct	Emotional	Security	
			Material	Social	
		Sex Instinct	Hidden Sex Relations		
			Acceptable Sex Relations		
		Ambitions			

REVIEW OF FEARS

"SELF"

COLUMN 1	COLUMN 2	COLUMN 3: Which Part of Self Was Affected?		COLUMN 4	Questions
THE FEAR:	WHY I HAVE THIS FEAR:			What is the exact nature of my wrongs, faults, mistakes, defects, shortcomings?	What was MY PART in all this? What did I do initially to get the ball rolling? How could I have done things differently?
			Frightened		
			Inconsiderate		
			Dishonest		
			Self-Seeking & Selfish		
		Ambitions	Sexual		
			Security		
			Social		
		Sex Instinct	Hidden Sex Relations		
			Acceptable Sex Relations		
		Security Instinct	Emotional		
			Material		
		Social Instinct	Personal Relationships		
			Pride		
			Self-Esteem		
			Prestige		
			Companionship		

REVIEW OF FEARS

COLUMN 1	COLUMN 2	COLUMN 3: Which Part of Self Was Affected?		COLUMN 4	Questions
THE FEAR:	WHY I HAVE THIS FEAR:	"SELF"		What is the exact nature of my wrongs, faults, mistakes, defects, shortcomings?	What was MY PART in all this? What did I do initially to get the ball rolling? How could I have done things differently?
		Social Instinct	Personal Relationships	Frightened	
			Pride	Inconsiderate	
			Self-Esteem	Dishonest	
			Prestige	Self-Seeking & Selfish	
			Companionship		
		Security Instinct	Emotional		
			Material		
		Sex Instinct	Hidden Sex Relations		
			Acceptable Sex Relations		
		Ambitions	Sexual		
			Security		
			Social		

REVIEW OF FEARS

COLUMN 1
THE FEAR:

COLUMN 2
WHY I HAVE THIS FEAR:

COLUMN 3: Which Part of Self Was Affected?
"SELF"

Social Instinct	Personal Relationships
	Pride
	Self-Esteem
	Prestige
	Companionship
Security Instinct	Emotional
	Material
Sex Instinct	Hidden Sex Relations
	Acceptable Sex Relations
Ambitions	Sexual
	Security
	Social

COLUMN 4
What is the exact nature of my wrongs, faults, mistakes, defects, shortcomings?

- Frightened
- Inconsiderate
- Dishonest
- Self-Seeking & Selfish

Questions
What was MY PART in all this? What did I do initially to get the ball rolling? How could I have done things differently?

REVIEW OF FEARS

"SELF"

COLUMN 1	COLUMN 2	COLUMN 3: Which Part of Self Was Affected?		COLUMN 4	Questions
THE FEAR:	WHY I HAVE THIS FEAR:			What is the exact nature of my wrongs, faults, mistakes, defects, shortcomings?	What was MY PART in all this? What did I do initially to get the ball rolling? How could I have done things differently?
		Social Instinct	Personal Relationships	Frightened	
			Pride	Inconsiderate	
			Self-Esteem	Dishonest	
			Prestige	Self-Seeking & Selfish	
			Companionship		
		Security Instinct	Emotional	Sexual	
			Material	Security	
		Sex Instinct	Hidden Sex Relations	Social	
			Acceptable Sex Relations		
		Ambitions			

REVIEW OF FEARS

"SELF"

COLUMN 1	COLUMN 2	COLUMN 3: Which Part of Self Was Affected?		COLUMN 4	Questions
THE FEAR:	WHY I HAVE THIS FEAR:			What is the exact nature of my wrongs, faults, mistakes, defects, shortcomings?	What was MY PART in all this? What did I do initially to get the ball rolling? How could I have done things differently?
			Frightened		
			Inconsiderate		
			Dishonest		
			Self-Seeking & Selfish		
		Ambitions	Sexual		
			Security		
			Social		
		Sex Instinct	Hidden Sex Relations		
			Acceptable Sex Relations		
		Security Instinct	Emotional		
			Material		
		Social Instinct	Personal Relationships		
			Pride		
			Self-Esteem		
			Prestige		
			Companionship		

REVIEW OF OUR OWN SEX CONDUCT & HARMS DONE

"SELF"

COLUMN 1	COLUMN 2	COLUMN 3: Which Part of Self Was Affected?			COLUMN 4	Questions
WHO DID I HURT?	SEX: Where Did I Unjustly Arouse Jealousy, Suspicion or Bitterness? / WHAT DID I DO? (SEX / HARMS)	Social Instinct	Personal Relationships		What is the exact nature of my wrongs, faults, mistakes, defects, shortcomings?	What was MY PART in all this? What did I do initially to get the ball rolling? How could I have done things differently?
			Pride			
			Self-Esteem			
			Prestige			
			Companionship			
		Security Instinct	Emotional			
			Material			
		Sex Instinct	Hidden Sex Relations			
			Acceptable Sex Relations			
		Ambitions	Sexual			
			Security			
			Social			
				Frightened		
				Inconsiderate		
				Dishonest		
				Self-Seeking & Selfish		

REVIEW OF OUR OWN SEX CONDUCT & HARMS DONE

"SELF"

COLUMN 1	COLUMN 2	COLUMN 3: Which Part of Self Was Affected?		COLUMN 4	Questions
WHO DID I HURT?	SEX: Where Did I Unjustly Arouse Jealousy, Suspicion or Bitterness? / WHAT DID I DO? (SEX / HARMS)	Social Instinct	Personal Relationships	What is the exact nature of my wrongs, faults, mistakes, defects, shortcomings?	What was MY PART in all this? What did I do initially to get the ball rolling? How could I have done things differently?
			Pride		
			Self-Esteem		
			Prestige		
			Companionship		
		Security Instinct	Emotional		
			Material		
		Sex Instinct	Hidden Sex Relations		
			Acceptable Sex Relations		
		Ambitions	Sexual		
			Security		
			Social		
				Frightened	
				Inconsiderate	
				Dishonest	
				Self-Seeking & Selfish	

REVIEW OF OUR OWN SEX CONDUCT & HARMS DONE

"SELF"

COLUMN 1	COLUMN 2	COLUMN 3: Which Part of Self Was Affected?								COLUMN 4	Questions
		Social Instinct		Security Instinct	Sex Instinct	Ambitions			What is the exact nature of my wrongs, faults, mistakes, defects, shortcomings?		What was MY PART in all this? What did I do initially to get the ball rolling? How could I have done things differently?
WHO DID I HURT?	SEX: Where Did I Unjustly Arouse Jealousy, Suspicion or Bitterness? / WHAT DID I DO? (SEX / HARMS)	Companionship / Prestige / Self-Esteem / Pride / Personal Relationships		Material / Emotional	Acceptable Sex Relations / Hidden Sex Relations	Social / Security / Sexual			Self-Seeking & Selfish / Dishonest / Inconsiderate / Frightened		

REVIEW OF OUR OWN SEX CONDUCT & HARMS DONE

"SELF"

COLUMN 1	COLUMN 2	COLUMN 3: Which Part of Self Was Affected?		COLUMN 4	Questions
WHO DID I HURT?	SEX: Where Did I Unjustly Arouse Jealousy, Suspicion or Bitterness? / WHAT DID I DO? (SEX / HARMS)	Social Instinct	Personal Relationships	What is the exact nature of my wrongs, faults, mistakes, defects, shortcomings?	What was MY PART in all this? What did I do initially to get the ball rolling? How could I have done things differently?
			Pride		
			Self-Esteem		
			Prestige		
			Companionship		
		Security Instinct	Emotional		
			Material		
		Sex Instinct	Hidden Sex Relations		
			Acceptable Sex Relations		
		Ambitions	Sexual		
			Security		
			Social		
				Frightened	
				Inconsiderate	
				Dishonest	
				Self-Seeking & Selfish	

REVIEW OF OUR OWN SEX CONDUCT & HARMS DONE

"SELF"

COLUMN 1	COLUMN 2	COLUMN 3: Which Part of Self Was Affected?				COLUMN 4	Questions
	SEX: Where Did I Unjustly Arouse Jealousy, Suspicion or Bitterness?	Social Instinct	Personal Relationships	What is the exact nature of my wrongs, faults, mistakes, defects, shortcomings?			What was *MY PART* in all this? What did I do initially to get the ball rolling? How could I have done things differently?
			Pride				
			Self-Esteem				
			Prestige				
			Companionship				
		Security Instinct	Emotional				
			Material				
		Sex Instinct	Hidden Sex Relations				
			Acceptable Sex Relations				
		Ambitions	Sexual				
			Security				
			Social				
	WHAT DID I DO? (SEX / HARMS)			Frightened			
				Inconsiderate			
				Dishonest			
				Self-Seeking & Selfish			
WHO DID I HURT?							

REVIEW OF OUR OWN SEX CONDUCT & HARMS DONE

"SELF"

COLUMN 1	COLUMN 2	COLUMN 3: Which Part of Self Was Affected?			COLUMN 4	Questions
WHO DID I HURT?	SEX: Where Did I Unjustly Arouse Jealousy, Suspicion or Bitterness? / WHAT DID I DO? (SEX / HARMS)	Social Instinct	Personal Relationships		What is the exact nature of my wrongs, faults, mistakes, defects, shortcomings?	*What was MY PART in all this? What did I do initially to get the ball rolling? How could I have done things differently?*
			Pride		Frightened	
			Self-Esteem		Inconsiderate	
			Prestige		Dishonest	
			Companionship		Self-Seeking & Selfish	
		Security Instinct	Emotional		Sexual	
			Material		Security	
		Sex Instinct	Hidden Sex Relations		Social	
			Acceptable Sex Relations			
		Ambitions	Sexual			
			Security			
			Social			

REVIEW OF OUR OWN SEX CONDUCT & HARMS DONE

"SELF"

COLUMN 1	COLUMN 2	COLUMN 3: Which Part of Self Was Affected?			COLUMN 4	Questions
WHO DID I HURT?	SEX: Where Did I Unjustly Arouse Jealousy, Suspicion or Bitterness? / WHAT DID I DO? (SEX / HARMS)	Social Instinct	Personal Relationships		What is the exact nature of my wrongs, faults, mistakes, defects, shortcomings?	What was MY PART in all this? What did I do initially to get the ball rolling? How could I have done things differently?
			Pride		Frightened	
			Self-Esteem		Inconsiderate	
			Prestige		Dishonest	
			Companionship		Self-Seeking & Selfish	
		Security Instinct	Emotional		Sexual	
			Material		Security	
		Sex Instinct	Hidden Sex Relations		Social	
			Acceptable Sex Relations			
		Ambitions	Sexual			
			Security			
			Social			

REVIEW OF OUR OWN SEX CONDUCT & HARMS DONE

COLUMN 1	COLUMN 2	COLUMN 3: Which Part of Self Was Affected?			"SELF"		COLUMN 4	Questions
WHO DID I HURT?	SEX: Where Did I Unjustly Arouse Jealousy, Suspicion or Bitterness? WHAT DID I DO? (SEX / HARMS)	Social Instinct		Companionship			What is the exact nature of my wrongs, faults, mistakes, defects, shortcomings?	What was MY PART in all this? What did I do initially to get the ball rolling? How could I have done things differently?
				Prestige				
				Self-Esteem				
				Pride				
				Personal Relationships				
		Security Instinct		Material				
				Emotional				
		Sex Instinct		Acceptable Sex Relations				
				Hidden Sex Relations				
		Ambitions		Social				
				Security				
				Sexual				
							Self-Seeking & Selfish	
							Dishonest	
							Inconsiderate	
							Frightened	

REVIEW OF OUR OWN SEX CONDUCT & HARMS DONE

"SELF"

COLUMN 1	COLUMN 2	COLUMN 3: Which Part of Self Was Affected?												COLUMN 4	Questions
		Social Instinct				Security Instinct		Sex Instinct		Ambitions			What is the exact nature of my wrongs, faults, mistakes, defects, shortcomings?		
WHO DID I HURT?	SEX: Where Did I Unjustly Arouse Jealousy, Suspicion or Bitterness? / WHAT DID I DO? (SEX / HARMS)	Companionship	Prestige	Self-Esteem	Pride	Personal Relationships	Material	Emotional	Acceptable Sex Relations	Hidden Sex Relations	Social	Security	Sexual	Self-Seeking & Selfish / Dishonest / Inconsiderate / Frightened	What was MY PART in all this? What did I do initially to get the ball rolling? How could I have done things differently?

REVIEW OF RESENTMENTS

"SELF"

COLUMN 1	COLUMN 2	COLUMN 3: Which Part of Self Was Affected?		COLUMN 4	Questions
I AM RESENTFUL OF:	THE CAUSE OF THIS RESENTMENT IS:			What is the exact nature of my wrongs, faults, mistakes, defects, shortcomings?	What was MY PART in all this? What did I do initially to get the ball rolling? How could I have done things differently?
				Frightened	
				Inconsiderate	
				Dishonest	
				Self-Seeking & Selfish	
		Ambitions	Sexual		
			Security		
			Social		
		Sex Instinct	Hidden Sex Relations		
			Acceptable Sex Relations		
		Security Instinct	Emotional		
			Material		
		Social Instinct	Personal Relationships		
			Pride		
			Self-Esteem		
			Prestige		
			Companionship		

REVIEW OF RESENTMENTS

COLUMN 1	COLUMN 2	COLUMN 3: Which Part of Self Was Affected?		"SELF" COLUMN 4	Questions
I AM RESENTFUL OF:	THE CAUSE OF THIS RESENTMENT IS:	Social Instinct	Personal Relationships	What is the exact nature of my wrongs, mistakes, faults, defects, shortcomings?	What was MY PART in all this? What did I do initially to get the ball rolling? How could I have done things differently?
			Pride		
			Self-Esteem		
			Prestige		
			Companionship		
		Security Instinct	Emotional		
			Material		
		Sex Instinct	Hidden Sex Relations		
			Acceptable Sex Relations		
		Ambitions	Sexual		
			Security		
			Social		
				Frightened	
				Inconsiderate	
				Dishonest	
				Self-Seeking & Selfish	

REVIEW OF RESENTMENTS

COLUMN 1	COLUMN 2	COLUMN 3: Which Part of Self Was Affected?		"SELF"	COLUMN 4	Questions
I AM RESENTFUL OF:	THE CAUSE OF THIS RESENTMENT IS:	Social Instinct	Companionship		What is the exact nature of my wrongs, faults, mistakes, defects, shortcomings?	What was MY PART in all this? What did I do initially to get the ball rolling? How could I have done things differently?
			Prestige			
			Self-Esteem			
			Pride			
			Personal Relationships			
		Security Instinct	Material			
			Emotional			
		Sex Instinct	Acceptable Sex Relations			
			Hidden Sex Relations			
		Ambitions	Social			
			Security			
			Sexual			
					Self-Seeking & Selfish	
					Dishonest	
					Inconsiderate	
					Frightened	

REVIEW OF RESENTMENTS

"SELF"

COLUMN 1	COLUMN 2	COLUMN 3: Which Part of Self Was Affected?			COLUMN 4	Questions
I AM RESENTFUL OF:	THE CAUSE OF THIS RESENTMENT IS:	Social Instinct		Personal Relationships	What is the exact nature of my wrongs, faults, mistakes, defects, shortcomings?	What was MY PART in all this? What did I do initially to get the ball rolling? How could I have done things differently?
				Pride		
				Self-Esteem		
				Prestige		
				Companionship		
		Security Instinct		Emotional		
				Material		
		Sex Instinct		Hidden Sex Relations		
				Acceptable Sex Relations		
		Ambitions		Sexual		
				Security		
				Social		
					Frightened	
					Inconsiderate	
					Dishonest	
					Self-Seeking & Selfish	

REVIEW OF RESENTMENTS

COLUMN 1	COLUMN 2	COLUMN 3: Which Part of Self Was Affected? "SELF"					COLUMN 4	Questions
I AM RESENTFUL OF:	THE CAUSE OF THIS RESENTMENT IS:	Social Instinct	Security Instinct	Sex Instinct	Ambitions		What is the exact nature of my wrongs, faults, mistakes, defects, shortcomings?	What was MY PART in all this? What did I do initially to get the ball rolling? How could I have done things differently?
		Companionship / Prestige / Self-Esteem / Pride / Personal Relationships	Material / Emotional	Acceptable Sex Relations / Hidden Sex Relations	Social / Security / Sexual	Selfish / Self-Seeking & Dishonest / Inconsiderate / Frightened		

REVIEW OF RESENTMENTS

COLUMN 1	COLUMN 2	COLUMN 3: Which Part of Self Was Affected? "SELF"															COLUMN 4	Questions
		Social Instinct					Security Instinct		Sex Instinct		Ambitions							
I AM RESENTFUL OF:	THE CAUSE OF THIS RESENTMENT IS:	Companionship	Prestige	Self-Esteem	Pride	Personal Relationships	Material	Emotional	Acceptable Sex Relations	Hidden Sex Relations	Social	Security	Sexual	Self-Seeking & Selfish	Dishonest	Inconsiderate	Frightened	What is the exact nature of my wrongs, faults, mistakes, defects, shortcomings?	What was MY PART in all this? What did I do initially to get the ball rolling? How could I have done things differently?

REVIEW OF RESENTMENTS

COLUMN 1	COLUMN 2	COLUMN 3: Which Part of Self Was Affected? "SELF"															COLUMN 4	Questions
I AM RESENTFUL OF:	THE CAUSE OF THIS RESENTMENT IS:	Social Instinct						Security Instinct		Sex Instinct		Ambitions						What is the exact nature of my wrongs, faults, mistakes, defects, shortcomings?	What was MY PART in all this? What did I do initially to get the ball rolling? How could I have done things differently?
		Companionship	Prestige	Self-Esteem	Pride	Personal Relationships	Material	Emotional	Acceptable Sex Relations	Hidden Sex Relations	Social	Security	Sexual	Self-Seeking & Selfish	Dishonest	Inconsiderate	Frightened		

REVIEW OF RESENTMENTS

"SELF"

COLUMN 1	COLUMN 2	COLUMN 3: Which Part of Self Was Affected?		COLUMN 4	Questions
I AM RESENTFUL OF:	THE CAUSE OF THIS RESENTMENT IS:			What is the exact nature of my wrongs, faults, mistakes, defects, shortcomings?	What was MY PART in all this? What did I do initially to get the ball rolling? How could I have done things differently?

Column 3 sub-categories:

Social Instinct: Companionship, Prestige, Self-Esteem, Pride, Personal Relationships

Security Instinct: Material, Emotional

Sex Instinct: Acceptable Sex Relations, Hidden Sex Relations

Ambitions: Social, Security, Sexual

Column 4 sub-categories: Selfish & Self-Seeking, Dishonest, Inconsiderate, Frightened

REVIEW OF RESENTMENTS

"SELF"

COLUMN 1	COLUMN 2	COLUMN 3: Which Part of Self Was Affected?															COLUMN 4		Questions
I AM RESENTFUL OF:	THE CAUSE OF THIS RESENTMENT IS:	Social Instinct					Security Instinct		Sex Instinct		Ambitions			What is the exact nature of my wrongs, faults, mistakes, defects, shortcomings?					What was MY PART in all this? What did I do initially to get the ball rolling? How could I have done things differently?
		Companionship	Prestige	Self-Esteem	Pride	Personal Relationships	Material	Emotional	Acceptable Sex Relations	Hidden Sex Relations	Social	Security	Sexual	Selfish & Self-Seeking	Dishonest	Inconsiderate	Frightened		

REVIEW OF RESENTMENTS

"SELF"

COLUMN 1	COLUMN 2	COLUMN 3: Which Part of Self Was Affected?				COLUMN 4	Questions
I AM RESENTFUL OF:	THE CAUSE OF THIS RESENTMENT IS:	Social Instinct	Security Instinct	Sex Instinct	Ambitions	What is the exact nature of my wrongs, faults, mistakes, defects, shortcomings?	What was MY PART in all this? What did I do initially to get the ball rolling? How could I have done things differently?
		Companionship / Prestige / Self-Esteem / Pride / Personal Relationships	Material / Emotional	Acceptable Sex Relations / Hidden Sex Relations	Social / Security / Sexual	Selfish & Self-Seeking / Dishonest / Inconsiderate / Frightened	

The Bigbook asks 3 times to test for self-will - the bondage of self

p67 Where had we been selfish, dishonest, self-seeking and frightened?
p84 Continue to watch for selfishness, dishonesty, resentment, and fear.
p86 Were we resentful, selfish, dishonest or afraid?

HONESTY

(Self-will) *(the opposite is)* (God's will)

Dishonesty .... Honesty
Resentment .... Purity

PURITY

Selfishness .... Unselfishness
Fear .... Love

UNSELFISHNESS

The opposite of dishonesty is HONESTY!

Honesty .... The "TRUTH" not "your" truth
Purity .... Motive: Is your motive pure?

LOVE

Unselfishness ... Helping Others vs Yourself Only
Love .... Joy, Oneness vs Separate, Shrink

"The 4 Absolutes"

Check out the Four Absolutes. These are the basis of the steps, there origin was founded on the basis that we would strive to each a place in time where we would live by absolute principle. However, being the humans that we are have found it far more convenient to dummy down the program and hold ourselves to lower and lower standards of accountability and responsibility for them. If you're the type that likes to get the most bang for their buck, then take a look at the absolutes and see the level of quality they can bring to your life for yourself.

1. **HONESTY**: By testing yourself against how honesty you really are in all of your affairs and by trying to increase the "degree" of the honesty you exhibit in all of your affairs, you will gradually, little by slowly, become a better person. People will trust you more and therefore show you more attention of a positive nature.

2. **PURITY**: To be pure in nature is to not carry ill-will for anyone in your being. When you carry these negative energies with you, others can sense them and they'll act and react accordingly. If you're intending to be loving, you will attract others who seek the same. Like attracts like. And this is what you'll experience.

3. **UNSELFISHNESS**: When you place the convenience and welfare of others before your own. The ego fears that this means going without, when in God's reality it means having more of what you really need. The steps teach us that helping others is joyful and we gain a missing element in our souls by doing so.

4. **LOVE**: is the essence of our Higher Power, this is the power that we lack when we are speaking in terms of powerlessness. To gain access to this power can only come to us by going through a learning and growing process which diminishes our fear of it and expands our desire for it, the steps are that process.

Order Your Workbooks Today
and Start a Workshop in Your Home Town!

By following the precise process outlined from the workbook, it will carry you and your AA friends through the 12 steps of Alcoholics Anonymous, Just like Joe & Charlie did it for over 30 years! You can rekindle the flame of the ol' timers who've lost their spark, burst the enthusiasm of the newcomers looking for a real solution and feel the flow of God in and throughout you as you and your friends are performing service work in carrying the message of recovery to yet others. This workbook and your Big Book are the basis of a rapidly growing movement growing up about you and will become the bright-spot in your lives as you watch countless others begin to recover from a hopeless state of mind and body. Catapult yourself into the fourth dimension!

Visit: www.JoeCharlie.com to get your copies today!

Need it, Want it, Do it!

Experience in print Joe and Charlie's dynamic way of carrying the message connecting you to the Big Book like know one else can.

You'll feel like they're right in front of you dispelling the Big Book with all of their southern charm and soft-hearted enthusiasm and wit for the love of AA and the Big Book!

Visit: www.JoeCharlie.com to get your copies today!

The Real Alcoholic
What Actually is a Real Alcoholic?!

There are only two conditions that MUST exist to be a Real Alcoholic, they are: (the hopeless condition)

1. Physical Allergy
2. Mental Obsession

• The Physical Allergy prevents any alcoholic from drinking any alcohol without developing a phenomenon of craving beyond their control.

• The Mental Obsession builds up a sense of irritability so great, and an insane reasoning so persuasive that it exceeds all will to resist.

Physical Allergy

An abnormal reaction to any food, drink or substance. The chemical reaction an alcoholic body has that produces anxiety and a craving for more alcohol.

Mental Obsession

A train of thought so powerful that it overtakes all other ideas, regardless of their importance. The obsession is so strong that the mind may also go blank or find insane reasons to perpetuate them.

**These conditions do not appear in the average temporate drinker. Just because you're addicted to drugs does not mean you're an alcoholic, or just because you drank heavily for years does not mean you're an alcoholic; if you can stop, stay stopped or moderate "at your will" you might not be alcoholic.

The Big Book *IS* meant to be studied, so that we become familiarized with its teachings and its principles; so that we can become awake and aware to our own actions, attitudes and behaviors, so that we can practice these principles in all of our affairs until they no longer become a 'hit and miss' struggle to do so, and become more of 'second nature'. Using Flash Cards will help the learning process. We are recommending that you check out **BigBookFlashcards.com** and see for your self this invaluable tool for learning the Big Book and its many Recovery Life lessons to behold.

Thank you Bill W. and Dr Bob,

Bill W.

Dr. Bob

Joe & Charlie's
Sobriety Prayers

Set Aside Prayer

God, please help me to set aside everything I think I know about AA, the 12 steps, the Big Book, my Program, Myself, and you God; so that I may have an open mind and a new experience with all these things, please help me to see the truth. Amen

Serenity Prayer

God, grant me the Serenity to accept the things I cannot change Courage to change the things I can, and the Wisdom to know the difference. Living one day at a time; Enjoying one moment at a time; Accepting hardship as the pathway to peace. Taking, as He did, this sinful world as it is, not as I would have it. Trusting that He will make all things right if I surrender to His Will; That I may be reasonably happy in this life, and supremely happy with Him forever in the next. Amen

3rd STEP

"God, I offer myself to Thee — to build with me and to do with me as Thou wilt. Relieve me of the bondage of self, that I may better do Thy will. Take away my difficulties, that victory over them may bear witness to those I would help of Thy Power, Thy Love, and Thy Way of life. May I do Thy will always!" AMEN

7th STEP

"My Creator, I am now willing that you should have all of me, good and bad. I pray that you now remove from me every single defect of character, which stands in the way of my usefulness to you and my fellows. Grant me strength, as I go out from here, to do your bidding. Amen."   (p. 76 BB)

11th STEP

(Prayer of St Francis of Assisi) — "Lord, make me a channel of thy peace - that where there is hatred, I may bring love - that where there is wrong, I may bring the spirit of forgiveness - that where there is discord, I may bring harmony - that where there is error, I may bring truth - that where there is doubt, I may bring faith - that where there is despair, I may bring hope - that where there are shadows, I may bring light - that where there is sadness, I may bring joy. Lord, grant that I may seek rather to comfort than to be comforted - to understand, than to be understood - to love, than to be loved. For it is by self-forgetting that one finds. It is by forgiving that one is forgiven. It is by dying that one awakens to Eternal Life. Amen."